LOST TO THE WORLD

Lost to the World

The Remarkable Story of a Buried Wartime Treasure

ALEXANDER LYNAR

MAINSTREAM
PUBLISHING

EDINBURGH AND LONDON

*To all of the Oettingen family, with my eternal gratitude for
having given me a new home away from home*

First published in Great Britain in 1998 by
MAINSTREAM PUBLISHING COMPANY (EDINBURGH) LTD
7 Albany Street
Edinburgh EH1 3UG

ISBN 1 84018 066 8

A catalogue record for this book is available from the British Library

Typeset in Berkeley Book
Printed and bound in Great Britain by Butler and Tanner Ltd, Frome

CONTENTS

ACKNOWLEDGEMENTS

Without the dedication and work of my wife Lolita this book would never have appeared. She is the one who actually wrote the book, not me. In school I never achieved more than three out of six for composition so I am totally incapable of writing a book.

It was Lolita who made sense of the memories which I wrote down and who converted my scrawl into an interesting and well-written (so I hope) text. Not only did she do this but she also typed and co-ordinated the manuscript. I cannot thank her enough for taking on this difficult and boring task. Her greatest achievement is that during the work she never got cross with me and we even had fun.

INTRODUCTION

Cling! Johann's shovel has bumped against something in the sandy earth, two metres down and a prolonged musical note, like the one from a tuning fork, resounds. We freeze. Silence falls; every head is turned my way, eyes flashing.

I would like my life to stand still at this exact moment and I wish that nothing would ever happen again. It is a sunny day, the rays of light dance across the woods, I smell the intoxicating fragrance of the trees, I am young and I am back home. In my mind I am a teenager again; the one who had to flee from his land at the age of 16.

The objects come out, one after the other, and proceed from one digger to the next, handled with the gentle care of lacemakers. It's incredible, fabulous, everything is there, practically intact, lying at the very spot where I buried it myself, half a century ago. The treasure! All the silverware and the porcelain my 19th-century ancestors have passed on to me through my mother. All that was required to entertain with proper decorum the crowned heads of their time.

I am the one who had taken the initiative to bury all that could reasonably be saved and who now is alive to retrieve our family inheritance – an inheritance that first the Russians, then the heads of Communist Germany and recently our very democratic government of reunified Germany have coveted and searched for during the past 50 years.

After a life of wandering the world having founded a happy family but always refusing to unpack my suitcases in any place beyond a few years, I am home at last; I don't want to leave any more.

*

I lived a sheltered if not serene childhood, the last of six children. My mother gave birth first to four girls and had to endure the exasperated sighs of her own mother every time. At the fourth, as my father and his mother-in-law were facing each other in petrified silence, the midwife exclaimed: 'There is another child coming, there is a twin!' It was my brother.

My mother wanted another boy as her own heir, the one she would make one hundred per cent a Redern. She thought she owed it to her family to make up for not having been a male heir. So, four years later she had me. She was set on making the necessary arrangements to have my name changed from Lynar-Redern to Redern when the war took charge of the destiny of us all, not only the name.

Mother was then grooming me lovingly but sternly to prepare me for my future role of guardian of the land rather than landowner. Indeed, in her mind the estate was to be transmitted, never to be sold. You had to make it larger, never smaller. Of the 35,000 acres she planned to pass on to me she made a clause in her will stating that I could not sell more than 700, whatever the justification. She hadn't hesitated herself to show the door indignantly·to the Goering emissaries who wanted to trade part of her forest against the same acreage wherever she fancied as long as it would be elsewhere. She thought she had succeeded in intimidating Goering but he probably kept his plotting scheme on hold and would have come back when less busy with other matters (we were in 1943).

In the following pages I have attempted to describe the background to the burial of the treasure, the times I have lived through and the story of how I returned after half a century to reclaim a little of my past.

Chapter One

THE LYNARS

The Lynar family originates from the north of Italy. The *Book of Florence's Documents* mentions it for the first time with 'Migliore, Conte di Linari, son of Conte Guido di Mutiliana' in 1347. The family traces back its origins through the Counts of Mutiliana to the Noble Wido from Thuringia, who wed a morganatic daughter of the Duke Otto of Saxony in 933.

Confirmation of this descent as 'Comes' (Counts) di Linari (a place near Faenza, Province of Ravenna) was given by the Duke Cosimo of Florence, of the Medici family, in a document signed in Pisa on 19 May 1564 for my ancestor Rochus Guerrino. After his arrival in Germany, he was registered as 'Count zu Lynar' in 1568.

Rochus, called Roch, was born in 1525 in Maradia, Tuscany, which was then part of the duchy (dukedom) of Florence, where the Medicis ruled. Florence was at that period the most important centre of arts and sciences. Very early in his life, Roch became a page at the court of the Medicis, where he was educated as any Renaissance nobleman was. He was talented in many fields, was a good officer and general, and at an early age became known all over Europe as an architect of fortresses. When he reached his tenth year of age, his father took him along to Tunis on a campaign, following an army of Emperor Charles V.

In 1540 Roch went to Paris with his brother, as a page to the court of François I and later Henri II. Henri II's wife was Katherine de Medici, who favoured her compatriots as her personal entourage.

In one of the numerous wars of the French kings, Roch lost his left eye. He was a colonel at 22 and general commissary of all fortresses in France at 24. He built the fortress of Metz and there he married Anne de Montot, a member of the Protestant faith. Soon after his marriage, he converted to Protestantism and that was the reason why he left France and went to work for Protestant princes in Germany, first for the Elector of Saxony, later the Elector of Brandenburg. In Brandenburg, he built the famous fortress of Spandau. He was much in demand throughout the rest of his life among the German princes and he travelled from one court to the next, being consulted as an expert in military, administrative and architectural matters.

At that time, services to the monarchs were rewarded with donations of land and money (much later, some smart king, presumably on the verge of bankruptcy, started giving pretty decorations to his followers instead of more costly privileges). So Roch had amassed quite a sizeable fortune, which later permitted his grandson to acquire a very large estate, Lübbenau in Lusace, a province which was first Saxon, then Prussian. The men served alternately in the armies or the services of Prussia, Saxony and Denmark.

Another colourful ancestor was Rochus Friedrich, a strikingly good-looking figure, who lived in the 18th century. He spent his entire life in the service of the king of Denmark, first as ambassador to Stockholm, then to St Petersburg, where he was rumoured to be one of Tsarina Elizabeth's lovers. Finally, he was named governor of Oldenburg, a grand duchy located in Germany but nonetheless then belonging to Denmark. He reigned for years over this land, happy to be independent and far from the intrigues of the court in Copenhagen. Alas, occupying such a position aroused the envy of some powerful enemies at the court. They accused him of having embezzled a large amount of money which was assigned to the army under his command. It is presumed he was innocent, as he was a very wealthy man, clever enough not to have risked his good name and position for a relatively small financial profit. He resigned his charge immediately and returned home to Lübbenau.

At the end of the 18th century, the family split into two branches: the counts in Lübbenau and the princes in Drehna.

*

Under Crown rule, the owner of a large estate could entail it and either all of the fortune or part of it could be included in the entail. The essential condition for the establishment of an entailed estate was that the male heir, generally the eldest son, would inherit the whole of the estate, the siblings getting only a yearly income during their life – they had no right to a share of the property.

The estate lord was more of a manager for his own heir than a real owner. He was not allowed to sell more than a certain portion of the estate, as specified in the foundation act of the entailed estate, and he had then to purchase new land for that portion sold. For a more important sale, the consent of the family council was mandatory.

To establish or dissolve an entailed estate, the consent of all the living members of the family was needed and the consent of the *agnates* was also required. The *agnates* are cousins of another branch, bearing the same name. They were eligible as eventual heirs in the event of the major branch becoming extinct. The dissolution would give them an indemnity to compensate for the remote chance any one of them had of becoming the heir apparent.

The advantage for the family was that the estate stayed in the hands of a sole person, generally the heir to the title. The estate would probably get larger with the years and centuries and it would at least not get smaller. Its value would give more power to the entire family. It was a guarantee as well against the danger that the fortune would be lost, as happened with my paternal ancestor, Prince Otto zu Lynar, after he dissolved the entailed estate.

For the state, that is to say for the kingdom at that time, there was the advantage of establishing an aristocracy deeply rooted in an important estate, permanently in the same place and wealthy enough in time and money to serve the monarch. The younger sons would of necessity go into the service of the king as they did not have money enough to live without working.

The first Prince Lynar, Moritz (1754–1807), was made a lieutenant when he was nine years old in the Foreign Regiment of Oldenburg where his father was the Danish governor. Franz II, who had his title of Emperor of the Holy Roman Empire removed by Napoleon in August 1806, made Moritz a prince in 1807. So, six months too late to become a prince of the Holy Roman Empire but just in time before dying in the same year. During his whole life span he collected land and purchased and sold thousands of acres.

Otto, the second Prince Lynar, was a man with a taste for art. He was a poet and a playwright. A liberal, he pressured the king of Prussia into giving his country a constitution in the years around 1840, a period during which the people all over Europe demanded more democratic governments.

Prince Otto's wife, Countess Louise Hedwig von Bosé, was the only daughter of Adolf Ludwig, Count von Bosé, former colonel in the Regiment of the Guards of King Louis XVI of France. Ludwig claimed to have received from Louis XVI the title of count when, disguised as postillion, he drove the King from Paris to Varennes. As the Postmaster Drouet stopped the King's coach and informed the Republican garrison who arrested the King and his family, Bosé pretended he had an opportunity to flee! Since then, he always signed his papers and documents 'Count . . .'. Germany did not recognise, much less validate such a dubious title.

The death of his 34-year-old wife and three of four sons tried Otto severely. He still had his eldest son, Alfred. Alfred, as keen on theatre as his father had been, met a ballerina from the Berlin Opera, Amalie ('Malchen') Senger. It was love at first sight for Alfred who married her in 1856. He was 36, she was 21. The King allowed her to bear the name of Mrs von Gollmitz. Alfred, with the consent of his father who could not refuse anything to his son, had wanted Malchen to bear his name and title but the rest of the Lynar family objected. Otto, Alfred and Malchen, on non-speaking terms with the rest of the Lynar family, retreated to the Drehna castle.

Amalie might have had talent for the stage but she was undoubtedly also gifted with grace, intelligence, charm and artistic taste so she was not long in acquiring an overpowering influence on her father-in-law.

Aged 37, in 1857 Alfred had a stroke that left him an invalid to the point that he had to be put under tutelage. One year later, giving way to his son's wish expressed before his attack and at his daughter-in-law's insistence, Otto named Amalie as his sole heir, leaving his son just the minimum required by the law. In 1859, Alfred had a second stroke and died a few days later. Otto then had his will registered in favour of Malchen before dying one year later, alone and miserable in his castle, cut off from his family and friends.

The ancestral estate and the beautiful castle of Drehna, which included a hereditary right to a seat in the Prussian House of Lords, were passed out of the family. The siren's song had been so overwhelming that the old man had not even considered the possibility of passing his fortune, at least his land estate, on to his brother, Ernst, the heir to the title.

Ernst, the heir apparent, had to take the blow and stay impassive as he received the congratulations of those who innocently thought he was lucky as he had had only a remote chance of inheriting in the first place, his four nephews having to die first. He had the last laugh on the occasion of the wedding of Prince William of Prussia, later the Emperor William I, in Potsdam. Ernst participated there in an ancient-style tournament and was asked what his motto was for the occasion. 'Everything for Her, Nothing without Her but Who is She?' was his answer under a thundering applause.

No doubt, contrary to the other family cadets who endured with no excess of enthusiasm the entailed estate, he cursed the fact that his brother had not been bound by it. An entailed estate would have forced his brother to pass it on to him altogether.

At 25, the pretty, scheming Mrs von Gollmitz found herself in possession of a huge estate, with no charges and no family obligations. Four months after the death of her father-in-law and benefactor, she wed a handsome young lieutenant, Baron Ernst von Eckardtstein, whose bed she had already been warming up before she was widowed. The couple sold Drehna in 1877. Until then, they lived in the castle. Apparently the baron hadn't a penny to his name and lived on his wife's providential fortune, having kept from the Army only the military uniform that brought him riches.

The baron's nephew described one of his visits to his uncle when he was a child:

> I spent several months at my uncle and my aunt's in Drehna. The old castle was sitting in the middle of a magnificent park. Several bridges crossed the moats, which surrounded the four-towered castle. Inside were all the modern facilities that the time could procure. Numerous paintings and works of art decorated the reception rooms.

The castle was packed with guests during the whole summer. When one would leave, another one would immediately move in. Most of the guests were illustrious personalities, interesting and witty, who sneered behind their hosts' back about the social claims of the baroness.

When the castle was sold the couple went to live in Potsdam in a luxurious villa. When her husband died, Malchen moved to Charlotten-burg where she ended her days in 1906 without having ever borne a child. It is a shame she didn't bear a Lynar descendant; we might have inherited in our genes some of her charm and her sense of intrigue.

*

My grandfather, Alexander, was for a long time a diplomat in Paris. Napoleon III befriended him and that was sufficient ground for Bismarck to choose him to escort the emperor to the fortress of Wilhelmshöhe, after he was captured in Sedan, and thus soften his humiliation.

When the war ended in 1871, Alexander returned to the embassy in Paris, now as a German, not as a Prussian anymore. In fact, the Germans were not very popular in French society circles in Paris after this war, and my grandfather could feel the ostracism. He found solace with the American Parsons family who stayed in Paris for a while. He married one of their very pretty daughters, Amelia.

*

Before he married, my father Ernst was a diplomat, in Rome and in London, after having served in the Regiment of the Garde du Corps, and moving to 'A la Suite de l'Armée', which was a privilege reserved to the high aristocracy and which allowed him to be automatically upgraded in the ranks of the army, without actually serving in it any more.

There was a photograph standing on my mother's chest of drawers of my father in his splendid uniform: over his chest and his back a silver cuirass with a golden eagle on it, white trousers with black boots that came up 15 inches above the knees in front. (My mother gave the boots to me during the war, when they were not available any more and we cut off the upper part. With that upper part went the elegance! It was no good anyway; they were much too stiff to be of any use riding.) The headgear was a helmet with a golden eagle with outspread wings on it. It was impressive, especially as the photograph showed my father as a young and very good-looking man, and he made quite an impression on the ladies in this attire.

In 1917, my father, recently married, went back to the front while my mother, pregnant since the first days of her marriage, moved to Görlsdorf, my family home. When she finally settled into married life, one or two years later, the whole household would commute between Lindenau, my father's estate and Görlsdorf for a two-year stay in each estate, 125 miles apart. We made what seemed an endless journey by car. My brother and I, shivering with the biting cold, sat next to the driver. Thus, neither of the two estates would be neglected. My mother loyally continued the same rhythm after my father's death until 1939.

My father liked to travel, particularly in the cold season. He would run away from the long, icy winters of our country. He often travelled to the United States, his mother's homeland, and to England. He was fully bilingual and could also speak French very well. Every year he spent a few weeks in Monte Carlo, on the French Riviera. Every time he felt like going away he would ask my mother to come along but she always refused, under the excuse of not being able to leave the children.

'What are the nurses for, then?' my father would mumble, exasperated.

But Mother was adamant. To the point that she never set foot in London in all of her life.

My father came back from one of his trips in February 1933 and, with a sombre look, addressed my mother: 'A fine job you have been doing while I was away! We are all going to pay dearly for this monumental stupidity.'

He was referring to the parliamentary elections of 30 January 1933 in Germany, which brought Hitler to power.

I have often thought it was probably better that he didn't survive to see the war. With his very straight character and his conservative, pro-monarchist, political views, his fate would have led him to be a passionate opponent against Hitler and Nazism. I am convinced he would have joined his cousin, Wilfried with whom he was very close, in the 20 July 1944 plot and that he would have been shot or hanged as Wilfried was.

My father was 59 years old when he died. I was five. I have a vague recollection of a very tall man who wore a hat. It sounds like the impressions of a five-year-old! For me, the youngest, he seemed intimidating, almost inaccessible and I believe he was rather embarrassed in the presence of small children. He was very gentle though and he would pick me up in his arms. He had a closer relationship with my eldest sisters. He was 43 years old when he married, having had a merry bachelor life at leisure. 'He was handsome, tall and slender and had exquisite manners which added to his natural charm,' a still very beautiful lady whispered in my ear years later.

The last images I have of my father are of him at the dinner table when he was already severely ill. He had cushions around him and was pale, yet composed. I vaguely sensed he was in a critical condition and I was very sad to see him in that state but I knew how to remain silent in front of the adults.

Then I remember his burial and, back at home, my mother, seated on the steps of the staircase, crying her heart out (she had also lost her mother a few months previously). I tried to console her, telling her – I think – that she still had all of her children who were going to do everything to alleviate her sorrow. My mother told my wife a different version many years later. She said that I put my sticky little paws around her face and told her with a convinced tone of voice: 'Daddy is dead, good for him, so I will have you for me alone!' I must say I prefer my own recollection to hers.

*

My father had a brother, George, and a sister, Jane. They both remained single and lived in the same building in Berlin, in separate apartments. They had lived with their mother, my American grandmother who died in 1924 and who never really mastered the German language. They often came to Görlsdorf for extensive stays and were a permanent fixture every Christmas, quarrelling non-stop. Uncle George smoked his first cigarette of the day only after dinner and then chain-smoked two packs before retiring to sleep. Aunt Jane owned a very old car, a yellow two-seater of some American manufacture. She was rather uneasy about driving it so she used it only for the trip to Görlsdorf from Berlin. She parked it outside, in front of the dining-room and left it there for her entire stay. She left one day to go back to Berlin while the rest of us were having breakfast. The car's engine started as usual with a thunder-like noise. An old friend who was visiting us and was stone deaf lifted his head, his hand in mid-air to reach for the bread, and said: 'Who would think you would get a tropical storm in Görlsdorf?'

Aunt Jane was a chess addict. As she couldn't find any opponent in the house, she played against herself for hours on end, staying up until four or five in the morning. We were instructed sternly not to make any noise near her apartment before noon. She pestered the cook before every meal and ordered him to make a special menu for her. She ate it and then proceeded to eat our menu as well. She was as thin as a thread. My poor mother couldn't stand her although she hid her feelings carefully. Aunt Jane must have reciprocated the antipathy and she adamantly refused to leave Görlsdorf with us when the time was ripe to flee. Sadly, she died through mistreatment one month after the Russian invasion of the castle.

*

My father adored Lindenau, a 16th-century castle in Silesia, which he had inherited along with an agricultural and forestry estate when he was very young. When he took possession of the castle, it was rather small and short on modern commodities. He added two wings to the principal body of the house, furnished it in French Louis XV style, redesigned the park and installed electricity, financing his renovation with a bank loan. It so happened that when he had to repay the loan in 1923, inflation had reached such proportions that the work cost my father in the end only ten per cent of what it was worth.

By the end of the 1920s, Lindenau had become a little Renaissance jewel. The main entrance opened on a vast hall on the wall of which was displayed a life-size portrait of my ancestor, Rochus Lynar, the fortress architect. He was represented in armour, with an empty socket where the left eye he lost in a battle should have been. The first time I had a real look at him I must have been around six years of age. I stayed a long time in front of the portrait, concluded he wasn't a person I would have sympathised with and stuck my tongue out at him before departing. After that, his nasty half stare following me would terrorise me. I used to run across the hall if there was no other way without looking at him, anxious to remain as little as possible in his company lest he would have me pay for my insolence.

Leading off the hall was the library. Shelves covered the walls up to the ceiling and one of the walls revolved to unmask the entry to the strong room where the jewels and silverware were placed. For me this secret device smelt of intrigue and adventure, as in adventure novels, and to this day I imagine scenarios on how the Russians must have uncovered this cavern filled with gold and silver.

My memories of my childhood in Lindenau are still very lively. It was often very hot during the summer. At the hated time of my mandatory afternoon nap, I would hear from my bed the noise the women were making, rattling their rakes on the sand, laughing and chatting. On Saturdays the paths of the park were cleaned for the coming Sunday. In the evening and in bed when it was still daylight I often could not sleep and I gladly listened to the hubbub of the grown-ups' voices on the terrace underneath my window.

Although Lindenau was an elegant castle, the moats sheltered impressive colonies of rats. One day my nanny had delegated her charge to a young blockhead. While the girl was babytalking to me to wake me up from my afternoon nap, as I was still a prisoner in my caged bed, a huge rat came to visit, climbing down from the window. It crossed the room and took refuge under my bed. Listening to the calls of her non-bravery and not to her too recent devotion, the young lady fled screaming. I stayed alone with my guest, yelling at the top of my lungs. The caretaker finally arrived with his dog, a non-descript hybrid as big as a fly. The diminutive dog murdered the big rat still stationed under my bed, in a Wagnerian pandemonium.

Apparently, I attracted rats. When I was eight, I went down to the cellar one day with the caretaker (it was not the same one as in Lindenau, though, we were in Görlsdorf). There was a big stack of coke in the middle of the room. Access to the cellar was through a corridor that circled it. On our way out, between the coke and the corridor, trapped in the circular gutter, four huge filthy rats were fighting to get free. When I started screaming the caretaker scolded me, saying: 'What, you are lucky enough to see the King of Rats and you want to run away? What a brave boy!'

They were four rats attached to one another by one single tail. I didn't appreciate much being introduced to the King . . . of rats, I'm afraid.

In Lindenau as in Görlsdorf, there was a Lutheran church. My great-great uncle had built the one in Görlsdorf. In each one, a gallery was reserved for us as patrons of the church. 'Patron', in the ancient sense of the word, meaning that it was his responsibility to pay for the repairs and general expenses of the religious community of the place. My brother and I, as well as my aunt and my uncle would go to the Lutheran temple every Sunday while my mother and my sisters would take the carriage to go to the Catholic church in the neighbouring town.

We had fifty *pfennigs* (approximately sixty pence) a week as pocket money. We were forbidden to buy sweets. In the village of Lindenau, there was only one little shop, which pompously read 'Goods from the Colonies'. I would buy some 'Brause Powder' there, an objectionable powder which, diluted in water made repulsive lemonade.

My brother, a cousin of ours, a pal and I had created a secret society. We sealed a pact with our blood and locked the document in a place accessible only through a hidden trapdoor. Apparently, someone discovered this priceless document much later, for my brother received a photocopy of it in the '50s.

In the village, there was a forge, with an open fire and a fan. I would watch how the blacksmith and his apprentices were shaping the horseshoes with red-hot iron and putting them onto the horses' hooves. I was afraid it would hurt the horses when the iron touched the hoof. A sizzling sound as from a frying pan was then heard and smoke would come out with a pungent smell of burnt horn.

The Lindenau estate of my father was small in comparison to Görlsdorf. After my father's death, my brother Ernst Wilhelm inherited it. As my mother wanted the whole Redern estate to go to me, she thought my brother would not have enough land. She wanted to be fair to both her sons, therefore she bought two additional estates, not too far away from Lindenau, so each of our shares would be more equal.

There was no separate administration of the Lindenau estate and the work was done in the Görlsdorf estate office. There was a permanent secretary in the courtyard building and a chief forester who was responsible for the Lindenau forest but under the supervision and orders of our Görlsdorf forest manager. The farms were leased, so they didn't require much work. It went without saying that all this common management would have to be separated once my brother was old enough to take his estate in his own hands.

While we were in residence in Görlsdorf, there remained only Mr and Mrs Limberg, the caretaker and his wife at Lindenau. They looked after the house and attended the occasional family member on a visit. The large house was then empty and silent and I had the feeling that both Limbergs, who had no children, were quite happy on the day the whole family – including a dozen servants – came for their two-year stay, although they had more work to do.

We used to arrive in the spring, when the luxuriant bushes of rhododendron were in full bloom. It was a magnificent sight. I, as a child, preferred Görlsdorf, less majestic but cosier and more intimate. But Lindenau had its advantages. We had the large cellars, lofts and more or less empty buildings in the courtyard to play in and more friends from the village. I missed the beautiful lakes of Görlsdorf for swimming in the summer but near Lindenau there was a large and pleasant public bathing establishment, which was fun too as there were other children to gather with. And, occasionally, there was a visit to Kmehlen, which was a real treat. It was another big castle, about four miles from Lindenau and was part of the estate. It was much older than Lindenau – a 13th century building, uninhabited for a hundred years. My friends and I roamed through the large, gloomy rooms, stripped of their furniture. We raised clouds of ancient, foul-smelling dust, looked into the moat and tried in vain to make the drawbridge work. We played knights and noble ladies until nightfall, when the coachman called for us urgently as he had strict orders not to leave us in the castle by night.

Lindenau was a village of small independent farmers, so our relationship to the families – which was like a family bond in Görlsdorf – was not as close. The village was much bigger; it had an official mayor and an administration. On 1 May every year, there was the big 'May feast'. On the little square, in the centre of the village, the 'May tree' was erected. It was a gigantic pole with a little tree fastened at its top, from which hung dozens of colourful ribbons down to the ground. A young boy or girl took the end of each ribbon and then, to the approximately melodious music made by the instruments of the village band that had mastered five or six marches, the young people danced around the pole. You could buy food, beer and lemonade inside two or three tents. Indeed, eating and drinking were the main entertainment. My family were the guests of honour, and my poor mother, once more, was expected to make one of her innumerable speeches. We pitied her but she didn't seem to look on it as a burden and delivered it with enthusiasm and merriment.

During the war, I would often go on my own to Lindenau to shoot deer. The deer were stronger and more numerous there than in Görlsdorf. It was always a treat and I was allowed to have one of the beautiful guestrooms which had fantastic four-poster beds and luxurious bathrooms. Mrs Limberg was a tiny fat ball of a woman and would cook for me. She was a remarkable chef as well as being a very nice and cheerful person.

I would get up at four o'clock, go hunting with a forester until eight, come home for a huge breakfast and go to bed again until one o'clock in the afternoon. Then lunch and more hunting. I had the feeling of not only being a grown-up but a castle owner as well.

Although Ernst Wilhelm inherited Lindenau I was the only one, out of the six children, to have been born there. In 1945, the Soviets arrived at the castle like grasshoppers invading a field of wheat and plundered the house. There wasn't a piece of the wooden floor or even a tap left after their visit. The castle was later used by the East German Government as a school for mentally handicapped children.

After the fall of the Berlin Wall my brother returned to Lindenau and, as the law prohibited recovering one's own property, he made a deal with a Swiss hotel company to transform the castle into a hotel. It would have been a good business and would have created quite a number of jobs, the place being situated between Berlin and Dresden. All the financing was established and Ernst Wilhelm offered a good price to the community, which had become, through nebulous channels, owner of the castle. The village council members however, most of whom were communists, refused to sell and the project collapsed. Now, four years later, they are willing to give the castle away for one symbolic mark, to the person who will install a home for old people.

I went to visit Lindenau with my brother a few years back. It was a devastating experience. The building itself as well as the park were in good shape. I toured the rooms, and in my mind's eye could clearly see again the beautiful furniture, curtains, tapestries, paintings, the grand dining-room where the big gatherings took place with the attendants in regal uniform standing behind my parents, my mother's cosy drawing-room and adjacent bedroom where I was born. Now I found myself walking in slow motion, as in a nightmare, through dilapidated, run down rooms, in an environment that had replaced past grandeur with actual pettiness through greed.

Chapter Two

THE REDERNS

A rnoldus de Redere is mentioned in the records in 1155, with the same coat of arms we still have today. He was a Saxon. Later the family can be traced to Brandenburg. In 1355, the Rederns purchased the Schwante estate, which remained in the family for almost 600 years (20 generations). Schwante was located near Berlin, too near for my grandfather's taste. The proximity implied constant involvement with court life and he felt overpowered by it, so he sold the estate.

In 1620, the Rederns acquired Görlsdorf, the grounds of which I am at last able to stand on again.

Of my more immediate ancestors, Count Wilhelm Friedrich von Redern, was born in 1802 in Berlin. He inherited vast domains near Berlin, most of them consisting of forests, agricultural lands, several castles, among them Görlsdorf, and the famed Redern palace in Berlin. This was a very large town house located at number one Unter den Linden (the Champs Elysees of Berlin), at the corner of Pariser Platz. Opposite, on one side, was the Brandenburg gate, on the other side the French embassy.

The palace was built at the beginning of the 18th century by Count Kamecke, who sold it in 1798 to Count Redern, Wilhelm Friedrich's father. At the time of Wilhelm Friedrich's wedding, the house was somewhat run down and was no more than adequate. It had to be modernised to meet the requirements of my great-uncle's numerous social obligations. He therefore asked Schinkel, the most famous Prussian architect of his time, to completely renovate the palace and to give it a new neo-classical façade. When the work was completed, the town house looked magnificent and worthy of the large collection of paintings, antique furniture and *objets d'art* that Wilhelm Friedrich already had in his possession and continued to collect all his life.

On the second floor, vast rooms were assigned for the continual receptions and balls my great-uncle gave after his marriage. A huge ballroom, fully coated with white marble, could contain 200 dancers. A long succession of receptions, balls and festivities began to take place, at which were entertained Europe's leading personalities.

Wilhelm Friedrich was very proud of his new home. He sent an engraving to Goethe, whom he had visited in Weimar a few years earlier. Goethe wrote to thank Redern for the picture, telling him that he would very much have liked to see the lively Berliners pass by such a superb house. Of course, he was invited right away!

In 1834, Wilhelm Friedrich married Bertha Jenisch, daughter of a very wealthy industrial Hamburg family. Around that time, Wilhelm Friedrich ordered a table service of 120 pieces in silver engraved with the Redern coat of arms from Odiot, the famed Parisian silversmith who made the banquet services of the most illustrious royal and aristocratic families of Europe. He also bought two Meissen porcelain services of more than 100 pieces each.

At the first appearances of the young Countess Redern at the court, she was greeted with a few poisoned arrows: 'What is your father's trade again, dear?' The young lady knew how to fend for herself: 'Wisdom and humour' she would answer suavely. When the emperor made her father a baron, that discouraged the critics. Gossips would whisper that her husband was living on a grand scale with his wife's money and bought property with his own. He was called 'the Count with the 99 domains'.

Gifted with a sure musical taste, Wilhelm Friedrich was friend and protector of some of the great musicians of his time and an old friend of Mendelssohn. He enlisted Giacomo Meyerbeer – who often played his compositions at the Redern palace – at the Berlin Opera. Meyerbeer wrote this letter of recommendation to Wilhelm Friedrich in favour of Wagner:

Your Lordship,

I take the liberty to send you the score and the book of the opera The Flying Dutchman by Richard Wagner. I already had, the day before yesterday, the honour to talk to your lordship about this interesting composer who, given his talent and his extremely difficult financial situation, would deserve twice that the Royal Theatres, in their role of protectors of the German arts, would not deny him access to their stages.

Your lordship was also good enough to promise me that you would confirm to him by a few words in writing the receipt of the score and your willingness to have it examined.

> Taking the liberty to bring this matter to your memory, I have the
> honour . . . Giacomo Meyerbeer.

The style of this note rings a bell in my mind: it is in the same style as
Wagner's numerous letters to King Ludwig II of Bavaria. Could it be that
he dictated it to the good Meyerbeer?

I found the following description in an old book:

> In Count Redern's house, artists were the prominent guests.
> Musicians, painters, sculptors, writers, philosophers, poets, actors,
> scientists, gathered at the Redern palace. Often the carriage of a
> famous guest was seen going through the gates to deliver its occupant
> for a stay of several days.

The poet Karl Imhermann reports from a journey to Berlin:

> Already in Potsdam I found a very obliging letter from Count Redern,
> inviting me to stay in his house. So I am now staying in this
> marvellous palace and can observe from my very room the animation
> of the elegant crowd in this part of the city.
>
> Excellent service, calm in my apartments, the opportunity to
> wander in the grand halls and to use the countless rare books of the
> library. Every evening, I enjoy a play at the theatre, where I have my
> seat in the Director General's box. The motto at the house of my host
> is to let me have total freedom. At 4 p.m., dinner is served. The guests
> are brilliant yet lively and pleasant. Should you not care to attend that
> meal, all you have to do is to inform the butler. I am treated with the
> utmost generosity and kindness and nothing is expected from me in
> return. I have met here personalities like Schinkel, Rauch (the
> greatest sculptor of his time) and Alexander von Humboldt. I met
> also many a member of the high aristocracy of Berlin. I've noticed
> they have a curious habit: they always start to speak French when
> they are among themselves. I thought I would be embarrassed,
> should they address me in that language, but they reverted
> immediately to good old German whenever they turned to me!

Apart from artists and scientists, Wilhelm Friedrich played host to kings
and the Emperor, as well as to international personalities and political leaders.
The huge white ballroom was often bristling with waltzes and polkas played
by orchestras of musicians in tails, the steps of the dancing couples sliding
making a muffled sound, the smell of the many flowers mixed with the ladies'

perfume giving an intoxicating fragrance to the room. Women were beautiful in their evening dresses, their sophisticated coiffures and their sparkling jewels. The men, attired either in their dress uniform with decorations and shining epaulettes or in evening dress of the 19th century, when men's clothes were still stylish, vied with each other to impress the ladies.

There was a life-size painting of my great-uncle in one of the drawing-rooms in Görlsdorf, in tails, with the sash of the order of the Black Eagle across his shirt. His beard was parted in the middle and combed to each side of his face, in exactly the same fashion that his revered sovereign, Emperor Wilhelm I had adopted.

Like his two predecessors – Friedrich Wilhelm III and Friedrich Wilhelm IV, Emperor Wilhelm I distinguished my great-uncle with every conceivable honour. He was named Director General of the Royal Theatres, Grand Chamberlain, Master of the Horse, General of the Cavalry and finally Grand Chancellor of the Order of the Black Eagle (the Prussian equivalent of the Order of the Garter in England).

If everything seemed to turn to gold for the Rederns in a material, professional and social point of view, on the private level the count and countess were living a tragedy: they were childless and were desperate. After 13 years, Bertha finally gave birth to a daughter whom they cherished and spoilt. Tragically, she died at the age of ten.

The couple were devastated. My great-grandmother, a very pious woman, said to her brother-in-law: 'Think that you will see her again in heaven!' But Wilhelm Friedrich answered with despair: 'But I want to see her again here, as she was, with her little pink dress and her big hat!'

There was a portrait of her in one of the reception rooms in Görlsdorf, showing her with long golden curls and long trousers with lace. In my opinion, she must have been a strangely hard little girl. She used to say to my grandfather, her cousin: 'You will have to marry me, whether you like it or not, so that the fortune remains in the family!' It is reported that, on her deathbed, she asked her father: 'What are you going to do now, with all your hard *thalers* (the Prussian currency)?'

The Rederns didn't have a direct heir any more. Wilhelm Friedrich established an entailed estate in the year 1880, but stipulated an exceptional clause in memory of his daughter: once and only once, a woman could inherit all of his properties and wealth, provided she had no brother. On this occasion, the Emperor wanted to give to Wilhelm Friedrich the title of prince. Wilhelm Friedrich declined with a respectful bow, answering proudly: 'Your Majesty, I have an old lineage of count, I wouldn't want my ancestors to turn in their graves and have a good laugh at the expense of the new prince.'

Wilhelm Friedrich died in 1883. His heir was his nephew Wilhelm, my grandfather.

Wilhelm, born a Catholic, had to convert to Protestantism to inherit from his uncle. He was morally torn by this obligation and his mother, the Austrian Princess Odescalchi, felt great sorrow over it. She spent the rest of her life thinking her son risked eternal damnation and feared that she would not to be able to be with him in heaven.

Wilhelm was a diplomat, mostly in St Petersburg and London. He was part of the Prince of Wales's (the future King Edward VII) inner circle and shared with him a fancy for gambling. From the English, he adopted their taste for bathrooms and had a dozen of them installed in the Görlsdorf castle. He had another passion: horse breeding. He created the Görlsdorf stud which was among the most important in Germany. Whilst in the Army, he had had an orderly called Schläfke, who had once saved his life. Together they discussed horses endlessly. Wilhelm had promised Schläfke that he would hire him if ever he started to breed horses. About 12 years later Wilhelm created his stud. Having lost contact with Schläfke, he put an advertisement in the newspaper and . . . Schläfke reported to him on the next day. My grandfather put him in charge of the stud and kept him and his family permanently.

Back in Berlin, Wilhelm married Marie Caroline, daughter of Prince Lichnowsky. The Lichnowskys were an old and very wealthy family, possessing huge estates located in Upper Silesia, where Germany, Poland and Czechoslovakia met. They were Austrian subjects until Frederick the Great of Prussia took Silesia away from the Austrian empress, Maria Theresa. They were elevated to the rank of prince in 1773.

Prince Karl Lichnowsky (1761–1814) and his whole family had an intimate association with Ludwig van Beethoven and Karl helped the composer in every possible way, taking him into his Vienna palace for years as well as into his castle in Silesia.

Beethoven had a very hot temper. One evening, in the presence of French officers of the Napoleonic army, guests of Karl, he went into a fit of rage, left the house and walked through pouring rain to the nearest town – some 14 kilometres away. Karl went after him in a carriage and finally overtook him, but had the greatest difficulty in persuading him to come back home.

Prince Felix (1814–1848), a good-looking young man with a full black beard, was known as an expert at driving carriages. He once made a bet: he boasted he could drive the left back wheel of a mail coach drawn by six horses over a *thaler* – a rather small Prussian coin – and won.

Felix was one of the very few aristocratic members of the first German parliament in 1848, in Frankfurt, very much on the reactionary side. One day, after the revolution broke out in September of that year, he went on an inspection tour of the troops who were fighting the insurgents. He was pulled off his horse by the populace, beaten to a pulp and shot dead.

Prince Karl-Max, whose sister was my grandmother, served in the same regiment of the Guard as Prince Wilhelm who was later to become Emperor Wilhelm II. They had a close relationship until 1914, the Emperor insisting that Karl-Max be sent to London as ambassador in 1912. Wilhelm I often attended the shoots on the Lichnowsky's estate in Silesia.

On Karl-Max's arrival in London, as he was being driven in a state coach drawn by four horses to present the British King with his credentials, the horses bolted and the official carriage, with my great-uncle inside, stayed in the gutter with not much style left. Some police officers came to his rescue and obliged by taking the place of the horses. It was in this undignified fashion that Prince Lichnowsky made his first visit to Buckingham Palace.

Karl-Max hoped to be able to improve relations between Germany and Britain and was convinced that he could prevent war between the two countries. Indeed he suceeded in smoothing matters quickly and he had an excellent understanding with Grey, the Foreign Secretary. Harold Nicolson said that almost never before had a foreign diplomat won so much trust and sympathy in so short a time. Karl-Max deeply believed that Britain would have liked nothing better than to live with Germany in good neighbourly relations. Unfortunately, all his endeavours were to no avail because, as he states in his memoirs, 'Berlin would not let him'.

When Karl-Max returned to Germany after the outbreak of the war, the Emperor and his entourage accused him of being a traitor to the German cause. He was made the black sheep of Anglo-German relations. When a memorandum about the causes of the Great War which he had written for the exclusive use of himself and a few trusted friends, became public during the war, through an indiscretion, and was then used by the *entente* in their propaganda against Germany, he was finished. He became a social outcast and had to endure the indignity of leaving the Prussian House of Lords. Until his death at the age of 68, he made every effort to re-establish his good reputation but couldn't achieve it. Thus, one of the few far-sighted German diplomats of that era, who foresaw the dangers of a great European conflict, died a broken man.

*

Wilhelm and Marie Caroline, my grandparents, had four daughters and only one son, named Wilhelm after his father, and known as Bubi. The Redern children were born and raised in the Berlin palace. Later, because of the difficulties encountered in modernising their residence, they settled permanently in Görlsdorf and sold their palace to Lorenz Adlon who had the venerable house demolished and built the Hotel Adlon on the site. The Kaiser, wanting to have in Berlin the most luxurious hotel in Europe, favoured the enterprise. My mother recorded for me a little about her childhood:

> I was born in the old Redern palace. The house contained numerous big halls richly decorated. The garden – which was more of a park – included a tennis court. We siblings spent a large part of our youth in those grounds and I cherish the memories I have from that happy time.
>
> To either side of the main entrance was a niche and in one of them, my great-uncle – my grandfather's brother – often used to sit. He would talk with a lot of people who passed by. The old man knew everybody and was very popular, almost revered.
>
> When I was a child, I could watch the procession of foreign visiting monarchs who passed our residence on their way to the royal palace from one of the house's terraces. I remember the first visit of Emperor Franz Joseph of Austria, since the Austro-Prussian war of 1866. That visit sealed the alliance between Germany and Austria. Our first emperor, the old Wilhelm I, was a very modest, unpretentious man, much liked by his people. At that time there were no bathrooms in the royal palace. When the Emperor felt like taking a bath, a bathtub was brought over from the nearby Hotel Reichshof. When the passers-by saw the cart with the tub driven down the Unten den Linden avenue, they nodded their head and acknowledged: 'The Emperor is taking a bath to-day!'

Bubi, an officer in the prestigious regiment of the Garde du Corps, was killed in August 1914 at the battle of Ypres. The exceptional clause in the entail, which had not even waited more than a generation to apply, fell on his sister Victoria, my mother. She was the eldest of the girls and inherited the entire fortune. She was 25 years old at the time. It was always a sorrow for Marie Caroline to see her daughter in the place of her darling Bubi and I think that my mother always felt guilty about it.

In 1917, Victoria married Ernst, Prince zu Lynar. By special decree the Emperor allowed the fusion of the names and titles of the two families to keep the Redern name alive and henceforth my father would be known as Prince zu Lynar, Count von Redern.

Around 1922, following the creation of the republic, my mother decided to dissolve the entailed estate so that she could give land and property to her sisters as well as to a cousin whom she hardly knew but who bore the name Redern. Here is what she wrote about the matter:

In the early 1920s, a law was passed which commanded the dissolution of the entailed estate at the death of the last owner. But those who would dissolve their entailed estate voluntarily before that would have the right to include their agnates in their sharing. As I thought it extremely unfair for my sisters to have nothing while I had everything, I decided on voluntary dissolution. Thus my sisters each got a good estate and a share of forest and I could still give land to relatives of the secondary lineage. There remained for me nonetheless more than enough and the Emperor gave me – with his usual tactfulness – the nickname of 'Grand Prize of Brandenburg'.

Unfortunately, it was one catastrophe on a world-wide scale that gave me my fortune, it was another one which took it away from me.

I was in Berlin in 1918 for the birth of my first child when the revolution began. There was no organised resistance by the authorities and chaos promptly set in. From the window of my mother's house, I could see the soldiers tear off epaulettes and decorations from officers' uniforms. My mother, my sisters and I were sitting together like a flock of intimidated chickens when suddenly a canon-bullet hit the entrance gate. We thought this was the end for us, when our old Polish butler came in to comfort us, an empty bottle in his hand: 'Em'ty pottle on rraight place on 'ead!' he said proudly, waving the bottle in a threatening gesture . . .

I was so happy cuddling my baby that all these events, even the flight of the Emperor to Holland, did not make too strong an impact on me, I'm afraid. I was glad that the war was over and that my husband didn't have to return to the front, whereas he was in despair over the political situation. When the *Kapp-putsch* surged (a weak attempt at revolution in 1920 from the right to re-establish the monarchy), he was full of enthusiasm. He boarded the train from Görlsdorf to Berlin, staying at the Hotel Bristol. When he left the hotel in the evening, a bullet shot by a sniper narrowly missed his head and killed a girl who was standing behind him.

A general strike was declared shortly after and signalled the end of the revolution.

My husband's mood was gloomy. On top of the political failure, he had to clean up his hotel room himself as there were no servants in sight during the strike!

General von Lüttwitz, to whom Ernst had been an aide-de-camp during the war, had been one of the leaders of the *Kapp-putsch* and therefore had to flee. Ernst offered him the loan of Glambeck, a small manor house located in our forest. I was fuming! My husband would be exposed to the worst difficulties if the police ever found out whom he was sheltering. I had to give the general a young maid to attend him who had never seen him on one of his earlier visits to Görlsdorf.

During this time inflation was galloping so fast that you had to do your shopping in the morning as prices would double in the afternoon. Our employees were paid daily, then rushed to the shop to get rid of the money. One businessman in Berlin had to receive an important sum of cash. It represented so much paper money that he couldn't carry it and he had to put it in a wheelbarrow. He went to buy one but by the time he had found it and paid for it, he had no more money left. The exchange rate of the US dollar went up from 18 thousand marks for one dollar in January 1923 to 40 billion marks in October of the same year. The old mark was then declared obsolete and a new one was created. Against all expectations it became a satisfactory hard currency.

Whereas the economy and the cultural life were blooming in the '20s, the political situation was catastrophic. Private armies of the pre-eminent political parties fought constantly in near civil war confrontations, strikes paralysed the economy, governments rose and fell every couple of months, and it was a terrible period in history. Then came the world economic depression, triggered by the American crash on Wall Street. More than five million people were out of work in Germany alone.

The national disarray led to the rise of Adolf Hitler. He vowed to rebuild Germany into a prosperous and respected nation and to put an end to the unemployment. I, myself, was seduced in the beginning by his promises to reshape our country without a war. We loved our fatherland and hoped it would regain its place in the community of the nations. It took me a few years to reach a frightful awakening when I realised that everything Hitler said was a pack of lies as he was, in fact, preparing for a new war.

Our religion – my father was a Protestant, my mother a Catholic – complicated matters enormously for us all. The Catholic Church is known for its severity regarding the children in a mixed marriage: they must be brought up as Catholics with the threat of excommunication for the

Catholic parent if this is not the case. There was an exception for Prussia because the Prussian State was of strongly Protestant faith and an officer who raised his sons as Catholics would be expelled from the army.

The head of a princely family was usually the protector of the churches on his estate. As he had a certain influence on the choice of the parsons, he could not be a Catholic. The Pope therefore made a concession to Prussia: in aristocratic families of mixed religions, the boys could be Protestants but the girls had to be Catholics.

Thus, my brother and I were taken to the church in the village for the Lutheran service while my mother and my sisters attended mass five miles away. I believed for a long time that it was the same in every family. My son is the first Catholic Lynar, the papal concession having been terminated and my wife being a Catholic.

When my brother was born in 1924, the local Catholic priest came to visit my mother and said, with a twisted smile: 'Oh, now we will soon have a baptism in my church!' My mother answered that she had promised at her wedding that her sons would be of Protestant faith and that the Church had given its consent. However, the local church administration contested this agreement. (It was a matter where money was involved because in Germany you pay an income tax for the Church of your faith. My brother, being the future heir, weighed a heavy load from a financial point of view.) Mother stood her ground and endured excommunication for a while until the case was brought to the Vatican Court of Justice, which ruled in her favour.

I used to ask my mother to tell me about life at court, as she remembered it. Seated at her feet in her sitting-room, I browsed through the photo albums while she was talking and I dreamt about all those people with decorations I had in front of my eyes. They would become alive with Mother's stories, some of which I later asked her to put in writing. Here is an example of what she wrote:

> In January the presentation of the families who constituted the court to the imperial couple took place. The ladies had a train nine to 12 feet long – my mother's was of velvet with silver brocade. After her death, I had a chasuble made out of it for the priest in Angermünde. I suppose it is still in the church. So attired, we would come, one after the other, up to their Majesties and make a deep curtsy.
>
> In the winter, we would go to the different court balls. Only old-fashioned dances such as the carré, the lancier and the French were played and, at the beginning of the ball, the Emperor and the Empress made what was known as the 'circle'. The Emperor would pass among the guests on one side, the Empress among the guests on

the opposite side. As the Kaiser stopped often to chat, the Empress, who was less exuberant, would be through with her circle long before him. She would then sit down on her throne and calmly wait for him. She was a very gentle person and a good mother.

My mother, as a countess, ranked relatively low at the court. So the Empress, who liked her dearly, gave her the title of 'Lady of the Palace'. She was given an enormous, atrocious brooch, which ruined every dress to her despair. My father had a higher rank as a member of the House of Lords and so had my husband and I, as prince and princess.

The social season opened in January. The first thing my mother, my sisters and I did was to take a carriage and go from one friend to another handing a visiting card to the butler at the door, without entering, as a sign that the family was back in town. One corner of the card had to be folded and you had to deliver it personally. No one would dare send a servant to deliver the visiting card – that would have been considered terribly ill mannered. It was a dreary assignment, especially if you consider that in January it was very cold outside, very often snowing and we were freezing in the carriage, not daring to move while my mother was with us. But as soon as she climbed down to ring a bell, we four sisters would poke at one another and wrestle gently to warm up. That was fun.

Our family doctor was the imperial family's doctor. When my sisters caught the scarlet fever, the Empress forbade the doctor to visit them for fear of infection. But the doctor, who was devoted to us, came all the same . . . at night.

In certain matters Empress Augusta-Victoria was very strict. For instance she would never have accepted a divorced lady in her presence and she did not allow the modern waltz in the imperial palace. On the other hand, quite unexpectedly, she demanded that the dresses of the ladies received at the court would be low cut and show the shoulders.

Guests at dinner usually sat at small tables. Pity the one who was a slow eater or was served last. He was at risk of having his plate taken away almost untouched for no one could go on eating when the Emperor had finished his meal. The Kaiser was served first and ate very fast.

After dinner, the young people would rush to the ballroom to dance the modern steps before the arrival of the Empress.

I was at the Court during Edward VII's visit to Germany. He could not stand the sight of the Kaiser. My father proudly presented my sisters and me to Queen Alexandra and we stole a few glances at her, as our education did not allow us much room for rudeness. She wore a wax mask on her face to hide her wrinkles. It was so tight she could not even smile at us. During that time Edward VII was seated on a throne, sulking, dressed in a Prussian hussar uniform which was too tight for him (at that time, heads of state on official visits wore the Army uniform of the country they were visiting).

My father, who had a great time while he was a diplomat in London, had often played cards with Edward VII when he was Prince of Wales. One day he won a big sum of money from the prince. On the next day, the Prince of Wales sent him an autographed photo instead of the money.

I was present when the Emperor gave his only daughter, Victoria-Louise, in marriage to the Duke of Brunswick, in 1914. At the end of the festivities, I was in the reception room and had a good look at all the monarchs of Europe – Tsar Nicolas II, the Kings of Britain, Belgium, Italy, etc. They were all there, chatting carelessly away. Nobody could have suspected that a few months later they would fight in a cruel war against one another. Queen Mary, who had had enough, called to her husband with a trumpeting voice: 'Come along, George!'

My younger sisters were often invited to see Princess Victoria-Louise when she was a young girl. Each time, a carriage from the court was sent to our house to drive them to the palace. My sisters didn't like the princess at all and tried every trick in the book to avoid going. So, when the butler answered the telephone and said 'Bellevue' (that was the name of the palace where the princess lived), both my sisters rushed out through the rear door and shouted: 'We are not at home!'

My recollections of my youth are very happy. We had a very cosy and closely bonded family life. I adored my father; we had beautiful homes surrounded by majestic trees and countless flowers. I trained as a nurse so, when the Great War started, I was immediately called upon to serve in a military hospital putting an end to that pleasant life. I shall never forget the moment when I saw my first wounded soldier. He had a deep wound in his throat. The thought that this dreadful hole had been inflicted on his body by another human being appalled me.

We always had a number of governesses. Sometimes there were three at a time, one English, one French, one German. We had to speak with each one in her own language as they were picked purposely because they did not know one word of another language but their own. This way, we learnt French and English. They generally couldn't stand one another and were bickering all the time.

I, being the eldest of their pupils, had to play the go-between to try and settle the argument.

My father was enormously interested in politics and was friends with numerous political personalities. Thus I remember Kiderlen-Wächter, the Home Secretary, von Bethmann-Hollweg, later Chancellor (prime minister) and Herbert von Bismarck, son of the Iron Chancellor. They were frequent dinner guests when we were in Berlin and came up to our bedrooms when it was time for us to go to bed and told us bedtime stories. Bismarck looked very much like his famous father (he was foreign secretary in his own right). With his powerful stature, his bulging eyes and bushy eyebrows, he personified the villain I read about in my childhood books.

In 1936, Mother went to Puetzchen, in Rhineland, where Milli and Meggi, my two eldest sisters, were boarders in the Sacred Heart convent for girls. She came to get her daughters and take them along to Doorn, in the Netherlands, to introduce them to the ex-Emperor, Wilhelm II. She planned to do the same thing with her other children in the future but the war prevented that.

Beforehand, Mother had solicited this audience with the one she forever called 'the Emperor' and promptly received an invitation from him.

The imperial residence in Doorn was of average dimensions, simple, charming, surrounded by moats. A butler greeted my mother and sisters and led them to a drawing-room where the Empress Hermine, Wilhelm II's second wife, born Princess Reuss, widow of Prince Schanaich-Carolath, greeted them. She was holding a red rose in one hand and extended the other to my mother, leading her, still escorted by my sisters, into a bedroom. She laid the rose on the bed, saying: 'For the Empress'. Empress Hermine was a modest woman and when she said 'the Empress', it was always to her husband's first wife that she referred.

Empress Hermine was a heavy woman, 30 years younger than her husband. My sisters kissed her hand without curtsying, which awarded them later a serious telling-off from my mother.

After taking possession of their rooms and settling down, they went down to the drawing-room where the Emperor greeted them. Milli and Meggi noticed the attachment Mother showed towards her ex-sovereign and the joy that she felt at seeing him again.

After dinner there were only three to four guests apart from my mother and sisters. After the meal, everyone sat in front of the fireplace and knitting *ouvrages* were distributed around!

The malformation of the Emperor's arm was quite visible although he tried to hide it. He was calm, pleasant, very different to the abrupt, curt, rigid militarist he was before 1918 – a perfect grandfather. There was talk of politics. It was the year when the Italians had a war going against Ethiopia and had chased away Haile Selassie, the Ethiopian King of Kings. 'He had the same fate I had!' said Wilhelm II in a sombre tone. The Kaiser was then a silent and sad man. His wife, although not very bright or witty, was nonetheless very solicitous and good with him.

My mother and sisters took their leave the next day, after a walk in the park with the Emperor who was adamantly intent in showing off in front of them his talents splitting wood, as he often did in front of his guests. All his life he had made pathetic attempts to prove that he was capable of the physical strain of the mightiest.

Hermann Goering visited the Kaiser in Doorn in May 1932. This visit took place before the rise of Hitler to the top and suggests that the Nazis hoped for a favourable opinion from the Emperor who still maintained quite an influence in certain circles in Germany. However, the Nazis and the Emperor were soon disgruntled with one another.

I had my own experience with the Empress. I was in Berlin with my mother one day to go to the dentist. The dentist had a great reputation but was pitiless where anaesthesia was concerned. In fact, he almost never bothered with it. Mother thought nothing of having a nerve killed without any anaesthetic, while I loudly objected. When we left the torturer's office, we bumped into an elderly, rather plump lady to whom my mother introduced her son. She looked very ordinary so I judged it improper to kiss her hand. Well, presently my mother dropped into a deep curtsy, to my greatest embarrassment. She was the Empress, the second wife of Wilhelm II. Mother didn't speak to me for two days! My sisters had a field day when they were told of the incident, so similar to their own misadventure. I felt that lady should never have taken the risk of going anywhere without a crown on her head.

*

Originally, Görlsdorf was a small, baroque manor, built in the 18th century. On the engraving made around 1850 which I have in my possession, the house sits in the middle of a beautiful park, created by a famous landscape architect, Lennè, with an artificial pond behind the house.

In the second half of the 19th century my grandfather, who thought the house was too small for his use, radically changed its aspect. He added another floor and a huge, hideous winter garden. I suppose that in those times, people needed a lot of space to accommodate their guests if they wanted company in this sparsely inhabited part of Prussia. As there were no trains or motorcars yet, it took a long time to travel even 50 miles. The guests and their servants stayed for at least a few days. One can perhaps understand that they needed help to slip into their formal regalia of uniforms, corsets, dresses and coiffures! So to have at least a dozen guest rooms was necessary. My grandfather added a dozen bathrooms in the '90s and installed the central heating in the first floor only, where the reception rooms were located It was not considered necessary in the bedrooms which were heated by way of stoves made of Dutch tiles. Upon my homecomings during the war, I would enter the house and sniff the particular fragrance generated by a mixture of old wood, ashes from the open fireplaces and incense that was burnt before the big dinner parties. It made me feel safe and happy.

In the last year of the war, while I was with the FLAK (anti-aircraft guns), Mother allowed me to sleep in one of the guest-rooms. It was a treat and I remember, in the winter, being awoken by a servant making a fire in the stove. I stayed cosily in bed (the beds were imported from England and extremely comfortable) and listening to the fire crackling, its glimmer softly illuminating the room. The warmth settled in slowly, crawling to my bed.

The aspect of the house changed a lot after the reconstruction, but the site, the park and the big trees remained. We children loved Görlsdorf and felt a bond with the house, much more so than in Lindenau, my father's house, which was much older and more beautiful.

The walls in Görlsdorf were very damp. In the beginning of the 1930s my mother decided to do something about it. Impressive machines were brought in by the chosen enterprise and began to saw the walls on the outside, at a height of about three feet. I was scarcely more than a toddler at the time but I remember I was struck that the walls of such a big house could be sawn like a regular tree. I was afraid that the wind would take the castle away. Behind the saw came a machine, which put in an isulating layer so that the dampness would not creep up any more inside the walls.

My mother maintained with great care about 20 horse carriages for all kinds of circumstances. The stables for the carriage horses adjoined the castle. We had, among others, an omnibus drawn by two horses that could carry eight or ten passengers and a stagecoach for 20 people. My mother had a passion for horse-drawn carriages. It was just as well for she was the worst of car drivers.

Mother was a real paternalist or rather a maternalist. She was devoted, body and soul, to those who depended on her. My brother, my sisters and

I often felt frustrated for she did not give us any special treatment. There was always someone who needed her more than we did. Come rain or sunshine, herself beaming with good health, she would go and visit the sick, the ones who needed to be comforted or the ones whose birthday was on that particular day. She was quite modern in her outlook. She was the head of a 35,000 acre estate, divided into about 16 agricultural farms employing around 100 people in each and 10,000 acres of forest, and providing a pension at retirement age for the workers, a roof for life and medical care through private medical personnel.

You could always count on Mother, loaded with gifts, at the time of births and birthdays. In Görlsdorf, the grandchildren of the people who had worked for us in the old days still have her framed photograph in their home and she has become a legend.

At Christmas, there was a big party at the castle around a 12-foot high tree, with distribution of presents to each member of the families. I could not sleep the night before, feeling sick with nerves because from the time I was eight years old I had to recite in front of this enormous gathering a long excerpt from the New Testament and I was terrified of getting stuck. Mother never suspected that this duty she herself considered an honour would make me so nervous.

Mother was hard with herself and sometimes with us when it came to principles she would not compromise on. But she always was a marvellous mother whom I adored and who made me forget I didn't have a father.

After the Christmas party for the employees, we children would wait outside the library door, tense and excited. Finally, Mother, ringing a bell, would open the double door. We would rush in but the torture of waiting was not yet over. Before we could have a go at our presents, we still had to sing 'Silent Night, Holy Night'. During the hymn, my eyes would search the room to try and guess which of the tables, every one of them covered with a white cloth, was mine, with all the gifts I had asked for. There was this gigantic Christmas tree, all alight with real candles. It was like a fairytale. Today our children want electronic games, in my time I wanted the usual electric train. I obtained a superb one I would add to at each Christmas. I was rather annoyed with certain uncles of mine who, to show me how it worked, played for hours with my train, thus preventing me from taking possession of it. I resorted to tears sometimes, which embarrassed everybody but me.

Chapter Three

CHILDHOOD

Mother's realm, over which she reigned with an iron hand, was well organised. It was divided into several departments headed by a director who reported to her.

Three heads of staff ran the household: the butler, the cook and the housekeeper. The butler, unlike in England where the butler rules over all the servants, headed only the valets. The cook had two or three assistants to help in the kitchen area. The housekeeper oversaw the chambermaids and was responsible for the linen, the guest-rooms and the cleaning of the whole house.

On the top floor were the large bedroom of the housekeeper, several bedrooms for the young chambermaids and for our tutors. The servants and attendants who slept in the house were all single; the other ones lived in the village with their families and commuted back and forth. Usually, however, they preferred to apply for another kind of work, which required less hours of presence although often more demanding.

When I was a little boy, the housekeeper impressed me as she always wore, fastened to her belt, a huge ring with the keys of every room in the house dangling from it. She told me a story I listened to with wide eyes:

A young bride asked her grandmother what she should do to have a well organised household to please her husband. The old lady gave her a box sculpted in a precious wood and told her to carry it around the house to every room, every day. She should never, ever open the box. The young lady complied and carried her box as she had been told, every day, to every room in her house, until she was so old and crippled she couldn't move around any more. She had maintained perfectly her household while she was able, to the great satisfaction of the large family she had produced. When she couldn't handle her chores any more, she gave way to her lifelong curiosity and opened the magic box. It was empty. She understood then what was the secret: visiting each room every day had allowed her to check and attend to every corner of her household.

The princess has been given the magic box, but shush . . . she must never know what you and I know.

She swore me to secrecy and I believed her for years as my mother attended personally to everything, even counting the huge piles of linen with the housekeeper.

The maids generally came from families who worked for us in one or other of our villages. For them it was a good job, not too strenuous, and they lived in much better conditions than at home. They all wore the same uniform, red for every day, black for formal occasions. They had a special bond with my mother who treated them a bit like her own children. There was affection between them and us much more than among themselves where some rivalry was always involved. The girls would always ask my mother's permission when they wanted to marry. In fact, although it looked like asking for permission, it was planning their future that they all had in mind. They could thus reorganise together the assignments, the living conditions, the wedding ceremony. Mother's personal chambermaid married George, the valet and while her husband was still fighting in the war, she came along with us on our flight. Her five year-old son was sitting very close to my mother in the tractor and once or twice complained loudly: 'Highneth, don't puth me!'

We children called the butler 'Mr Ehrentraut' while my mother addressed him by his first name, Alfred. Although he was already rather old, he waited on us at table, attended the guests as well and was responsible for the silver, the china and the wine cellar. He had two or three younger valets under his command. In that department, also, my mother made a yearly audit, comparing a huge list with the stock of silver, china and wine. It was not out of suspicion but rather to check on the repairs for the silver, replacements for the china and glasses and to make a note of the wines which had to be drunk or stored and the ones which had to be ordered. Every evening after dinner, Ehrentraut came in with a slip of paper on which he had noted the bottles that had been drunk during the day. Mother scribbled 'FSTLR' on the slip (abbreviation for Princess Lynar-Redern). We teased her about that name we tried to pronounce: 'efssstttlllrrrr'!

The head gardener was in charge of the vegetable and fruit garden which was to provide its products for the 25 to 30 people who lived in the house as well as for the care of the park and its flowers and lawns. Four or five young men assisted him and if they were still unmarried, they ate at the house with the servants. Mother was careful to avoid amorous relationships between her young maids and married men and was secretly happy, I presume, to see the sparkles in the glances the young people would steal from one another or romances blossoming. There were several hothouses to shelter the flowers that grew there during the winter. We also grew melons and grapes, which was quite an accomplishment as in our region we had plenty of snow and temperatures down to -30°C.

We were not allowed to enter the hothouses and for me the order was enforced as I had been diagnosed as having an allergy to one species of flower inside. I frequently roamed the area, waiting for one of my sisters or my friends to come around and then tried to persuade them to go in and get me the fruit I wanted. On the other hand, we had permission to eat all the different kinds of berries that grew in the garden. They were not sprayed with insecticides, pesticides or any of those substances the modern world has devised so it was not necessary to wash them before eating them. We loved to gather and eat them on the spot – juicy and warm from the sun.

In the stables, adjacent to the house, reigned Mr Kohlmorgen, the riding master. There were always four or five riding horses. We all rode, except the youngest of my sisters, Netti, who was afraid of riding.

There was Bella, Mother's horse, reserved for her sole use, as it was the only mount that could be ridden side-saddle. This way of riding has now almost disappeared but it was very pleasant-looking. The special saddle had a big protruding bump on one side. The lady's attire consisted of a long black skirt, white corsage with cravat, boots, bowler hat, gloves and stick. She was heaved onto her saddle by some helping hand, put her legs on each side of the bump so that they were on the same side of the horse, the leg in front being slightly bent.

Then there was Perle, a tall half-breed, for my elder sisters and Snow White, my pony. My brother, being away at school most of the time, had to make do with whichever horse was available when he was home.

Kohlmorgen had a coachman under his command, assigned to drive the carriages and the carts for all sorts of chores in the park and the garden. On special occasions, when Mother went on a drive with guests, Kohlmorgen was on the box, dressed in full regalia – light-brown livery with matching top hat. His long whip straight up in his right hand, he sat proudly, motionless, waiting for the party to be helped up into his coach.

Petrol was not available for private use during the war and we had to resort to horse-drawn carriages. But even before the wartime restrictions, we used the horses a lot, as the dirt tracks in the fields or the rides in the forests were unpaved, therefore impracticable for motorcars.

Mother drove her one-horse carriage every day to go to her office and let herself be driven by the coachman in a two-horse carriage to check the fields and the forest. She took me along sometimes, which I didn't particularly like – except if we went into the forest – because she took advantage of my inability to escape to give me a lecture on agricultural management and that bored me stiff. She often asked me in a stern voice to name the species of cereals we passed. In the summer, when the grain was tall, the answer came easily, but in the spring, how on earth could I know when there were only a few sparse and thin tufts barely showing? I then got the dressing-down I dreaded: I should follow the example of Ernst Wilhelm who apparently was much more interested in agriculture than I was, and was *so* good at naming plants. 'So be it,' I would mumble bitterly. 'But Ernst Wilhelm is four years older than me!'

'You're just jealous and incompetent,' she said cruelly if I had committed the crime of being careless about agricultural matters. In fact, she often forgot the age difference in her desire for me to know everything concerning the estate.

The garage was next to the stables. My mother and father each had their personal car and, as my sisters were still too young to drive before the war, we had a large family car, a Maybach. It was a huge limousine, which could carry eight passengers and had a 12-cylinder engine, the same that was used in zeppelins. Heating did not exist in European cars at the time, so in winter you had to be smothered in fur coats and blankets. The Americans, having a more practical side to them, were quick to discover that the engine could easily heat up the car as well as make it move.

Opposite the garage was the coach-house with about 20 carriages – some of them 100 or more years old – all in good working condition and looking impeccable. It was a favourite playground for my friends and me. We sat solemnly in the different carriages and pretended to drive to see the emperor, all dressed up in the grandest uniforms made out of the rags we could set our hands on. I always insisted on having a patch over on my left eye, whatever the uniform, whatever the colour of the patch and on being called Roch, identifying with my ugly-looking ancestor and hoping to scare my friends as much as he had scared me glaring down from his portrait. In fact, to my secret despair, my pals laughed their heads off when they saw me with a green or multicoloured patch over an eye that sneaked out bleary and red when the ill-adjusted patch fell off.

The stud played a major role at Görlsdorf, particularly for my mother and Buttel. My sister had inherited from our grandfather, who created the stud, a passion for horse breeding. Mother and Buttel made almost daily visits to the stud and discussed with the manager the development of the yearlings, the foaling of the mares, auctions, etc. I sometimes went along but grew bored after a while with that endless babbling. They knew at least 40 horses by name, plus their descendants and recognised them immediately at first glance. I was content to watch the horses canter around the paddocks and then be guided into their boxes at night, always two to a man. I would go into the stables filled with their soothing smell and listen to them munching and snorting,

When I was still a little boy and as soon as I could understand that Görlsdorf would be mine one day, I magnanimously told Buttel she would be manager of the stud. So, later, when I saw her so immersed in everything concerning the stud, I always felt secure that she would stay with me for the rest of our days. After my father's death, my mother stopped training horses and running them under our own name, and concentrated on breeding only.

The most important part of Mother's responsibilities was the general administration. Her office was located in a large manor house in Greiffen-berg, a small town, four kilometres away. Mr Schoch, the general manager, was a living symbol of honesty and correctness. He had in him all the good qualities of the old-time Prussian civil servant.

Mr Schoch had been with the Rederns since before the First World War and was entirely devoted to the family. He was trusted to the point of having general power of attorney; that is to say, he theoretically had power to sell the whole estate without informing the owner. There was only one shortcoming: he was not very modern and didn't know a thing about agriculture or forestry (he was the boss in those departments as well) and was steadfastly against any change. Apart from book-keeping, Mother had more knowledge than he had about every department of her estate and she must have felt frustrated at times as she liked to make improvements and understood the need for them. However, she left him in charge until he retired, at the age of 65. He was given a considerable pension that was paid entirely by Mother's pension fund, as were the pensions of everyone who had been on her pay roll. Mr Schoch was not a member of the state pension system. He lived in the manor house, which also housed the offices of the administration, with his wife and two daughters, in spacious quarters. He was always very stern, almost solemn, but I was so used to him that I didn't even try to avoid him. I considered him more or less as a familiar piece of furniture and never listened to what he said until one day when he said to Mother in my presence: 'And how is your eldest, His Highness Prince Ernst-Wilhelm, the *good* child?'

Mr Schoch's wife and daughters were rather haughty and put on airs, availing themselves of Mr Schoch's position. That is probably why the daughters remained single. No postulant was good enough for them.

When finally Mr Schoch retired, Mother hired a new general manager, Mr Koch. She made sure he had a degree in agriculture and was very much in on the latest improvements in this field. Mr Koch was so efficient that Mother had no difficulty, after the war, in obtaining an equivalent position for him from friends of hers in Schleswig-Holstein.

When he took charge at Görlsdorf as general manager, my mother changed the organisation to ensure that Mr Koch would be responsible for the agriculture department and Mr Marquardt, the chief forester, for the forest department. Mother had the overall supervision and she held her part with the utmost energy.

We administered entirely only four of the sixteen farms we had – between 1,500 and 3,000 acres each – the other ones were leased. Mother tried in vain to take back a few of the leased ones but, as the tenants had been on the land for generations, it was near to impossible to terminate a contract, especially as the farmers made a very good living.

Every one of the four farms under our own administration was headed by a farm manager, himself a learned agriculturist. The farm buildings were very big as we had large numbers of cattle and many horses. Most of the labour in the fields was still done with horses that drew the plough. I have in my possession a list which shows that on one of the farms, there were 109 horses, 248 head of cattle, 1,200 sheep and 850 pigs!

Until the First World War, our estate was very profitable. After the revolution in 1918, there were great changes in the German economy. It became more liberal; there was more competition in the agricultural field with foreign countries for the international market. The salaries rose but the profits did not and the financial situation took a nose-dive ten years later with the world-wide economic crisis. Costs rose sky-high and the payment of pensions became an enormous burden. So, in the '20s and early '30s, our net income went down substantially. Mother decreed her own austerity plan, which she applied for two years. She packed up the whole household, including four or five servants and the house-teacher, closed the castle and transferred the lot to the Swiss mountains where we stayed in a chalet. I don't know whether she or anyone ever compared the costs but I don't think it resulted in saving much! But we enjoyed skiing.

On 6 December, St Nicholas' day, St Nicholas himself (usually Mother's secretary) paid us a visit, in full Father Christmas regalia, complete with white beard and bag full of toys. In Switzerland, the custom was slightly different. On the first occasion, I was four years old, Mother's secretary was in Görlsdorf and she was too busy to take such routine matters in her own hands. So we were graced with a visit by St Nicholas. All right, but his costume was pure white instead of red with white fur adornments and he had Crampus in tow. Crampus, according to the Swiss tradition, is the devil. He was dressed in a hide with long black hair, had big, bright green eyes and two long red horns were protruding out of his head, as if they were incandescent. He carried two long, thick chains, which he shook, growling that he would use them to tie the bad children and take them along with him. Never having a clear conscience, even at that age, I was petrified and remained deadly silent for a second, then my shrieks of terror must have alarmed the whole neighbourhood. Crampus exited, more shocked than even I was. What a dreadful experience!

The depression receded and by 1932 it was over. But my father died two years later and although our finances were in better shape, Mother cut down drastically on her social life. She never stopped having the house full of guests, however.

*

I hated eating when I was small. Therefore I was very thin and was mockingly called 'Gandhi' by my sisters who switched to *Käschen* 'little cheese' when I began to be very pale in the face. I grew weak and was carried around in the park in a little cart instead of being allowed to walk and run. I remember having in my hand the toast I was supposed to have eaten at breakfast and wasn't allowed to leave. I constantly offered my piece of soggy toast to anyone coming along but had no success, not even with the dogs. I threw the toast once or twice in front of them but they just sniffed it, looked at me with reproach and were off. I was scolded, had to pick up the toast again and wait for the next catch.

It was declared that I needed a change in climate. My father decided we should spend two months in the Mediterranean climate and thus spare me (him?) the cold German winter. He left in reconnaissance and we followed by train, Mother, Buttel (who pouted at the prospect) and me. In Marseilles, France, we took a boat to Palma de Mallorca. My father was there to greet us, a tall figure on the waterfront. He came along to the small boarding-house Mother had chosen (she was still on her savings plan) and declared: 'This island has no trees, bushes or flowers, it's as bare as the palm of my hand. I'm not going to stay here.' And off he went on the next day, leaving us three behind.

There was practically no tourism on Mallorca in those days, and our boarding-house was the only one in the village of Cala Radjada. Today there are endless hotels and crowds of tourists there and Palma's airport is the busiest in Europe during the summer.

Foreign currency in the '30s was extremely difficult to obtain in Germany and by the time we had to come back home, Mother was very short of cash and so we had just enough money to book two bunks on the Marseilles – Berlin train. Buttel and I had to share the same bunk. We slept, as Mother directed, in the opposite direction. That was all right for Buttel because I was small but I had to spend the night with her feet in my face. Anyway, from that time on I started to develop a huge appetite and I am not too grateful for it. When my son was at the same age I was then he said to me: 'Daddy, is there no way to become strong and big without eating? Life would be so wonderful if we (!) didn't have to eat!'; I didn't raise an eyebrow. I knew his appetite would all too soon match mine.

Life at home, after my father passed away, was simple, especially compared with the style my great-uncle and my grandfather had maintained. It was due in a large extent to the fact that my mother didn't care much for entertaining on a grand scale for herself alone. The men in my family had always served as diplomats until they inherited family homes. They had to live in the capital cities of Europe, in prominent social circles. When they retired, they lived half of the year in their house in Berlin where they entertained a great deal. Mother was quite content to live as a country squire on her own estate, surrounded by her friends and children. We lived comfortably, in a big house, attended by many servants but definitely not in the style of certain South German princes, who maintained an army of footmen in livery, even after World War II.

My daily routine included lessons with my tutor at home and in town for my Latin classes, homework, and sports. I was too young to take my meals with the grown-ups so I ate alone with some governess. I got to see Mother in her drawing-room after dinner when she was alone, and played with my toys in her presence for an hour or so while she went about, listening to the radio. Mother retired early as she got up at dawn so I was asked to hop into bed when I felt I should have been allowed to play for at least two hours more.

We very often had relatives visiting, mostly Mother's sisters and their families, as they lived near by. The house was then filled with playmates for me and the atmosphere was merry. Later, when my eldest sisters were grown-ups, there were parties for them and they invited their friends from Berlin for weekends. A lot of sporting activities were involved: tennis – we had a court in the park – swimming, riding, and bicycling. During the war, the house was often full of young officers – flirts and friends of my sisters.

We had the shooting as well. Many old friends of my parents were invited during the rutting-season of the stag and spotted deer. The house filled with guests and the daily schedule was changed: a first breakfast at 5 a.m. was followed by another one at 10 a.m. after the stalking. Everybody was again back home for lunch and back to the woods after siesta until 9 p.m. Dinner was at 10 in the evening.

In winter, we had many guests for the deer and wild boar hunting. The dinner parties were the big events and I witnessed them only from my watching post, crouched up the staircase. The ladies wore long dresses and displayed sparkling jewels; the men were in dinner jackets. The reception rooms were brightly illuminated, the dining-room table was beautifully set and the candles blinked softly in their silver candelabra. The fragrance of incense, perfumes, flowers and wood burning in the open chimneys was intoxicating and contributed to the festive atmosphere. I observed all the goings-on including the ballet of the servants passing cocktails and the guests being introduced. I tried to take in everything so that I would be a perfect host in times to come.

Every now and then, we took the family car and descended on Berlin like a flock of ravens on a cherry tree. Sometimes it was only for the day – a one-and-a-half hour journey only thanks to the short-cut through our own gate to the highway. Sometimes we overnighted in the town in a small hotel on the Kurfürstendamm. I loved those trips when the dentist was not the target. I liked the hustle and the noise of the great city, going to the restaurant, sleeping in a hotel bedroom . . . Mother's lawyers, doctors, dentists were all in Berlin. In Görlsdorf, we had only Dr Brown, a general practitioner. He was a friendly middle-aged man and had an enormous paunch. We called him when we had a cold and he arrived in a one-horse buggy. I don't think he ever prescribed anything more sophisticated than aspirin but his presence had a soothing effect on Mother and us.

When I was around seven or eight years old, during our two-year sojourn in Lindenau, four of us six children caught scarlet fever and the house looked like the quarantine department of a hospital. My sister Netti and I, who were not sick, were not allowed to enter the rooms of the others. However, as they were treated to much better food than we were, I often sneaked into their quarters to eat what was left on their trays. I never caught the disease.

Buttel caught diphtheria on top of the scarlet fever. She was transported to the hospital and for a week hovered between life and death. Mother made her usual vow in times of anguish: not to smoke for an entire year if Buttel recovered. Buttel survived and we all suffered when we saw the distressed glance Mother stole at her cigarette box after the meals.

Life was peaceful at home. However, we had such a big household that it needed a team of about 20 people, under the direction of a butler. I recall that on the servants' floor, in front of the strong room, there was almost permanently a valet polishing the silverware which was my great-great uncle's and was engraved with the Redern coat of arms. My grandfather had brought it along from his Berlin palace. Before a big gathering, this valet would make a round of the house with a pan filled with incense that would spread a mysterious and intoxicating perfume.

I was fascinated to see him rub with such application objects already so clean and shiny. They would become instantly powdered white and tarnished. He would polish them with a choice of different pieces of cloth, then put the objects carefully back in the place assigned to them in the strongroom. I used to think he was the best of us all because he would not cheat although he must have been half-dead with boredom. He was the one I would try to get to come and play with me. But as he usually refused, I would stay less with him than with the older servants because he didn't know how to tell me stories as they did, didn't have their patience and never gave me any sweets. Besides, I hated the sulphuric smell of the liquid polish that would bite my nose.

The forest was one mile away from the castle and at the mating season, I would go to sleep listening to the roar of the stags calling one another to the fight. I closed my eyes and felt I was one of the animals wandering in the woods. I smelt the damp, sweet scent of moss and the leaves cracked smoothly under my hooves as I imagined I was a stag. If I imagined I was an owl then I plunged from my branch sweeping the air softly with my heavy wings in a velvety whisper.

I was put on a horse, as my siblings had been, when I was five and I was given a pony mare. As she was white like snow and as I knew the tale I called her . . . Snow White. Snow White seemed gigantic to me then. She had a very hot temper, as ponies often have, and wouldn't allow anyone but me on her back. When the riding master insisted on trying to ride her, she sent him flying to the ground, to his intense humiliation and my shrieks of laughter. Although she shrank as I grew, she stayed always so tall for her breed that I suspect the horse trader to have sold a half-bred pony-giraffe to Mother. Her size allowed me to ride her until we went into exile.

As soon as winter was over, when the bright green grass was already growing between the snow patches, I went for long rides on Snow White, in Mother's company or more frequently with our riding master. The oak and the beech trees were drying their wet branches on my cheeks and my neck, as I brushed past them.

We would occasionally encounter herds of stags, up to 50 animals sometimes. We would stop and observe them at leisure. The wild animals let the horses come very near, even with the riders on their backs. The crows, usually so suspicious, would simply step aside, without taking flight, giving us just the necessary room to pass by, as long as we didn't have a gun, of course. That reminds me of one of our guests, a maharajah of exquisite courtesy, even as far as animals were concerned. He clapped his hands at the shoot, finding it was bad manners to shoot a grazing stag.

To those poetic rides, I preferred by far my bike escapades with my pals from the village, the sons of my mother's employees. We would swim in a lake and cruise in a small rowing-boat when it was summer, or play in the big park where there were several little houses with a hundred eyes inside to spy on us.

When it was winter, we went skiing behind a horse-drawn sleigh, two of us, one on each side of the track. The hissing of the sledge on the snow, the wind whipping our ears, the ringing of the bells on the horse's harness, which gave rhythm to our race, enraptured us. Folded on our skis, clinging desperately to the reins, my buddy and I felt like Olympic champions. When, by misfortune, my numb fingers would let go – the 'enemy' would never remind me to wear gloves – rage, humiliation and despair mixed violently in my heart. I had to bear the scoffing of my rival while the sleigh was stopped for me. Sweating in the cold, breathing heavily, brooding over vengeance, I would come back to the sleigh with the help of wild gesticulations to unglue my skis from the snow each step of the way.

In summer, we had picnic parties on the lake shore. There was a wooden shack there, where my dinghy was parked. A long footbridge overhung the lake. One day, when I was four years old and didn't yet know how to swim, I took advantage of the relaxed alertness of the grown-ups at nap time to go and inspect the water, taking the edge of the path as an observation post. Sure enough, I fell into the water and sank. My gurgling and the bubbles, which subsequently surfaced, attracted the drowsy attention of an uncle who was good enough to fish me out of the lake.

Mother insisted strongly that we learn how to swim at an early age. To stimulate our good-will, she would offer a bike to the one who could pass with success the swimming examination. It was required that the bicycling candidate swim for 15 minutes under official control. That method worked wonders, and by the age of five we had the bike.

Cycling was indeed our favourite sport and an indispensable means of transportation to go to play or to get to the neighbouring little town.

In the summer, I would escape as soon as my classes were over (I had a private tutor at home until I was 12) and pedalled for dear life to the village. I would make a discreet toot-toot with my bike horn in front of the first house where I had a friend, he would come out in a flash and together we pedalled at full speed to the next friend's house. When there were four or five of us, our gang was complete and we started our expedition with a round of sweets that I offered regally when I had funds, relatively willingly as I was forbidden sweets. I must say that if I wasn't the wealthiest in our children's kingdom, I wasn't the tightest with money either. Unfortunately, I received my weekly allowance (one dollar, a mere nothing, even at that time, for someone who had as large-scale needs as I had) on Mondays and, already on Tuesdays I waited in dire destitution for the next Monday.

My friends from the village and I were not aware of a social difference between us. To be sure, I had the luck to live in a big and comfortable house, to go to a better school and to have plenty of other advantages that they didn't have but, as they were satisfied with their home and their lives and preferred their freedom to my obligations, there were no feelings of envy on their part. They were perfectly natural with me and we were thoroughly at home together. For me, they were all Mother's children too, in a way, I was just privileged to be closer to her, but we were all more or less one family. We were children in our own world, closer to one another than today's children and putting a high value on friendship because in the countryside, without friends, you would have died of boredom.

To go to the lake in a carriage with Mother gave me an intense feeling of exhilaration and sharpened my senses. Crossing the woods of pine trees made me see a thousand shades of green in the sun's heat, the aroma from the trees intoxicated me with innumerable flavours and the grinding of the wheels on the sand was a melody to me. Unfortunately my mother spent more time controlling all the movements of the horses and carriages than on rides and I often felt frustrated. Furthermore, she would get mixed up sometimes and, at the very moment where I was tumbling down the stairs to go to my appointment with Snow White at the stable, I would find the coachman at the bottom of the stairs, in full regalia, top hat on the head . . . waiting to take me to the dentist. I don't recall any time where the mistake was the other way around.

There wasn't at that time running water in the village houses. The women, a yoke on their shoulders with a bucket at each end, came to fill them up at the manual pump on the little square in front of the house which, in times past, was a little inn that my grandmother had closed lest the employees would be tempted into excess drinking. In this house now, Mother gave evening parties for the women and, in October, the Harvest Feast took place there in a thanksgiving for the crop. I was allowed to be present there for an hour. It opened with a speech from Mother and I was apprehensive that she would suddenly stop in the middle, not finding the words any more.

We owned all the houses in the village but in fact, the families lived in them, generation after generation, as long as one of their members worked on the estate. They didn't pay any rent, of course. They were paid partly in goods (wood, food, etc.). They worked either in the forest department or on the farms and stayed all their lives with us.

Mother employed a full-time nurse who would constantly shift between the different villages to cure the old and the sick. Mother herself spent a great deal of her time visiting the elderly as soon as the administration of the estate gave her some freedom. She got up every morning at dawn, took a spartan breakfast prepared the night before so that she wouldn't wake up the staff, took her one horse carriage (during the war we were not allowed to use petrol for private vehicles) and went to Greiffenberg, two and a half miles away, where her offices were located. After she had crossed the park, she would arrive at the big gate with a bronze stag on either side. She would then yell ritually at the top of her lungs: 'Mueller!' The gatekeeper, a pensioner who lived in a pretty little lodge next to the gate, would come out with a lot of gesticulation by way of salute, a broad smile on his face and would open the gate.

We children were sometimes seething that our mother spent more time in the office or visiting people than with us. We had the telephone as a rival too. The manager or the chief of the forest very often chose mealtimes to call and it was endless chit-chat while we put on sulking faces.

Mother had planned to renovate all the houses in the village, to have water laid on and bathrooms installed as early as 1939. The war put an end to the renovation as it had just started. The remains of the canalisations are still visible today, even more than the ruins of the castle.

In 1919, Mother had created a mutual insurance to provide a pension for the employees and workers on the estate, for the widows and the orphans and to give assistance in case of sickness. The employee paid one per cent of his salary to the mutual fund and received 75 per cent of his salary after 40 years of work. If you think that several European countries have created their Social Security system only in the '30s or '40s, you might say we were pretty progressive at home.

In my mother's mind, the property wasn't hers; she ran it for the next generations. One wouldn't sell anything, one would keep everything and whenever possible one would expand the estate. For Mother, the family and the estate passed on by the ancestors were the paramount values in life. And she was convinced that, together with wealth and property came the obligation to take care of one's employees from their birth to their death. Contrary to the industrial world, there were still strong bonds between employers and employees in the countryside.

Today, 50 years after we were expropriated and 15 years after Mother's death, there are still many people in the villages of our former estate who knew her when they were children and they remember her with kind feelings. When I came back to Görlsdorf after the fall of the Berlin wall, one of my childhood friends told me: 'When it was my birthday, I told my mother as soon as I woke up: "Have me look beautiful, today the Princess will come to visit me and bring me a present!" She never missed the appointment.'

Mother, too, remembered everyone vividly. Our childhood tales were extracted mostly out of her memories and we loved those stories. I still recall the story of the coachman her parents had when she was young. One of his most important chores was to drive every day to Angermünde – the nearest town that had shops, as there weren't any in the village at the time. Every morning, the house occupants, including the cook, the butler, the housekeeper, etc. approached him and told him what they wanted him to buy for them from the town. As the coachman was illiterate, which already at that time was a rare exception, he could not make a list of his errands. However, he never forgot a single one of the dozens of orders he received. He had developed such a memory that he remembered easily every item, its cost and how much money everyone individually had given him. He was the most respected and trusted of the whole household.

In the village of Görlsdorf, there was a tiny building made of rough stone. It was the jailhouse. Nobody had ever seen an inmate in it. Why was it there, then? I can't picture Mother having that kind of house built.

A little further away was the school, a small house that sheltered the schoolmaster's apartment and a big classroom. The eight grades were all taught in the same place. Adjoining was the house with Mr Hahn's office. He was my mother's personal secretary and we children adored him. He made practical jokes with us and we wouldn't tell on one another. I looked for red chestnuts in October because he paid me ten cents a pound. I wondered what he was doing with all those chestnuts. Today I think he spread them again under the trees so that I would find them on the next day and I don't wonder any more why I found some under the oak trees. He impersonated Saint Nicholas on 6 December and arrived with his long robe, a white beard hiding his face, carrying a huge bag of gifts. I was always scared of him. Later, when I was around eight years old, I recognised him because of his East Prussian accent. But as soon as I was in front of him, I forgot everything and quivered like a plate of jelly.

Mr Hahn lived with his wife, my ex-governess, in a very pretty house at the end of the village and I often went to visit her. She gave me homemade raspberry syrup and bitter green apples in August.

The rest of the village consisted of four long one-storied houses. Two families lived in each one. There lived my two playmates, Horst and Willie. A thousand yards away, there were four more houses that my mother had recently built. We called them 'the new houses'. They sheltered a few employees, among whom was the riding master.

Near the castle there was 'the white house' where the chauffeur and the cook, Rühmling, lived. Rühmling looked like a tiny ball. Every afternoon, after lunch, he walked from the castle to his home, very dignified and straight so as not to lose an inch of his height.

Beside the cook's apartment in the white house was Bensch the chauffeur. Ernst-Wilhelm and I were very fond of him. He taught us car mechanics, especially for the big 12-cylinder Maybach. Bensch wasn't very tall but he was unusually strong and even when Ernst-Wilhelm was 14 he lifted him up with his little finger.

Adjoining the white house was the washhouse. Primitive washing machines existed already but the ironing was still done with hollow irons of cast iron which were stuffed with pieces of white-hot metal heated in a coke container.

A little further away, in front of the indoor riding school where I rode in winter, a little wooden Scandinavian house was situated, where the butler lived, an Englishman by the name of Prentice. He had never learnt how to speak German and had a pronounced cockney accent. He didn't aspirate the 'H' while talking and we had a hard time not to chuckle as he said 'Your Eyeness' to Mother. When he left, Ehrentraut, an old valet of ours, took his job. His wife was stone deaf. Fate was cruel with this poor couple. They lost three of their four sons from tuberculosis, for which there was no cure at that time.

Rühmling, the cook, was my friend. I adored going down to his beautiful kitchen, entirely covered with Delft tiles, an army of copper pots and pans hanging on the walls. I crossed the ante-kitchen where the vault was located, a real room where a man could stand, which sheltered the silverware and the china of the official gatherings. I went straight to a small table and consulted the book in which Mother inscribed the everyday menus and I watched the cook with his creations, and giving snapping orders to his two female assistants. He didn't tolerate with good-will anybody in his kingdom, only I was always welcome.

Sometimes Rühmling showed me how to cook. I was allowed to make two recipes alone: scrambled eggs and mushrooms from the wood, with parsley. There were plenty of mushrooms from June to October in the woods and I picked them myself. My harvest must surely have passed a thorough inspection but nobody ever had such poor tact as to do it in my presence and I have no recollection of having poisoned anyone. Rühmling was always cutting his fingers while cooking. I thought it was part of the job so I was careful to cut my own fingers every time. I was delighted and proud when my blood started showing and it didn't hurt a bit. Rühmling handed me over a plaster without a word and I felt we were blood brothers. Anyway, with the quality of the food Rühmling prepared for routine meals, nobody would have suspected me. I was allowed, as well, to make sweets with sugar and cream . . . mmm, delicious, so much so that they were the only ones I was permitted to eat.

We killed a pig three to four times a year. It was always an occasion to party. A butcher came to help the cook for the event. They made different kinds of sausages, pâtés, hams, etc. I watched, hypnotised, how the animal was cut and how the sausages were made. At dinner, there was the *Wellfleisch* on the menu, the offal of pork and the fresh liver sausages. It was so savoury that my mouth waters just at the remembrance of it.

Adjoining the kitchen there were two big cool chambers where the carcases of entire wild boars and deer were kept. Aside from the dining room of the senior servants – the governess, the butler, the valet and the riding master – the other employees from the castle and from the gardens and the stables, ate in a second dining-room where there were about ten of them seated at the table. The cook had had to prepare meals for at least 20 people at every sitting. That annoyed him and he certainly did not put his best talents to use for such a boring routine. He was happiest and very proud to display his best craftsmanship when there was a formal dinner.

My father, unlike my mother, had been a refined gourmet and he appreciated good wines with the knowledge of a connoisseur. When Mother came back from a dinner party where she had gone on her own, he used to tease her: 'What was on the menu, again?' And without waiting for the answer, he recited: 'Oh yes, I know: meat, vegetables, dessert!' True, Mother never remembered what had been on her plate.

When my father was alive, the food was good at home. When he died, the quality crumbled down several degrees. When the cook went on holiday, my grandmother's old cook, Mrs Jamnick, would come out of her retirement and take active service until he was back. We children were delighted for, as a true Austrian, she would make dream desserts. My favourite was the *Schmankerdel Eis*, a vanilla ice cream (real, proper vanilla, the ice cream was marked out with tiny black dots) in which she threw pieces of crunchy pastry and she would spread the whole thing with chocolate sauce. Jamnick was of the old school, where food had to be rich and abundant. She used to throw a pack of butter in the oven when she needed a lively fire to sear a dish. During the war, that way of cooking would greatly upset Mother, butter was so rare! When there were only a few minutes left before mealtime, she could become very nervous. It was dangerous for the kitchen maids to cross her path then or to talk back to her. She threw pots and pans at them in blind fury and the girls complained bitterly about the treatment Mrs Jamnick subjected them to.

Next to the kitchen were the wine cellars where thousands of bottles of Bordeaux and Burgundy lay. My grandfather used to order his wines by barrels in France and the wine was bottled at home. As Mother drank only water and we were too young to drink wine, it stayed quietly on its shelves during many years. The bottles were all more than 50 years old.

*

We had a sizeable area of fishponds in our forest. Carp and tench were raised there. During the whole of spring and summer, the ponds were full of water and we often went duck shooting in the evening, when the birds came back to the water for the night. At the end of the autumn, all the ponds were emptied, with the exception of one or two, by draining the water out. The fish would gather in a corner of the pond, in the last water. They would be picked up in landing nets to put them in pools to sell them. The ponds that were not emptied were the deeper ones. They would not freeze to the bottom, especially as a river crossed them. It allowed the survival of the ones that would repopulate the ponds in the warm season. I tried to be present as often as possible when those different operations were scheduled. It was fascinating to see a big pool of water vanish in a matter of hours and I liked seeing the fish wriggling in the nets. I could spot the long pike that lived in the permanent ponds. Sometimes our forester Wiechmann would fish one . . . with a rifle and I was mighty glad because it was the only fish I found edible at home. In fact, fish was served at meals every Friday, always boiled. I hated Fridays. I once passed a piece of fish under the table to a cat I had rescued in the village just for that purpose. I had forgotten to warn her and her pleased 'meow' had me caught red handed. The cat was not re-invited and I was served a second helping . . .

Mother was ahead of her time as far as vitamins were concerned. She would fill us everyday with fruits and orange juice that we would gladly wolf down. She had a harder time with the castor oil – 'for the vitamin D, darling!' – which had a horrendous taste. But we missed the castor oil, too, during the war.

Behind the castle ran a small river, the Welse, which crossed the lake in the park. When I was a child, it was full with crayfish that were caught in trap nets. During the summer, we had big parties with fresh crayfish just picked out of the river. In 1935, the crayfish plague killed them all. Normally they should be reborn after ten years but, in the meantime, we were thrown out on a more permanent basis.

*

The English or Swiss governesses would follow one another alternately. Miss Haff and Miss Marshall were the two English ones and I couldn't stand them. Still, I learnt English with them all the same. In the end, I had a ravishing young Swiss, Zabeth. I liked that one a lot. Besides being pretty, she was sweet and cheerful, not like those cantankerous spinsters who were there before her.

Rara, my nanny, occupied a special position. She had never married, being a devoted Catholic in a resolutely Protestant environment. She stayed with us for at least 20 years. She was a wonder; she had never gone to college but gave us lessons in every field until we were 15 or 16. When I reached high school, she studied Latin all by herself so she could give me classes. I learnt so much and so well with her that, when I had to take my admission examination for the boarding-school at 13, I was admitted in a higher grade than the one my age deserved.

Rara was a fantastic nurse when we were sick. And, if I couldn't go to sleep, I would knock on the wall (her bedroom was next to mine) and she came with a glass of sweetened water. When I heard the ringing of the spoon in the glass, I would immediately fall asleep. I loved Rara with all my heart. We took her along when we fled and stayed very close until her death.

For a time, we had a tutor, Dr Lintzer. He was a young man who had just proposed to a young lady. He caught the mumps with us all and he was terrified as he pictured himself becoming impotent just before getting married. We thought he was comical.

It was a great event for us children when we were allowed to participate in a formal dinner. Most times the grown-ups would relegate us to the children's quarters. It was not bad either when it was an official dinner for, in the general excitement, our guards would not watch over us too closely and we took advantage of that to get up to some pranks. Mercy on the one who had punished one of us recently! I would not tell on the others but I had my little battery of retaliations. For the English I would lick my hand and run it on the clean plate of my victim, I would blow my nose in her napkin and pretend afterwards I confused it with my handkerchief or, if I was lucky enough, she would stand up while dessert was served and I could discreetly rub the seat of her chair with custard or jam. What a disappointment if we were served yoghurt on that day! By the way, I still loathe yoghurt today; maybe the origin can be traced back to that.

Mother would never punish us. She only wouldn't come and say good night to the culprit. It was a punishment we found extremely painful. Her authority would never be challenged by anybody but it must be said that she didn't use it much. She was adamant sometimes, though, about having us speak French in the dining-room. 'Speak French!' A deadly silence fell immediately. When I was a child, I thought it meant 'Shut up'. So, when a row would settle between my sisters, I shouted at the top of my voice: 'Speak French! Parlez Français!' Everybody thought it was so funny that nobody volunteered to explain. I was very humiliated when I discovered my mistake and, on top of that, I had to endure the teasing of my sisters who are still laughing today about it.

*

From the time I was a little boy, I went regularly to our forester's house. Our forest of 10,000 acres was divided into six parts of which the manager had the general direction. He lived seven miles away and had the impressive title of Master of the Woods. Having stalked the boars all his life, he had taken on a strong resemblance to that animal.

Each one of the six parts was under the responsibility of a forester whose duty was to supervise his territory, dividing the work between the lumberjacks, telling them which trees to cut down and monitoring the planting of the new trees. He was responsible, furthermore, for the hunt and shot deer when they became too numerous or when there were too many complaints from peasants about the damage caused by the animals in their fields. Finally he prevented poaching and escorted the guests at the shooting.

For the 'Görlsdorf partition', Wiechmann was the forester. He lived in the outskirts of the village, beyond the railway, in one of our forester's houses which was big and comfortable and on the threshold of the woods. As every forester's house did, it displayed a stag's antler on the front, under the roof, with our coat of arms. The internal walls were covered with deer, stag and boar trophies.

Wiechmann was the volunteer mayor of our village and he took care of the paper work on top of his own work. Ten years later, under communist rule, there was one mayor and two assistant mayors for the same amount of work, all paid full time. I was very fond of Wiechmann. He was gentle with me and taught me with great patience, along the years, the secrets of nature and hunting.

After school and lunch, I jumped on my bike and rushed to his house. He unhooked his three-barrelled gun and we went into the woods. He named for me the different trees, told me their age, the height they were expected to reach; the life span of each species, when they would be cut down, how the trunks were converted into cubic metres, their destination – to sell or to keep for our sawmill. He showed me how the new trees were planted and how you protected the young ones from being eaten by the animals.

We would leave together for the forest and tried with cautious steps to stalk boars and deer. Wiechmann taught me how to follow a trail, to remain in a hiding place or behind a bush for hours without moving. I was stung by thousands of mosquitoes and the itching turned me sometimes half-crazy. I wondered – without daring to ask – if Wiechmann was stung too. Maybe he didn't feel anything, he remained so motionless. His parched skin had me in awe and envious.

We observed all the animals in the woods. It was especially exciting at the time of the mating season. I often saw stags defy one another to fight with that sort of bellowing which is so resounding that it seemed to me that the earth was shivering under me. It is Wiechmann who awoke in me the love of nature, of its woods and its fauna. I am grateful to him for this special relationship I have with the forest, for the deep bond I still feel with it, stronger than for the rest of the universe. It was with Wiechmann that, after years of schooling in everything regarding the hunt, I was able to shoot my first stag.

Tradition had it that we began hunting at ten years of age. I began with a compressed-air gun, then when I reached 11 I was allowed to shoot my first deer. At 14 we could shoot our first stag and participate in the hunting with *battues*. We were shown our place for the *battue*, generally in a forest with high trees but facing small very bushy ones. It was in December or January. It was often -20°C in the snow and we had to stay hidden, sometimes four hours in the same place, without moving. Bitten by the intense cold, I missed the mosquitoes of my summer stalkings. After four hours I once saw a big boar sprinkled with snow come out of the bushes like a legendary creature. It was breathtaking.

The bag would be displayed in front of the castle, the animals in rows. Twelve or 14 foresters in uniform played the bugle with a different tune for each species of animal, then the salute to the prince and finally the *hallali* resounded. Then we had tea in the library in front of the gigantic chimney, with sandwiches, scones and pastries.

A forbear had the library lined with the portraits of all the Electors and Kings of Prussia, from the 16th century to Friedrich III. It wasn't very artistic but was instructive for me who learnt them by heart for school. After tea, it was bath time. A hot, scented bath that we longed for. In the evening there was a gala dinner. I have an image from the time of my father: his personal gamekeeper, Michaelis, in impeccable uniform standing behind him, had as his sole duty to stay put for the duration of the dinner. My sister Meggi, who was eight or nine years old, thought he was magnificent and targeted looks and glances at him but he never changed expression.

Mrs Wiechmann was very nice. When we came back from our excursions, she often gave me a snack, obviously much better than the one I would get at home. To be fair, I have to say that every child finds the food better tasting if it is not from home, and I was no exception to the rule but with a few better reasons than most!

The Wiechmanns had a daughter they worshipped. She died of acute joint arthritis when she was 15. Her parents' despair, albeit discreet, was appalling.

The stud was located 400 yards from the castle. It was the one my grandfather had founded in the 1880s. The buildings dated back to that time and were maintained with pride. The paddocks where the horses grazed were circled with hedges that would blossom with flowers in summertime. I loved to go to the stud, particularly in the evening when the horses were in their boxes eating. That environment enthralled me, the strong smell of the horses, the soft sound of their mouths peeling away the hay from the rack and chewing it rhythmically.

Boy, my father's mount during the First World War, followed his master everywhere like a dog. He outlived my father for a long time for he died only when he was 34 years old, a more than venerable age for a horse.

Our stallion was called Tullus Hostilius. He was a superb dapple-grey horse, very tall. During his period as a racehorse, he had broken a leg. That put an end to his career. He had a slight limp but was very imposing and I was a bit shy in front of him.

In my youth, there were very few tractors on the farms. Our fields were large (up to 180 acres) and rather flat. The work was done with what was called a steam-operated plough. A steam engine was placed at either end of the field, pulling a huge plough with 12 or 14 ploughshares back and forth. Seated on the top of the plough, a worker drove it so that it traced a straight path. The steam machines were heated with wood, and that represented a sure advantage during the war, when diesel was very scarce.

In October, Mother would send me to a farm to help with the harvesting of the potatoes. It was very hard work that I loathed, but Mother insisted for she thought I should know first hand all the work concerning agriculture and forestry. I had to be on the grounds at seven o'clock in the morning. We walked behind a machine that extracted the potatoes. We had to pick them up and throw them in a basket. It was usually raining and it was already quite cold. The earth stuck in thick balls under our shoes, which made walking rather strenuous.

When a basket was full, a man would come and empty it on to a cart. We received a ticket worth five *pfennigs* (one cent) a basket. With around 25 tickets per day, I was a wealthy but miserable child. The only pleasure of the day for me was the coming back home in the evening.

*

Fortunately, during my childhood some picturesque guests came, adding spice to our everyday life and taking the attention away from our manners, good or bad. Moreover, knowing it was in our best interest to behave, we usually demonstrated some courtesy, at least for strangers. I remember an old friend of my parents, Field Marshal von Mackensen, a hero on the Russian front during the First World War, who materialised in Lindenau as well as in Görlsdorf. His visits took on the decorum of a state visit, the whole village participating with dances, trumpets and drums. I remember the Field Marshal as an old man who always wore the black uniform of his regiment, 'the death head hussars', and with all his decorations spread on his chest. German field marshals never retire so he was allowed to wear his uniform and to be assisted by an aide de camp. I wondered how the field marshal could bear to wear his uniform and those giant boots which looked so uncomfortable every day but I thought he looked so magnificent that I always tried to be next to him when he was being photographed!

My aunt Meggi was a frequent guest whose visit I anticipated with eagerness. She was my maternal grandmother's sister. She had married an Austrian count, Karl Lanckoroncki, whose family originated from the Austrian Galicia. In fact, the Lanckoronki were Polish but rarely lived on their land, preferring to reside in Vienna, as my uncle was a famous intellectual figure in Viennese cultural circles.

Aunt Meggi, under a rather stern appearance, was the nicest person on earth, particularly with me whom she called *das Manderdel* ('little man' in Austrian). She was very, very old looking and very small, with a funny accent. Without leaving home, she had changed nationalities five times during her existence: German, Austrian, Polish, German and once more Austrian. Those successive nationalities were the consequence of the political situation resulting from the multi-ethnic Austro-Hungarian people. My mother would visit her regularly in Vienna after the war, defying the risks she was taking by going to Austria, and that worried me a lot. Austria and Vienna itself, as Berlin, were still divided into four zones and Aunt Meggi was living in the Russian zone. We were refugees of the Russian zone in Germany and thus enemies of the People.

*

When I reached ten years of age, I had to be registered in the books of the local council in the neighbouring town of Angermünde as *Jungvolk*, 'young male'. It was not fashionable to be a Nazi sympathiser in our region. In our village there was one single man, named Stolzenberg, who openly declared himself as Nazi. He held an obscure position in the N.S.D.A.P., the German National Socialist Workers Party. He was a man of 50 something years, one-legged with a wooden leg, like the pirate in the adventure books. When I met him on the street, I would make the Nazi salute out of cowardice, as was ordered by the Party, to avoid trouble but being careful not to have witnesses.

Nobody liked that man because on top of all that he was considered a renegade. Until 1933, he had been a Communist, then a Nazi and after the war he changed his political colour again and became chief of the village's Communist Party.

The boys of my age were supposed to get together once every two weeks, dressed in a uniform of a brown shirt, shorts and a boy-scout-like scarf. Our mothers had the right to choose our shoes and were sometimes quite imaginative.

I think there was only one gathering. It took place at Görlsdorf, in the open. We played games in the woods; we were half a dozen, left to our own fantasy, as Mother wanted no part in those masquerades which she silently objected to. We had great fun but, already less skilful than the others, I twirled warrior-like my *schlagball*, a sort of baseball bat, which fled away from my hand and landed with a smashing sound on the nose of one of my colleagues, breaking it. Stunned, I wanted to bring him back to my house to have his injury dressed but he kept crying and screaming he wanted to go back home.

'I want my mum!'

'But mine will cure you better.'

'It's not true, mine is much better than yours!'

I had to surrender to such a convincing argument and took him home. I wasn't very proud, my buddy was obviously hurting and he kept cursing at me. His whimpering became a piercing shriek as soon as his house was in sight.

After stuttering my apologies, whining a little myself and shedding a few tears, I left, my pride in shambles, to get *my* mother who immediately sent the doctor and arrived herself, loaded with toys and sweets which got a far warmer welcome than me . . .

Chapter Four

YOUTH

When I was 12, I was sent to the Birklehof boarding-school in Hinterzarten, in the Black Forest, 14 hours by train from home. It was a democratic, modern establishment, where the classes mixed boys and girls. Although élitist, the everyday life was rather austere.

The Birklehof discipline was based on a very solemn 'honour system'. Our honour guaranteed our honesty and our goodwill but left us some room for harmless nonsense, thank goodness.

When there were concerts or theatrical performances, we were forced to observe several minutes of silence at the end, supposedly to meditate but which unavoidably gave way to uncontrollable laughter. Our music teacher, a famous pianist, would make her entrance at those functions in elaborate evening dresses with a tragic expression painted on her face rather like a priestess about to make a human sacrifice. All this pretentiousness seemed to me to border on the ridiculous.

I had, by the way, a tendency to find opera, theatre and cinema rather comical because of the pomposity it seems to display. I had ample time to laugh myself silly at the antics of movie actors during my summer holidays at home the first year I was in Birklehof. In 1941 the U.F.A., the almighty state production company, asked permission from my mother to shoot a picture at Görlsdorf. The scenario was based on the true story of a Baron von Langen, who was badly injured at the end of the First World War. He was sent back home, almost entirely paralysed. Through tremendous training and willpower, he was able to walk again and then ride and win the most important jumping tournament of the time, the Grand Prix of Geneva.

Mother gave permission to use Görldorf and opened – for free, needless to say – the doors of her domain as it was a film promoting the virtues of courage and determination

The U.F.A., with a considerable retinue of equipment and people, settled in for almost three months. When I arrived home from school I was thunderstruck but overjoyed with the noise and disorganisation which had overpowered the castle and joined the crew every day. The scenes involving the stars were shot up to 30 times, especially the love scenes and I would pity the poor actors, having to kiss so many times in a row. The director and all the members of the staff were very nice to me. Only the star, Willy Birgel, one of the greats of the time, was arrogant and allowed no one – certainly not me – to forget his status. He was comically torn between his snobbery (after all, he was a princess's guest!) which made him bow and kiss hands at random in the house, and his will to impress people. He was appallingly ridiculous and seemed to me much too old, whatever his efforts, for his Romeo role and, shame of shames, he didn't know how to climb on a horse, much less how to ride. He had a stunt actor do all the scenes with his mount, except for the close-ups and even then, he seemed to be afraid that the horse would bite him. Maybe he hadn't read the plot before accepting the role or hadn't realised his limitations.

My buddies and I followed the camera teams around and, hidden in the bushes, made fun of the stupid dialogues. Birgel had an aunt in the story, played by a nice old stage actress, and we chuckled at their interpretation of how blue-blooded people behave.

I had to leave long before the shooting was over. When I left Görlsdorf, I felt I was taking my leave from the new owners. They were more at home than I was.

After the war, I succeeded in laying hands on a copy of the film. It allows me to see today on the screen Görlsdorf, the castle, the stud and the forests as they were before the 1945 débâcle. The film is in black and white but for me its colours are rich in every shade of nature's palette.

There was no supervision in the classroom during exams at Birklehof. It was unnecessary because with the honour system nobody cheated.

To each one of the most deserving of the pupils – I am proud never to have joined that group – was given a pocket book with his mandatory programme and his personal one (optional but only in what that dummy chose as supplementary torture), on which he wrote every day a plus if he had achieved the goal he had targeted for the day, or a minus if he had missed. The poor fellow had to show his pocket book now and then to his tutor. Honour system or not, apparently trust had its shortcomings. You had to deserve the uniform as well and some school sins would have you stripped of it. I always had the uniform because that was one shame I couldn't bear but sometimes I had to clutch to it with my claws.

Just before Christmas, the school authorities picked a fir tree in the middle of the woods and had it decorated and lit with candles. At twilight, the whole school looked for the tree in the forest. The search usually lasted a long time and that increased our pleasure in gathering around to sing Christmas carols.

There was a curfew at night, at a different hour depending on the grade. For mine, it was ten o'clock. We were four per room with two per room for the inmates of the senior years – the 'big ones' – to whose group I didn't belong. Often I went on reading under my blanket once all the lights were out, with the twinkling flash of an electric torch. But my conscience spoilt the fun, because in so doing I was transgressing the honour system. Still, I wasn't remorseful enough to inscribe it on a copybook.

At one time, I had a roommate who was said to have fits of somnambulism. Once when there was a full moon and while I was sound asleep, he left his bed and went up to the roof through the window. There he walked back and forth for a while, under the terrified stares of the teachers called by a star gazer. Then he slipped and fell into the schoolyard. He got away with a broken arm. His waking up was quite unpleasant, though. Not mine, I slept like a log until the morning call.

The food was inedible at Birklehof, partly due to the war, partly so that we learnt that life is no bed of roses. I wasn't picky because the meals at home had been a good rehearsal, but at Birklehof they served on a regular schedule the three vegetables I couldn't swallow: kohlrabi (I'm glad for you if you don't know what that is), turnips and beets. Sure enough, they turned up all the time in the menu. There was no way I could elude them because there was a teacher at every table. He ate with us and he was the one who filled our plates. We were forced to eat everything. Was I at a torture at mealtime! During the week for breakfast we were served porridge, prepared with water instead of milk. It was no treat either. Fortunately, there were the Sundays where we were allowed muesli.

It was strictly forbidden to receive parcels from home containing food. We were all supposed to endure the hardships equally. Obviously many children came from families who lived in big cities and had no access to supplements of food as we, the peasants, did.

Our favourite sport was hockey on grass. Our school team was good and took part in numerous competitions. I played too, like everyone else, but I was murder for my team. I was scared of this unfriendly and hard little ball which knocked more than one down senseless before my eyes.

In winter, we went skiing in the hills of the Black Forest. It was very good skiing but not overly attractive, as we had to hike up the rough way. There were no ski lifts to drag you up the mountain with a glass in your hand, as today, and we had to pant and sweat on the way up and freeze on the way down. Each one of us had a different pace and everybody had to wait for the late ones – I was one of them – so late that the skilful as well as the clumsy had plenty of time to turn to ice.

Some of my friends and I would sometimes get up secretly in the middle of the night to go and raid other pupils from a dormitory in the next building. It spiced up a bit the everyday routine and gave us the illusion of kicking discipline in the shin. It was forbidden, of course, but as our fights would generally consist of not too loud pillow battles, the authorities would look the other way. Once we took away all the left foot shoes of our 'foes'. It caused a mighty stir but we got away with only a light lecture.

In June 1942 the school sent me for a few weeks to help a farmer to harvest. I was delighted and preferred that a thousand times to lessons. I was outdoors, in the sun, the work was not too hard, and for snacks the family pampered me with crusty bread spread with real butter and the renowned raw ham of the Black Forest, goodies from which we were long deprived and contrasting dramatically with the less than edible diet of Birklehof. I was given cool cider to drink and it was delicious but had alcohol in it. I had to monitor my intake – in case anybody at school noticed!

My siblings had had an uneventful schooling in Birklehof but now we were reaching mad times. We children were perhaps even more aware of it than the adults. The new laws rained down and their friends were upset and disoriented. Their whispers would stop when we were around. They had practically no control any more of our future. The women were red-eyed, the men, even the very young ones, were all in uniform. They were the same people who ruled our lives with authority and knowledge before, whom we trusted, respected and turned to for comfort. Now they were stripped of their right of parental decision, they had to run endlessly from one place to the other, queue up for a mountain of paperwork, shut up or else bring on their family the worst consequences, teach their children how to lie, how not to rebel.

The Director of Birklehof, Mr Kuchenmueller, (nicknamed 'Cake') had taken the responsibility of keeping the few 'half-Jews' who were in the school. It was an act of courage as the Nazis almost closed the school. He ran into the worst difficulties and, in the end, those pupils were forced to leave anyway. Birklehof was almost shut down and the pupils concerned were taken away.

We had a classmate, Eckfried Heissmeyer, whose parents were high-ranking in the SS and the Nazi Party. But we were more impressed by the fact that he had severe diabetes and had to inject himself with insulin every day.

I have a vivid recollection of a boy in my class whom our director had to send home. His name was Eberhard Schmidt. Three of us protested loudly. The only thing we were able to do in the end was to accompany him to the station and carry his belongings. Neither he nor we knew what the future had in store for him but we were stunned all the same by this incomprehensible injustice. I realised for the first time what it meant to be born a Jew in that time and place.

Eberhard was a brilliant pupil, quiet, popular, and who played the violin superbly. I know that he was sent to work in a factory in Freiburg and was denied the right to go on with his studies. We were given a mild scolding when we came back from the station. 'Cake' explained to us there was nothing that we could do against the orders except put everybody at risk by our attitude. In fact, not because of us but probably because he was judged untrustworthy, he was forced to apply a Nazi educational programme.

Birklehof was nationalised at the beginning of 1944. It had been expected the year before and in fact Mother had called me home in the summer of 1943, before the change in the boarding school policy. It was not to have me pampered. I was sent to Angermünde's high school. Five miles back and forth, biking, mostly in the cold, the snow and the night. I didn't realise then that it was happiness.

A Government order prevented me from enjoying that happiness for more than six months. Under a decree in 1943, every schoolboy reaching 15 years of age had to enter the F.L.A.K. (Flieger Abwehr Kanone) as auxiliary soldiers. In between, I had become a Hitler Youth, as I was informed by official mail. At home, a disapproving silence greeted my promotion. I was about to be 14 years old. I had to go to another forest with the same guys I had met for the unforgettable gathering when I was ten.

This time we played cops and bandits. What a joke! Under the eyes of our mothers – nobody had had a father around for quite a long time – we had to play innocent games in a paramilitary uniform. The underlying statement was that in the Army, into which we would be drafted barely one year later, we would be treated as children in just the same way. Well! What a surprise!

True, we were sent to class at the F.L.A.K., but it was on top of fighting in the war. School during the day, war during the night. Sleep? If there is time. Play? Never.

*

My eldest sisters, Milli and Meggi, were respectively 19 and 18 in 1937. They had reached the age of going to their first balls. The goal for the girls at that time was to find a husband. My mother was a good Catholic and was closely watched by the clergy of her faith who did not intend to lose one more sheep of the Lynar-Redern family. She owed it to them and to herself to have her daughters make their debut in Rhineland or in Bavaria where they would have the opportunity of meeting suitable young Catholic men because in our region almost everybody was Protestant. Thus, during the last two years before the war, they appreciated the invitations they received from West Germany. My poor sisters, Buttel and Netti, were still too young to be included in the festivities. The war took away their turn which never came back.

In 1939, Meggi married an officer in the Luftwaffe, Count Karli von Hoensbroech, who was killed in action in 1941. The Hoensbroech family originated from part of Holland that belonged to Spain until 1648, that is to say until the Westphalia Treaty which put an end to the Thirty Years War. Since then the Hoensbroech heir bore the title of Marquese. Karli had four brothers. Three of them were fighter pilots during the war. 'Be careful to fly very low, my darlings,' recommended their mother, 'and slow down on the curves'.

In spite of the poor lady's warnings, three of her sons crashed at the front, a fourth died of cancer around 40. The fifth lived as a recluse among his brothers' memorabilia and died before his time too. Ernst-Wilhelm, my brother, left for the Army in 1941 and only came back four years later but safe and sound.

After Meggi was widowed she started studying law in Freiburg, living with Buttel who studied maths and physics. Meggi, as a war widow, didn't have to do mandatory work but Buttel had to serve six months in an armament factory in Pirmasens, Sarre and in Silesia. Her supervisor, having learnt that she was already two years into scientific studies, came to her once she was in grease up to her eyebrows. She was handling a machine to manufacture grenades. The supervisor offered to take her into the planning office. She refused in not so many words, with no excessive courtesy. In this infamous work of death, the least evil was to have as little responsibility in it as possible. Poor Buttel, she lived then all by herself in a furnished room with no heating, in a town where she didn't know a soul. When she was discharged in 1942, she joined Meggi and together they went to go on with their studies in Breslau, because this town was less gloomy, they had many friends and relations there and, paramount to all, it gave them a little respite away from the bombing over Berlin. They came back the next year, however, to enter university in the capital.

One week before Christmas 1944, my eldest sister, Milli, married Count Ignaz von Hoensbroech, a cousin of Meggi's husband, and had her wedding in Görlsdorf. The war was raging, the Russians were already close. The atmosphere for the wedding was depressing. During the past summer, on the fateful date of 20 July 1944, Milli went with our cousin, Karl-Max Schaesberg, to 'Paulchen's bar' in the afternoon. It was a small, old-fashioned place, in Berlin, where Paulchen welcomed swarms of young officers and young girls every day. He knew every one of his regular customers, cheered them in time of brooding, listened to their problems and when asked gave good advice. When the place was full up, he locked the door, went to his cellar and brought out bottles of wine and liquor, much-appreciated goods in those months.

As Milli and Karl-Max sat down on their bar stools that afternoon, Paulchen approached them with a gleeful expression on his face: 'The pig is dead! I'll get my best bottle to celebrate, wait here!' He then bolted to the staircase leading down to the cellar, leaving the two wondering what he had meant. He reappeared soon and uncorked the wine while Milli and Karl-Max asked him what the commotion was about. 'Hitler, of course, they killed the bastard this morning!' Hitler outlived Paulchen's joy and Paulchen vanished some time later. He was never seen again.

In February 1945, my sister Netti, Ernst-Wilhelm's twin, was working as a nurse in the hospital in Angermünde. She was engaged to a Navy doctor, Wolf Steffan, who was serving in the hospital in Aurich, near Bremen. She had a release to get married at the end of March in Bremen. The problem was to obtain the necessary papers, which, in time of war, especially then, were near impossible to get in a short time. An old friend of ours, Philipp Boeselager, who will appear in this book a few times more, came to the rescue. Through his connections, he solved the matter. Mother packed a massive trunk for her daughter with everything she would need, including wedding dress, cutlery, china and the food for the wedding meal. Philipp then drove Netti and her trunk to the railway station. There they inquired when the next train was to Bremen. 'There is one in five minutes, when there will be one after that is anybody's guess.'

So Philipp and his driver rushed to the platform with the heavy trunk on their shoulders and shoved it with my sister into the train which was already in motion.

Netti got her wedding but nobody in the family was able to be present at the ceremony which took place in Aurich.

Chapter Five

MILITARY LIFE

I received my draft order for Wilhelmshaven, on the North Sea. We were about 50 kids in naval uniform, drafted as auxiliary soldiers for the anti-aircraft guns. We were to man four batteries of four old cannons of 8.8 cm each, 12 miles away from the town, under the orders of a captain and half a dozen non-commissioned officers. A few elderly privates were in charge of our schooling. Those in authority were way beyond retirement age but didn't try much to act as grandfathers to us.

I caught the flu just before I had to leave. As it was forbidden to report when sick in case one contaminated the others, I arrived in Wilhelmshaven two days late. The end of the world: 'His Lordship gratifies us with the honour of his presence . . .' yelled the non-com.

He sent me three times in a row to the hairdresser, had me do all sorts of chores during the first days, and then calmed down completely, even saying: 'If you are the one in charge, today, there is no need for inspection.'

I thanked my first teachers for teaching me discipline.

Part of the time assigned to schooling was spent teaching us to identify the planes that flew 30,000 feet above us. The aim of our gunfire was not so much to target the planes – our equipment and ourselves were not exactly adequate – as to force them to stay at a very high altitude.

We soon became so tired that we would no longer answer the roll-call, not to mention how to make out the difference between a fighter and a bomber . . . However, we were quick to learn how to sleep with open eyes. What a parade of glassy looks must have faced the teacher! One night, in spite of the shrieking alarm calling us to the guns and the stampeding of my roommates – we had to be in full attire in one minute – in our bunker which sent back an echo like a battery of drums, I didn't wake up. The petty officer who came to get me barked routinely but did not punish me. I wasn't the first to whom it had happened.

At the F.L.A.K., we were allowed to receive parcels of food because what we had to eat in the Army was absolutely revolting: generally some black bread, wet inside, for some reason, sausage branded 'rubber sausage', and a coffee substitute which foamed because it was sprinkled with bromide to soothe the crude dreams of the raw recruits.

I received from time to time a parcel from home. It usually contained eggs and sugar. I shared that precious food with my roommates so, on the days a parcel arrived, there was no shortage of cooks to prepare the mixture of eggs and sugar to make a kind of omelette, very filling, which seemed to us a treat from the gods.

Every two months we had four days' leave. When I was back at Görlsdorf, I was immersed in a heavy atmosphere, quite different from what I had known, without really understanding what was going on, as nobody volunteered information.

For me, the trip back and forth took two days. I had to change station in Berlin, usually on foot because all means of transport were stormed and immediately overloaded. There were hours of waiting, of trains being postponed, of cancellations. When a train did finally show up, it was crowded up to the steps. I would have held on to the bumpers with my teeth, though, to return home. Once, I must have looked so desperate, running until I had no more breath behind the train catching speed, that two soldiers inside hauled me through the lavatory window and pulled me up. I slipped and broke the window with my left knee which was deeply cut in the process. There was blood everywhere. I was quite embarrassed, especially as I knew that my blood doesn't coagulate easily but didn't want to say so for fear of discouraging people to hand me down some cloth to mop up this torrent. I was much more annoyed with the sight of my torn and soiled uniform than by the injury.

After two hours, I finally arrived in Angermünde. Nobody expected me because no one ever knew if or when I would have a leave and a train. My mother was called from the station and I waited for a good half-hour, time for her to put a horse to a carriage as we didn't have petrol for a car. I had lost a good amount of blood and must have looked very pale. Mother didn't waste too much time in welcome or in whining and drove me directly to the hospital. Six stitches later we were released.

It was dreadful to see this hospital filled to capacity with wounded soldiers lying in every place available. They had war wounds, I had a leave wound. I was ashamed to have monopolised a doctor and to have to go back to the hospital every other day for the dressing and not to be able to go back at the regular time to my unit.

When I went back to the F.L.A.K., one of my colleagues, a son of

General von Treskow, approached me, wax-coloured in the face. He stated: 'My father has been killed at the front.'

A few days later, he wasn't there any more. His father had been a member of the 20 July 1944 plot against Hitler. He was on the eastern front when the news of his imminent arrest reached him. He positioned himself where the fire was the most intense and stayed erect. He fell almost immediately. By his death in combat, he probably hoped to spare his family the *Sippenhaft*, the general imprisonment in a concentration camp and the confiscation of their properties. Unfortunately, that wasn't the case.

In mid-December 1944, I successfully passed the examination for naval officer candidates. I had applied because it was the fastest means to become an officer and, paramount to that, to escape the eventual draft into the SS. An official letter informed me that I would be enlisted in the Navy between 15 April and 1 May 1945. I would be notified of the exact date in due time.

I was discharged from the F.L.A.K. one year and one week after I started. Two weeks in Görlsdorf to change kits and off I went, this time for the R.A.D. (*Reicharbeitsdienst*, or mandatory service for the Reich), stationed one hour by train from Berlin, on the west side. The R.A.D. consisted of a military training, with no weapons in my time. Conceived originally to keep the unemployed busy in public works, it had become a pre-military drill. We were handed not a gun but a shovel on the shoulder (there were no guns left but shovels, shovels, mountains of shovels). At our age, we felt humiliated to carry that shovel. So much so that we had to walk with a shovel, to march in step, to present . . . SHOVEL! And to clean it, polish it, treasure this d . . . d shovel, while our fathers, brothers, uncles, cousins, to whose rescue we eagerly wanted to go, were falling by the thousands at the front.

There was a very tense atmosphere in the R.A.D. The bullying was a non-stop occurrence between peanut political factions. I was often approached by provocateurs who tried to make me talk against the Regime. They couldn't fall on worse ground. I was briefed and very much warned by the different officers who were showing up all the time at home, especially after that fatal day of 20 July 1944, to be suspicious of everybody and to shut up.

One day the biggest fat guy of a team of nitwits threw a filthy and rusty shovel in my arms and ordered me to clean it. When I refused, he told me with a sardonic smile: 'Great! That will give us a good reason to come and pay you a little visit tonight.' Not being very bellicose, I didn't sleep a wink. They never showed up! Gathering a courage that I feared I lacked altogether and preferring certainty to doubt, I said in a light tone to Fatty on the next day: 'You and your friends didn't come last night, should I still wait for you?' He shrugged and muttered a few grunts. A pal told me in a hushed voice: 'He couldn't convince the others.' I felt comforted that he didn't think he was strong enough to slug me on his own.

My stay in the R.A.D. lasted six weeks. Six very cheerful weeks: constant inspections of a miserable shovel and a horrible brownish uniform (help, my bedecked ancestors!), intense cold and food that didn't dare be named so (bread without bread but black all the same, sausages made of . . . what? I'm still wondering). Ah! The sweet homely evenings spent, fingers stiff, mending our socks, multicoloured because of the threads of different wools!

On our last day in the R.A.D., 26 March 1945, we were called one by one and each one of us received his marching orders, for the real war, this time. An oppressive silence, thick with the pains and the mourning each one of us had already had to bear and still feared, fell upon us. We were 16 years old. Out of 200, we were only a handful to have been accepted as candidate officers in the Navy, not because we were the best but because most of the raw recruits had only frequented elementary school.

I stood outside the barracks, where two officers sat in an office with long lists in hand. When one of us heard his name shouted, he entered the office, white in the face. The sentence fell with one word: 'SS!' It meant his routing orders were to join a SS unit immediately. It was equivalent to a death sentence. He knew what treatment the Russians had in store for the SS, yet this youngster was shoved against his will into the hated black uniform.

By the time the names beginning with L were reaching the very last name – mine – I was on the verge of fainting. I overcame my panic attack to go inside when my name was called and reached for the paper the officer handed me. I read: 'Call at the Navy post in Stralsund on 1 May.' What a burden was lifted off my shoulders! Being a candidate officer of the Navy, I had escaped the SS incorporation *and* I had five weeks leave at home! All the other ones had to leave directly and immediately for the front, in the SS units, not the ones that spread terror but the ones who went to get killed, without glory or medals, a tributary of the disgrace and shame that surround those ominous initials. We, the midship candidates, were ordered to go back home to wait for our destination orders . . .

*

I still have in my mind's eye the picture of my mother, seated in front of the radio (I know now that it was on 3 September, 1939, the day Britain and France declared war on Germany). She suddenly began to cry. She had lost her only brother in the 1914 war, now her sons were threatened. She told me later that her brother and all the men in Germany had gone to war singing, but that it was quite different in 1939. Then everybody had sombre hearts. With the enormous losses suffered by every family during the First World War, people couldn't have any illusions about the damage that this one would cause. Even the most fanatic followers of Hitler had to be worried. For those ones it was one thing to go to fight at the front, another thing to crush entire populations of defenceless civilians under their boots.

In 1944, while my brother was in the Army (tank regiment), my sisters had a hard time, studying at the university and at the same time working in a factory or at the hospital, doing their mandatory service for the Reich. At home, my mother gave shelter to friends or relatives in difficulty and everyday they became more numerous.

For two or three years, Admiral von Löwenfeld, then retired, lived at Görlsdorf. His wife, Dorothee, grand-daughter of Chancellor Bismarck and a close friend of my mother, was much younger than the admiral and was doing mandatory work. At that time every German, man or woman still fit and not fighting at the front had to help the war effort. Labour was cruelly needed in every field for there were ten million men in the Army. Mother had offered her hospitality to the admiral so that he would be sheltered from the incessant bombing of Berlin. He had been sent into retirement in 1919 and was more than 65 when he moved to Görlsdorf. He was sure the Nazis wanted to kill him, first during the Roehm *putsch* in 1934 and then after the 20 July 1944 plot

We all were very fond of the admiral. Uncle Wilfried, as we called him, was a small man, with shining white hair. He stood very straight. He had enormous feet and he was the first one to laugh about them, saying they were 'very practical for balancing on a ship in rough seas' or 'so as not to fall while walking, I must either stand back or bend into a skiing position'.

When he arrived from Berlin, we would run to hug him and he encouraged us to plunge a hand into the big pocket of his coat. Every child fished out a little present. He allowed me sometimes to be present when he was shaving. It was fascinating: he had razors like the ones a professional barber used. He possessed eight of those, from the best steel, 'one for every day of the week and an eighth to give a day off to the seven others', he would say. He pretended not to be able to find sleep if he hadn't drunk a whole bottle of wine before going to bed. Actually, I suspected he liked to pat the bottle, as sailors do.

He was the only man in the house and I had almost a grandson to grandfather relationship with him. Up to the point that, to oblige my mother, he undertook the task of enlightening me about the facts of life, blushing like a schoolgirl, before my departure to the F.L.A.K. I thought I would choke on my repressed laughter. I was 15 and my buddies in the village had taken care of my sexual education, with the help of rather graphic sketches, long before.

One day at the F.L.A.K. we received an inspection visit from the Admiral Commander of the North Sea fleet. He asked to talk to 'Count Lynar'. I moved forward, cringing, and my ears so hot I thought they would pop out of my head. The admiral was all smiles and compliments and he told me he had served in the old times under Admiral von Löwenfeld who had signalled him my presence in Wilhelmshaven, etc. The more he talked, the redder I became, seething to have been pulled out of anonymity. I had to bear the teasing of my fellow men and of the non-com. and complained loudly to Mother, making clear that her relatives and friends should please forget me and leave me alone.

For a few weeks, a very highly ranked SS general was quartered in the house. He was one of those unconditional Nazis and had played an important role in breaking the uprising of the Poles in Warsaw. He acted as if house and property belonged to him. One day he complained to my mother that he could not sleep in the morning because of the noise of the lawnmower working in the garden at ten o'clock! Thank goodness he left fairly soon and was replaced by a real general. After the war, he somehow found out where my mother lived and wrote to her asking for what we then called *persil-schein*, detergent certificate, that is to say he wanted my mother to certify that he never was a Nazi! Needless to say, she did not answer his letter.

During the war, we had Baroness von Richthofen as a guest in Görlsdorf. She was the wife of a nephew of the 'Red Baron', and was stationed in a headquarters in Berlin. He would come to visit his wife when he had leave. The baron had a face with pronounced features, and was so tall and stocky that we named him 'King Kong'. He was one of the few people who never hid his hate of the Nazis. As early as 1940, when Germany was piling up the military successes, he openly stated, in our family circle, his conviction that Germany would lose the war in the end and would drag its people into a disaster. He told us he didn't have anything to do with the regime and had no intention of getting killed for a cause he loathed. He actually succeeded in surviving, one of the few of the classes 1920–24. From the classes 1920–21, only one man out of four survived. There were families so wiped out by the war that it would take on the proportions of a Greek tragedy. Friends of ours, the Schall-Riaucourts, had eight sons. Five of them were killed at the front. After the war, the mother was travelling by car with two of her remaining sons. They crossed a zone of manoeuvres of the Belgian troops and a tank collided with the car. Both sons died and the mother survived once more. She still had one last son. Prisoner of the Russians, he came back home only years later and then died of the hardships he had endured. The poor woman went on living only to mourn her sons.

*

On 21 July 1944, Uncle Wilfried came down for breakfast with a dark expression on his face and announced: 'Hitler will have us all killed because yesterday's plot failed and half of those who took part in it are aristocrats.' I was at home on a leave for two days. I learnt later that out of the several thousand people who were arrested as participants in the conspiracy, half of them were aristocrats and most of them were put to death. About 20 of them, caught on the spot, were shot immediately. Among these was Count von Stauffenberg. The others, including my father's cousin, Count Wilfried zu Lynar, arrested a few days later, were hanged at a butcher's hook. Uncle Wilfried had a wife and six children. One of the boys was killed in the war, the other one became a parson. After the war, I learnt that many relatives and friends of ours who had taken part in the plot were not found out at the time. That means that the other conspirators, the ones who had been caught, did not tell on them, even when tortured. We are all proud of the ones who died and we are all grateful to them for their heroism.

My sister, Meggi, who lived in Berlin, was at that time in pain with a bad back. She consulted regularly a doctor who had Heinrich Himmler, head of the SS as a patient. The doctor reported to her the threatening words proffered by Himmler: 'I heard that the Lynar pig, one of the conspirators against our Führer, has a very wealthy cousin. We are going to take care of her.' Supposedly, the doctor protested that the Lynar family was loyal to the Führer with the exception of that one black sheep.

In the days following the attempt against Adolf Hitler, we realised it was not at all a plot by 'a small group of officers', as Hitler qualified it, but a true conspiracy which involved men of all political tendencies, from the ultra-conservatives to the Communists and many officers from the aristocracy.

Ley, one of the heads of the Nazi Party, made a speech full of hatred on 22 July 1944 and declared that the State was going to eliminate 'those blue-blooded pigs' in the nick of time. It seemed that Hitler would also have liked to apply the 'final solution' to the aristocrats but at that moment of the war there were too many officers from the aristocracy. They were covered with decorations for 'bravery in combat and services rendered to the fatherland', esteemed and sometimes worshipped by their troops and by the people. Hitler didn't dare deal with them at that time, but if he had won the war, the purge would have taken on the extent of an elimination.

Nobody dared speak about the conspiracy. Therefore we learnt after a long delay about the hanging of my uncle, aide-de-camp to Marshal von Witzleben who, in the event of the success of the plot, was to become the head of state. The Boeselager brothers, from a family very close to ours, and Minister Popitz, uncle of my future brother-in-law, Wilhelm Moessinger, were also among the conspirators.

Among our relatives and friends, a certain number of conspirators succeeded in slipping through the holes of the Nazis' nets. One of them was Axel von dem Bussche, first a suitor of Meggi, then one of my great friends, another was Ewald von Kleist, a classmate of Buttel's.

Axel von dem Bussche was, at 25, a captain in the infantry serving at the front in Russia in 1941. He was a handsome man, very tall, and his moral value was as obvious as his courage. He attracted everyone with his exceptional charm. In October 1943 in Russia he saw a detachment of SS kill a group of Jews. He felt a decisive shock. He spoke to his intimate friend, Count von der Schulenburg, about his decision to join the resistance. Schulenburg put him into contact with Colonel Count Klaus von Stauffenberg . Axel volunteered for the coup, which was being set up against Hitler. On the occasion of a presentation of new uniforms to Hitler, Axel had to come forward, jump on the Führer, keep him against his chest and explode the bomb he had in his pocket. They would have been blown up together in a deadly embrace.

Axel was provided with a bomb and he took the train for Wolfschanze, Hitler's headquarters in East Prussia. When he arrived, he went to the cantonment of the visitors to wait for the order to appear in front of the Führer. Axel waited for two days and three nights in a tiny room, aware of the sure death he had ahead. He didn't want to sleep his last moments and he fought against drowsiness, seated in an armchair, making the balance of his life in his head. The balance of a life of 25 years is quickly over and on the third night he fell asleep. In the morning, when he woke up, he was informed that there had been a bombardment of the train and the car containing the uniforms had burnt. The presentation was therefore cancelled, the attempt postponed. Axel went back to the front. While packing, he was wondering how on earth he could get rid of the bomb. He could not leave it in his room and he didn't have time to bury it in the neighbouring woods. He took it back to Russia in his military pack and put the pack in his personal cupboard. He had no immediate opportunity to get rid of the 'thing' and, in the fire of action, forgot about it.

Three months later he was severely wounded in the leg. He had already lost the thumb and the forefinger on his right hand in combat the year before. He caught gangrene and they had to amputate the foot, then the leg up to the knee, then up to the groin. He was operated on in Berlin in an SS hospital. When he awoke from the anaesthesia, he saw a cupboard in front of him and, on top of it, his military pack. It was customary to send their personal belongings to the wounded in the hospital where they were treated. Therefore, the bag was routinely forwarded to the hospital in Berlin. Axel assumed nobody had inspected it, as everybody around him appeared unconcerned. When he heard on the radio Hitler's speech on 21 July 1944, he knew he would be interrogated. He couldn't reach his sack, as he was in no condition to move, nor ask anybody to hand it over to him or to get rid of it, but he succeeded in reaching his address book on his night table. At night, while everybody was asleep, Axel ate his address book.

On the next day, the Gestapo reported. There was no better alibi than to have been having a leg amputated, even for the Gestapo.

While the thugs were questioning him half-heartedly, they had their back resting against the cupboard, with that ill-fated grey bag that Axel had been watching intently since he woke up. The guys went away after a thorough look at Axel's papers.

A few days later, one of his most trusted friends came to visit and went away with the implicating evidence. Axel couldn't play his role of human bomb any more. The mission fell on another conspirator's shoulders – Ewald von Kleist. Again the presentation of the uniforms was cancelled; the war was beginning to demand, even from the Nazis, less frivolous gatherings.

*

I took the train from Berlin to go back to Görlsdorf on 27 March 1945, after I was discharged from the R.A.D. Between Berlin and Angermünde I saw the flashes of the artillery fire at the front, on the other side of the Oder, a few miles away from our estate. The sky was almost devoid of planes as the Russians did not have many to spare for the conquest of that piece of land, already almost theirs, and the German fighter planes had too much to do on the western front to disperse their forces on that side.

I found the headquarters of the Oder Army lodged in the castle. It soon became clear that the arrival of the Soviet troops was only days away. With all that had been reported about the occupation of Germany by the Red Army there was no alternative but to escape. Mother had a conference with the Commanding General of the Army Corps and he assured her that he would give her a safe-conduct to be able to leave. Without that document, it would have been suicidal to flee as the Party had given the order to stay put 'until the final victory' and all the ones who left were shot for 'defeatism', including the people who only made plans to flee. The newspapers were recounting those executions on a daily basis.

In the region of Görlsdorf, the front was more or less stable for a few weeks when the Soviets broke through in the north, near the Baltic Sea and in the south near Berlin. However, there was the risk that they would make a junction behind our back and encircle us. It was, then, vital to run away while the road westbound was still open.

In March 1945, a colonel who was aide-de-camp to the commanding general and who afterwards became a well-known figure in horse-breeding and whom my sister met often, told my mother: 'Get your daughters out of the way before the Russians arrive!' Plenty of horror stories were heard about the way Soviet troops were treating women.

Philipp Boeselager, who belonged to the Supreme Command Army (O.K.H.), passed through Görlsdorf at the time. Always obliging, he used his connections to organise two wagons for us to load a number of mares from the stud to transport them to safety in the West. He told my mother: 'This is a unique opportunity to save some valuables from the Russians. You can load paintings and furniture with the horses. There will be no risk in these wagons.' My mother had a typical reaction: 'It's not allowed, I won't do it.'

Milli and Buttel came to Görlsdorf, supervised the loading of the mares and travelled in the same wagon with the horses. The journey lasted four days. Milli, who had wed in December 1944, was four months pregnant at the time. The most comfortable place she could find to sit was a cushion of straw she would gather in a corner of the freight carriage. She was glued there most of the time, frantically knitting baby clothes. Sometimes and for no apparent reason, the freight train came to a halt that could last a few hours. Several times, Allied planes attacked the train with machine-gun fire. Then everybody had to leave the train and run for cover. One old man in the next wagon was shot dead when he could not run fast enough to find shelter.

On arrival in Lubeck, Buttel left the train to try and get some food. When she came back, the train, horses and pregnant sister were gone. She had no clue about the direction the train had taken, much less where its next stop would be. It took her hours to find out and more to find transportation to that point. Finally, after an entire day of worries and pleas for help with the railroad employees, she managed to re-join the convoy. As most of the railroad tracks were destroyed, the train made improbable detours to reach its destination. Instead of arriving from the south, it went north into Denmark, only to retrace its way south again. More air attacks on the railway stations where the train was stopping forced its passengers to seek refuge for hours on end in some cellar, waiting for the plane to leave the area. After the raids, the problems were arduous, with the station and most of the tracks destroyed. Milli and Buttel succeeded in getting to Altenhof and were there to greet us when our own convoy arrived, seven days later.

There was one very young officer attached to the general at Görlsdorf. He flirted a bit with my sisters and we never heard of him again until last year, when Buttel and I were attending a conference on the problem of the expropriations in Eastern Germany. There, an elderly gentleman approached my sister and said: 'The last time we met was 50 years ago, when we had a little party in Görlsdorf, the day before you and your sister left with your horses!'

I received my marching orders. I was supposed to report to the port of Stralsund for 1 May and was confined at home until then. There was the chance as well that, when the Russians started their attack, I would be called upon locally at the *Volksturm*, a ghost army composed of old men and children to face the final battle. I went through periods of anxiety at home, thinking that, after I had worked hard to escape the draft into the SS, I was going to die on the Russian front, a few days before the unavoidable end of the war.

Around 8 April, I awoke feverish, nauseated and weak, with a splitting headache. One look in the mirror reflected a definitely yellow face. The army doctor lodged in the castle confirmed my diagnosis: I had hepatitis. That disease, the consequences of which dragged on for a long time, saved my life. It gave the general who occupied our house a reason to give me the authorisation to leave with my mother, as I couldn't report to the military with a contagious disease. It could not be a false pretence not to comply with my military obligations as my lemon-coloured complexion was sufficient proof and made people stay away from me. Obviously, nobody could afford to be debilitated at a time where the situation outside was critical.

I spent my last days in Görlsdorf in bed most of the time. I heard the news of Roosevelt's death on the Nazi radio. In a desperate attempt to convince the German people that there was still a chance of winning the

War, the Nazis compared the President of the United States' death with Catherine of Russia's, which marked the turning point in the Seven Years War and the salvation of Frederick the Great. Even at my age, I was able to judge that those transmissions of propaganda were not only ludicrous but also criminal, considering the hopeless military situation in which we found ourselves. The great majority of the German people thought as I did.

Chapter Six

THE RUSSIAN ADVANCE

In a slightly calmer state of mind I awaited the authorisation to leave. Mother organised our flight. She had a tractor prepared and thoroughly checked, as well as the trailer it had to pull.

We were taking along about 15 women and children, families of our employees. There were two criteria for the selection: first, my mother chose young women with small children, as they were the ones most exposed and vulnerable to danger from the Russian soldiers. Second, they must have some connection, relation or friends in western Germany where they would find refuge. It was unthinkable to dump them along the way and we could not arrive with our full load at our destination, where it was kind enough on the part of our hosts to take into their household such a heavy burden as it was.

The absolute priority was to make room for as many people as possible so we were only to bring along one small bag. All that had been ours for centuries was going to be gulped down by the Russians just as an ocean wave destroys castles of sand. I remembered my childhood books, still fresh in my mind, full of stories of treasures hidden by or from pirates.

First, together with Wiechmann, my forester friend, we pondered on what to do with the guns. I was rather attached to them. They were of excellent quality, among them a pair of Purdeys left to my brother and me by our father.

We resolved to dig a hole in Wiechmann's garden, wrap the guns in oilpaper, bury them and hope for the best. We knew from reports of refugees that for the Russians to find a gun, even an air-pressure gun for children, was enough reason to shoot the owner.

During the years following the war, I forgot about the guns. Wiechmann had passed away and I had other priorities on my mind. After the fall of the East German State, I became friends with the new forester at Görlsdorf, a nice young man, very keen on hunting. He told me that sometime in the 1980s, he had dug a hole in the garden to bury some new pipes. At some point, he stumbled on our hiding-place. He told me: 'I saw the vestiges of eight guns. All that was left were the barrels, the wooden parts had thoroughly rotted. I still could imagine the quality of the guns and was sad to have to throw everything away.'

With the guns out of the way, I hatched a plan a few days later to save at least a few valuables, my ancestors' silverware and china, from the cupidity of the Barbarians. To do so I had to obtain permission from my mother, and that was a feat in itself. First, she was so busy that I almost never saw her and never alone, second because the operation represented many risks for little chance of success. I finally managed to see Mother privately one evening when she came to give me my medicine herself. Absentmindedly she gave me a blank cheque.

For two days everyone on hand in the house, under the direction of Ehrentraut, our old butler, packed the contents of the vault room in newspaper and wood wool and stuffed it in 13 old wooden wine crates. Mother seemed totally unconcerned by what we were doing. She interfered only once: it was to forbid us to pack the silverware and the china that we currently used: 'I don't want to be cheap with the officers who are presently under my roof and who offer us their protection. I can't picture myself burying my possessions and leaving them to eat out of their mess bowl.'

One evening she sent for a small metal trunk, upholstered inside and out and equipped with a lock. She shut herself in her apartments with it. When she came out the next day, she had the trunk placed with the other crates. I had found, with the help of our trusted Wiechmann, a place in the woods, accessible, not too far but isolated enough so that it would not be spotted from a road or a path.

*

On 20 April, on a night that should have been black but presently was red with the war so close, we loaded the crates onto a two-horse cart. Walkhoff, the caretaker, Beutel the coachman and I plunged into the woods where Wiechmann was waiting for us at an agreed spot. A light, thin, even rain was falling, licking our faces. It had a salty taste. We dug two holes, seven feet deep, a certain distance apart from one another. The ground was sandy and easy to dig. We set the little coffer and the crates containing the silverware in one hole, the other crates in the second hole. Then we proceeded to cover the holes with the earth and hid them with foliage. The whole operation took most of the night. There was an eerie atmosphere in that part of the forest. The four of us worked in silence with the discreet light of a torch. In the distance, the roaring of the military trucks from the front lines could be heard and we could discern the rays of their headlights. The sky was striped with the flashes of the guns giving out a staccato, deafening sound. We didn't pay attention any more to the whistling of the bombs, which exploded in the distance without startling us.

I was clearly aware that we were not only hiding a material treasure but severing our roots. It was my heart I was burying in those woods, and Mother's heart. And where to go to? What for? To live? To die?

My mournful disposition was probably because I felt so rotten physically for I never looked back with regrets after that night until I came back, 50 years later. My memories were intact, I realise now that they are not as painful but I avoided calling on them.

We returned to the village, still silent. We said a goodbye to one another loaded with unspoken but overpowering emotion. I never again saw any of those three trustworthy and honest men who hold forever a place in my heart. They contributed to make from my youth a spiritual wealth and my modest material fortune of today. They never uttered a single word about our secret, not even to their closest family and took it to their graves.

Wiechmann, the forester, worked a few more years under the new regime. After he retired, he lived in the village. When they questioned him about 'the treasure', he pretended not to remember where it was buried. It was probably a deception. He was the most trustworthy of the trusted. He died soon after, without giving away the secret, even to his wife.

Beutel, the coachman, died immediately after the war and we lost all trace of him.

Walkhoff, the caretaker, lived until a very old age. He was mentally disturbed in the end. He often talked about the treasure, said he had to find it, 'Because the Princess will come back soon and everything must be ready for her.' He would sometimes slip away to go to the woods but didn't remember the spot where the treasure was buried. He died without revealing the secret. His two daughters, both very old, are still living. We visit them sometimes; they have become slightly senile as well. Horst's mother (Horst was my childhood buddy) had taken care of Mrs Walkhoff before she died. That is how she learnt that a treasure was buried in the forest, she suspected vaguely in which area. But I am dead sure that without the map it would have been impossible to find it, except by an extraordinary coincidence.

Upon returning home, I went immediately to Mother in her sitting room. She was alone in front of the fireplace. The expression on her face was so aloof that she seemed a stranger.

In the evening, I drew a map of the area where we had buried the crates, from the notes I had scribbled on a small piece of paper in the woods, with the light of the war. I suspected I wouldn't be back for a long time, maybe never, but I hoped that one day some descendant of mine would go back to his ancestors' land and I wanted him to find a trace of his past, even such a meaningless one.

I thought that after 20 years the forest would be unrecognisable. Therefore, I measured the distances on the ground with the hunting stones as markers. They were square stones, five feet long, planted vertically in the earth, emerging only three feet above it. On each side of each stone, to help the hunters to get oriented, was inscribed a number showing the four corners of a square department of the forest. I had thought that those stones deeply rooted in the ground as they were, would be very difficult to unearth and that there was a great chance that they would be left in place.

Effectively, half a century later, they were still standing in the same places.

*

On the evening of 25 April 1945, I made a grand tour of every room in the castle to say goodbye to my home and to see whether I could find one or two souvenirs to take away in my pocket, rather like a child who doesn't want to leave without his teddy bear. But I was a grown-up now; the only right I still had was to flee or to die. I was treated as a man too soon; I had had to wear a uniform for such a long time. And, only when Germany was crushed and humiliated was I taught what pride and honour there is in victory. And now the Army was retreating, it had given up 'its children' and I must run, along with women, children and old people, from the enemy I was taught to confront but had never seen, away from my home, away from my life. I was lost, sick and alone with anxieties that I certainly wouldn't add to my mother's own. Deep down in my soul, I knew I would never again see my home, the witness of my happy and careless youth. I was going away from my roots, away from the place that had been designed for me by my forbears.

I began with the children's floor, the big room where we took our meals and where I took my classes. Next door, my bedroom, where I had so often voiced loudly my protests against the intrusion of a bat through the open window in the summer, then my brother's bedroom, my sisters', Buttel's and Netti's and Rara's, all so familiar and yet already fading away. One floor down I crossed Mother's sitting room, where we gathered in front of the fireplace to listen to the radio during the war and heard the frightening news from the Russian lines getting closer and closer with so much speed. Sometimes it was the voice of that demented Hitler, whose rantings would make our hair curl. I laid my hand on Mother's writing table, on her armchair, on the table next to it, empty now of the silver trinkets I would always handle or play with. Where was my little heart-shaped piano? Where was my little carriage with its coachman? They would have been small enough to find room in my pocket. I dragged my feet to leave the room, glancing one last time at the park through the balcony. I entered the bedroom and stopped in front of the dressing-table. I used to play seated on the floor, while Mother was putting on her make-up before dinner. Her perfume, 'Soir de Paris', always scented her apartment.

When one of the children had his or her birthday, he or she was allowed to sleep in Mother's bedroom. A small bed was set for the occasion and when it was my turn, I had the pleasure of going to sleep in her presence and to find her there when I woke up. The day's hero also had the right to choose the lunch menu. The choice was excruciating, between roasted pigeon and chicken in supreme sauce. If I wasn't satisfied with my selection, I still had another birthday coming . . . next year.

Across the bathroom I entered what had been my father's apartment and had been redesigned as two rooms for my eldest sisters, Milli and Meggi, since the war. I walked down the corridor to the guestrooms, which each had a name: the two Rose rooms, the two Carnation rooms, the room with the balcony, the Schleich room (a doctor-painter, friend of my parents). Then my Aunt Babich's room for when she would grace us with a visit. Her bedroom and bathroom, the bathtub included, were entirely panelled and there were old English engravings on the walls in both rooms. On the first floor was the big hall with the double-revolution staircase, then, straight on, the winter garden where we had coffee after meals and where I had to come and say hello to the guests, which I dreaded as does every child who hates to be hugged and kissed by strangers. From the winter garden, where the palm trees stood high, there was a splendid view over the park and, behind the castle, to the lake where a melancholic white swan glided. The female had died and her mate adamantly refused to remarry, charging nastily any candidate to her position, however pretty and attractive she might be.

Farther away were the succession of reception rooms with the big familiar portraits of my great-uncle with an identical beard to Emperor

Wilhelm I's, and of his eight year-old daughter in a pink-laced dress, the vast library, where we had our Christmas parties, the imposing dining-room with its display of the silver trophies our horses won at the races, where I had my first drink of schnapps for my 12th birthday. I pronounced redundant obscure philosophical sentences such as: 'Life is so-o dull, forever getting up-school-eating-going to bed . . .' which occasioned loud, merciless laughs. Next, the breakfast room, where the family gathered in the morning under a gigantic 18th-century portrait of Court Marshal Redern. And finally my grandfather's sitting-room, dark, with tapestries, that had been untouched since his death in 1909.

Around midnight, after a last dinner, we took our little bags, our coats and a few trinkets which could be stuffed in our pockets and waited in front of the castle for the tractor which soon arrived with the trailer already filled to capacity with women and children. The wife of one of our managers, who travelled alone, had brought four big suitcases along and had spread them generously on the knees of the other refugees, although she had been given the same instructions as everybody else. Mother was fuming but couldn't gather the courage to tell her to leave her belongings immediately. It was a real nuisance for the whole trip, however. A little Mercedes was tied to the trailer. There was no petrol for it but Mother wanted it, partly to be able to fill it with luggage, partly because she hoped to sell it later. Besides, the person who would be at the wheel would be a person less in the trailer. We tried to tell her that she might be miscalculating as the car could attract envy long before our arrival in a safe place. 'The lack of petrol will discourage the thugs!' answered Mother stubbornly. She was right.

We said goodbye to Uncle Wilfried, the retired admiral, who wanted to protect our flight and had to stay anyway, as no man, whatever his old age, had the right to flee. A few days later he left with the rest of the village people, in horse-drawn carts, when the Nazis finally gave the order to evacuate the region. He made it to the west, found his wife who had fled Berlin, and we had many reunions with them afterwards.

We hugged tightly our old servants who had chosen to stay and climbed on board. The tractor shivered and moved on heavily, taking the path of the Snake, so called because it displayed many curves.

Before the first turn, I stole a last glance at Görlsdorf, which was neatly distinguishable against the sky, illuminated by the artillery fire. The castle stood tall and pink, the most beautiful home in the entire world. Then it faded slowly away and among blinding flashes and with the sound of the guns which made the earth shudder, we entered a life that was to consist for a long time of deprivations, sorrow and fear for our loved ones.

Chapter Seven

ESCAPE

Mother had approached a Polish prisoner from the mandatory service a few days before, to ask him whether he would agree to drive our tractor. He had immediately accepted.

Poles wore a 'P' (for Pole) on their coat, partly to make flight more difficult for them, partly so that the Germans would not fraternise too much with them. Mother had applied the same treatment to foreign workers as to German ones. They seemed relatively satisfied with us, given that they were away from their land and worried for their families in a hostile country engaged in a merciless world war.

The tractor was an old model, powerful but designed to pull carts rather than to play the role of tourist bus. It managed ten miles an hour, at the most. It didn't have a starter. We had to heat the engine with a blowtorch for ten to 15 minutes to start it. It was such a complicated operation that we avoided stopping the engine for stopovers of less than two hours.

I have in front of me the little piece of paper on which I had planned the itinerary of our flight that I always kept. We had to avoid the roads and the big cities because I feared we would be drowned in the traffic jams caused by the refugees from the east and the military trucks of the Army backing away. The distance we had to cover was 255 miles and I had written down the mileage between each city.

I was at the wheel of the Mercedes and I couldn't help but feel slightly proud to drive a car, even one pulled by a tractor, and even if I was nauseated and very uncomfortable between the bags and all kind of rubbish around me. In fact, I was rather like a child on a merry-go-round but my dignity spared me realising that. I pictured myself driving a racing-car and daydreamed about my future as a racing pilot. Mother came to take my place a few times but she could not be less welcome. Either she would wake me up from my dreams or I felt so weak that to change places was too much of an effort. To tell the truth, I did not get a chance to forget about my hepatitis with the diet I was observing and that we all had to share, like it or not. We had only bread, sausages and . . . fat, greasy pâté. When I was too cold, I would secretly gulp down a shot of schnapps. The alcohol had just enough time to reach my stomach and come back up but with this back and forth movement inside, I was at least a little warmer!

Very few were the ones who were lucky enough to have a vehicle in which to flee. Many poor people threw themselves on the road, walking, surrounded by children in tears, exhausted with cold, hunger, fright and weariness before they even started their journey of despair without so much as a wheelbarrow. The ones who had carts pulled by horses could not feed their animals, whose corpses were abandoned to rot along the roadside while their owners, not in much better condition, left their bags and tried their last chance on foot, in utter destitution. Most of them had a long way to go, strenuous and dangerous for they originated from the farther away eastern provinces. The roads were icy and choked with crowds of refugees. For weeks, people progressed slowly in the snow, without any means of obtaining food or medicines.

East Prussia, already encircled by the Soviet army, was cut off early from the rest of Germany. To get out, you had to find a place on a boat and try an escape by the Baltic Sea, along the coasts.

A mother with five children I met on the road, told me she had been offered the opportunity of boarding the *Wilhelm Gustloff* at Koenigsberg harbour, on the Baltic Sea. She declined, as she could not leave on that very day. The ship was torpedoed and sunk by a Russian submarine as it was leaving the harbour, with more than 5,000 refugees on board, mostly women and children. No one escaped.

We listened to bits of pathetic stories as waves of people arrived alongside us, pushed by the crowd, then they would fade away again, in front or behind.

We had brought with us what medicines we had left so that we could be of help along the road. We had had a choice to make and there had been less room then for extra food. It was apparently the right option as we had not even a single aspirin left on arrival and we had the joy of seeing some tragic faces light up with relief.

We had had a heated discussion at home, Mother and I, concerning the choice of provisions. I wanted food provisions, she had replied: 'You are always hungry and have a gigantic appetite, my son. And if you don't eat it all, the others in the trailer will. We are headed for problems. They will not fight for bandages and we will be able to bring all the medicine we have left for the same volume as for one day of extra food.'

Sadly, I had to admit her reasoning was sound, and I agreed with all my heart.

We saw prisoners from the concentration camps, in striped rags. The roads were clogged sometimes as we were forced to park or stand aside while those pathetic figures, famished and weak, with haggard eyes, passed along. They dragged their skeleton-like bodies in files of two, framed by SS, going west. It was the first time that I had seen with my own eyes that the rumours about the camps were founded.

I learnt later that their guard-torturers had got the prisoners out from the concentration camps in the east of the country so that the Russians would not find them. Now those guards didn't dare release their prisoners so that they, the guards, could run away, under the stares of a hostile crowd, fearing to be assaulted and lynched. They had their fingers on the triggers of their machine-guns which they let wander in the direction of the civilians. They could still use their guns to intimidate the people around but they well knew they were poison. If they put them down, they would be jumped on, if they kept them they would be of no use to find bread.

Perhaps now I should say something about how Nazism and politics affected me as a German.

Our family unit was not much involved in politics, unlike many of our relatives and friends. The reason was that there was no adult male at home, as my father died when the Nazis came to power and my mother had no father or brother any more. I guess I can be grateful to God about it now when I see the incredible impact the condemnation of their husbands, fathers, sons or brothers had on their loved ones. They say you never recover from such a blow. My uncle's son became a clergyman. I think he was the wisest, as faith helped him deal with those dreadful feelings that eat away at you: hate, rage, humiliation, sorrow combined with utter despair and distrust in mankind at large.

My mother was nationalistic to begin with, like most people of our social upbringing at the time. She was seduced at first by the idea that Hitler would re-establish the position of Germany as a great power with a strong economy, a position lost by our country after the Versailles Treaty. She wasn't long in changing her opinion radically in view of the bellicose tendencies of the new regime. Her true nature was Socialist and she remained so until she died although no one among us ever sympathised with her opinions, so she kept them to herself. 'With the Socialists there will not be another Hitler, at least,' she would say defiantly.

What did we know about the crimes against the Jews? We were aware that the Nazis persecuted the Jews. We knew of the 'Nuremberg laws' which forbade the Jews to practise their trade and to marry non-Jews. We knew that several of them had fled Germany before the war when the conditions were getting more difficult every day for them. I think that very few of them as well as ourselves foresaw the danger that was lurking, however. Now it was impossible for any German, Jew or not, to leave the country as we were at war with the rest of the world and not one nation gave visas to Germans. What we didn't know was that murder was involved, mass murder. I remember the shock I had when I saw for the first time someone wearing the yellow star. It was in the subway, in Berlin, in 1943. The image remained imprinted in my memory because I felt shame to be a German and to accept that. Later, I sensed a responsibility in the fact that I remained silent and I am not proud of my cowardice. I don't think, even now, that my young age was an excuse. We were all made adult and responsible at a very young age during the war and I am therefore guilty too. I imagine it is shame together with helplessness and fright that silenced most of us. We wanted to find our excuse in believing the official version, which stated that the Jews would be transferred east to settle in new territories as had been done for the American Indians. There was no glory in accepting that, however; people are not cattle to be parked.

The genocide which began in 1941–42 was kept top-secret by the Party and, because the extermination camps on a grand scale were located in Poland and Ukraine and not in Germany, the people had little idea of what was going on. Many Jews, even the ones who were already in the camps and heard rumours, would not believe them. My wife's father, who was a French cavalry officer, was locked up in three different stalags during his five years of imprisonment. He had been taken prisoner in Metz, Alsace, in 1939 and his entire unit killed their horses before surrendering. In the camp, they had better information than the Germans, as they always had a clandestine radio and they listened to the BBC every day. All the same, my father-in-law, still with us today, says they never suspected anything and the first hints they had were after they were freed.

When this ignominy was made public after the war, and was proven with written documents, photos and films, I wasn't innocent any more. I had seen prisoners from the camps on the roads during our flight, and although they were probably political prisoners and not Jews, they had no human shape left.

*

Every now and then on our journey Nazi dignitaries passed us by, first in their brown Party uniform, in the end in plain clothes as they thought it was wiser to throw away their uniforms. They would push us to the side of the road and pass at full speed, blasting their horn. They had petrol.

A refugee we met on the road told us he had seen in a town several sacks loaded with money bills of 100 and 1,000 marks, just abandoned on the side of the street. Nobody picked them up as it was thought that a few days later that money would be worth nothing at all. Still, in 1948, the banks accepted that money for conversion into new marks for ten per cent of its value.

It took us three days and three nights to cover the distance. We were travelling at night, by stages of eight to ten hours. By day we stopped, in an isolated place if possible, under some trees to have shelter against the low-flying fighter planes that sometimes would shoot at us. We ate and slept in our trailer and went out only for our natural needs in the woods – which were plentiful on our route, fortunately – where the foliage would hide our confusion. I had an acute awareness of the brutality of this change of life for my already ageing mother who had crossed, in a few minutes' time, the threshold from luxury to absolute poverty. As far as I was concerned, I was at last appreciating having been trained in the army in difficult enough conditions to have been somewhat toughened against hardships.

Next to the fighter planes, what I feared most was that some Party official would stop us in a village. The officials had all become almost mad with fear and rage. They were terrified of being captured and judged by the Soviets at the end of the war and we were at risk of them requisitioning the tractor and the trailer. We would have been defenceless, and with no means of transport the Russians would have been on us in a matter of hours – they were advancing at lightning speed.

The SS or the military checked us at every street corner. Luck was with us. Our little caravan of women, children and one teenager – armed with a certificate from the official doctor and the written agreement of the general – who felt responsible for his small party, went on with not too many difficulties. What a relief it was for us all when we crossed the Schleswig-Holstein border! We knew that that province was going to be occupied by the British and that would surely be better than by the Soviets.

Our Polish driver delivered us at our destination, 200 miles in the opposite direction to his destination in Poland. He did it with dedication, as if it were a normal thing to do. He could have chosen to go directly back home and that would have been a disaster for us. No one else could have driven the tractor, which pulled a heavy trailer and still another car behind for there were only women and me. Not one of us knew how to operate that tractor and I was still weak with this 'jaundice', as people would say at the time, which refused to go away.

We said an emotional good-bye to our lifesaver and Mother gave him the reward he deserved. He left, walking in the direction we came from. Our eyes followed him for a long time. He was marching, cheerfully, towards those Russians, hellhounds for us, angels of deliverance for him.

Did compassion that was shown successively from one side, then from the other between him and us, represent a lifebuoy or a bridge between two enemy worlds?

*

In the evening of 30 April 1945, a speech from Admiral Doenitz was broadcast on the radio: 'The Führer fell in the Berlin Battle. He named me chief of the temporary government . . .'

The speech was recorded and broadcast from the town of Flensburg, in Schleswig-Holstein, within a stone's throw of where we had taken refuge. Only on the next day did we learn that Hitler, far from falling on the front as the millions of Germans he had sent to get killed for contemptible reasons, had cowardly committed suicide at the very last minute before being caught, huddled up in his bunker.

I was thunderstruck. I brooded a lot, asking myself questions I didn't have the answer to. His last but one act of war had been to kill the woman he had married for the circumstance. Was he aware that his trusted Goebbels would do even better just after him, adding the murder of his seven children to his wife's before killing himself? Did the wives agree? Had they any choice? Did they or the children have any political say or carry any importance? The Protector of the Nation . . .

Deep down I had always known that Hitler would never agree to surrender, to take responsibility for his crimes in the face of the entire world. If only he had committed suicide earlier, even only a month earlier! There would have been hundreds of thousands fewer deaths. But the Führer was a blood-thirsty, paranoid and megalomaniac criminal. He thought that if the war was lost, the German people would be to blame and therefore didn't deserve to survive.

What an enormous relief for us all! No more fear of new tricks, new nightmares, new lies. No more Gestapo and SS rule. They soiled Germany forever. We didn't realise it immediately because we didn't know the extent of the crimes committed in our name but, at the bottom of the heart of each one of us, there started to grow this terrible feeling of guilt which had to be passed on to our children after us, then surely to our children's children.

Chapter Eight

POST-WAR LIFE

When we arrived at Altenhof, the estate of Countess Reventlow in Schleswig-Holstein, the Countess and her daughter, Marie-Louise von Bethmann-Hollweg, daughter-in-law of the last Chancellor of Wilhelm II, and intimate friend of my parents, greeted us with extreme kindness and warmth.

We heaved a deep sigh of relief and at the same time, an intense feeling of gratitude overwhelmed us. We were however deadly anxious about our loved ones. We couldn't get any news from them and we had to bear those worries and the pain of having left all that was our reason to live. It was out of the question to try and get relief by communicating our feelings when there was nothing we could say to one another to relieve the pain. We were conscious, however, of having been blessed with enormous luck. We had arrived safely, with neither injuries nor breakdowns, we had escaped from the Soviet troops who were breathing on our heels and of whom we knew what brutality and savagery was to be expected.

It was a large number of us who ended up at our generous hostesses': first my mother and me, later our estate manager, our riding master (they were immediately hired at the Countess's estate and stayed there until they retired) and my nanny Rara.

My sister Meggi had gone back to Berlin because she hoped to obtain her graduation in law but she had to leave a few days before us. In fact she had waited until the very last minute, when there was only one road still open westbound, the Soviets already circling Berlin. She left with Irmgard Zarden, daughter of a State Secretary and friend of my sisters, who had been jailed previously by the Nazis. Here is what Irmgard wrote about her flight from Berlin to the West:

In April of 1945, Meggi and Wilhelm (her future husband) stayed with me in my aunt's villa in Grunewald. I had lived there since my release from prison in July 1944 . . . I had had my backpack ready for weeks but had not yet decided to leave Berlin. Meggi and I resolved to go to Görlsdorf and get potatoes and peas. In the early morning of Friday, 20 April (Hitler's 56th and last birthday), we set out from the Grunewald station. The Russians were near the Oder and we thought we had time to get to Görlsdorf and come back.

After changing trains many times, we arrived in Görlsdorf in the afternoon.

We could hear the noise of the battle taking place on the Oder and the tractor was ready to leave.

That night in Görlsdorf, we had a memorable dinner. There were a number of other people, relatives and friends at the table, and the old butler proceeded to serve the choicest wines from the cellar, as they would have to be left behind. We tasted from many bottles of old vintages. To this day, I remember an 1896 Burgundy! Whatever was left in the bottles was poured away.

As the noise of the battle was heard closer and closer, we went to bed after having decided to leave very early next morning, fortified with 100 pounds each of potatoes and peas. Before we departed, Meggi's mother still tried to persuade her to stay and leave with the tractor.

We left with our load in a horse-drawn buggy, changed trains many times but arrived safely in the afternoon at the Grunewald station. The trains were full of soldiers who helped us up and down with our 'hand luggage'. There was a general atmosphere of confusion because of the Russians getting closer and closer to Berlin. In Grunewald we could hear some rumbling battle-noise. I took the handcart from the house and thus we brought our precious load home. A feat considering that the Russians were by then at the outskirts of Berlin.

On the next day, Sunday, 22 April, my mind was made up. I would leave for the West at nightfall. Meggi and Wilhelm couldn't bring themselves to leave yet, but, as the noise of the battle became deafening, they decided to come along. We gave the potatoes and peas to the cook who had attended us so well in my aunt's house and was the last person to stay behind. It proved life-saving for her in the coming months.

We left at 12.30 a.m. on a pitch-black night and stumbled through the Grunewald. Wilhelm wore his black tank uniform with his iron cross, his arm in a make-believe sling (he had a real wound on his body but it didn't show). We were stopped repeatedly by military patrols who were on the lookout for deserters who would be executed by hanging on the spot, but we had concocted quite a believable story: Wilhelm had been in a military hospital and was now trying to find his unit.

At dawn, we were on the Nauener Heerstrasse, the last main road out of Berlin that was not yet occupied by the Soviets. Strangely enough, the only people leaving were military with horses and wagons, a striking contrast to the beginning of the war when the military used tanks and Stukas, the famous planes which fell 25,000 feet down from the sky at lightning speed, dropped their bombs and were off again so fast that no anti-aircraft guns had a chance to strike them. Except for us, there were no civilians on the road. The Berliners had obviously left or decided to stay in their homes and guard their belongings.

We were given rides now and then from the soldiers, which were welcome since our loads were heavy. As the army was leaving Berlin, the roadside was packed with Volkssturm, young boys not older than 15. One of them said: 'The Führer is going to manage, General Wendt and his army will come soon.' There was indeed a General Wendt, but his army had long since disintegrated and these poor youths were eventually killed by the Russians.

Our destination was Schleswig-Holstein, via Mecklenburg, where we had a friend. It took us several days to get up there. Some small town in Mecklenburg had just been almost wiped out. The British had attacked V-bombs, loaded on a train at the railroad station.

One morning, at the end of April, we rang the bell at our acquaintances', in Eutin, looking bedraggled and dirty by then. Our hosts were not exactly jumping with joy but had to let us in. We stayed for a while after getting ration cards. One day, shortly before the end, I saw Heinrich Himmler, the almighty head of the dreaded SS, in a simple military green coat, sitting in the dining-room of a hotel, looking as green in the face as his coat. A few days later, he commited suicide by poison.

As I learned 50 years later, the night we spent in Görlsdorf was the night Alexander buried his treasure.

Wilhelm, in the meantime, had left Meggi to get his discharge from the Army. A few days later, Meggi was walking along with Buttel in Eckernförde, a small town next to Altenhof, when they saw for the first time a few grey automobiles with a white star. The Allies had arrived and occupied the region without a shot. For a few weeks, we lived in a strange situation as the German troops, still armed, and the British circulated peacefully side by side. Suddenly, a German military car stopped in front of my sisters and a German officer jumped out to embrace Meggi. It was Wilhelm, together with another German officer, Lix Oettingen, an old friend of his he had been reunited with by chance a few days earlier in the hospital.

In 1946, Wilhelm married Meggi and Lix, Buttel. Chance had it that Buttel found a Catholic husband without Mother's socialising. Lix radiated such kindness and attentions that everybody loved him immediately and he was soon and forever my best friend. For Mother, he could have been from outer space and she would have given him her blessing all the same. His first common point with me was hepatitis. He got it in Stalingrad and thanks to it he was able to leave that door to hell. We both had a lot of gratitude towards Santa Hepatitis.

In Altenhof, we were installed in the guest-rooms, large and sumptuous, decorated with antique furniture and precious French tapestries. It was a time when every house was packed with refugees (it was worse later, when twelve million people from the Polish part of Germany and several hundred thousands from the Russian zone poured over to the west side of the country in the latter part of 1945) and when there was a great shortage of food. Our hostesses usually succeeded, nonetheless, in providing us with adequate meals. Unfortunately, after a few weeks, the Chief Commander of the British Forces of occupation decided to invite himself in and to establish his headquarters in that beautiful castle. We had to leave this new home which had greeted us with such kindness and generosity but we all kept forever in our hearts feelings of affection and gratitude for our hostesses.

For my mother, this fabulous hospitality has been instrumental in helping her survive the horror of what the war meant for her in the end. Contrary to most women, she had never left home when she married, she even became the owner of it. The end of the war, with the loss of her land which had been in the family for over 300 years, was the end of her world, of her life. I know she was in agony over it although I never heard her complain.

*

We were rescued in another castle, not far from there, at Princess Heinrich's, the widowed sister-in-law to Kaiser Wilhelm II. She was a sweet old lady, sister of the last Tsarina who was murdered in 1919. She became adamant and pitiless, however, when the subject of Anna Anderson was brought up. Anna Anderson spent a great part of her life trying to get recognition as Anastasia, the youngest daughter of Tsar Nicolas II.

'I've seen her for a few days,' said the Princess, 'and I talked at length with her. I can guarantee she is not my niece.'

We couldn't take advantage for too long of the Princess's hospitality. Buttel and I left then, to try and find the different members of our family, not knowing anything of what had become of them. There was no telephone and the mail was not to be relied on. We made a trip of roughly 500 miles, hitchhiking from northern Germany to Rhineland and Milli's in-laws. It took us three days to complete the journey because there were very few cars. Their occupants were willing to help and stopped. The difficult part was to find food and a roof because there was a curfew from ten o'clock at night until six o'clock in the morning and you were shot at if you were out in-between. On the return trip, I was alone and once hopelessly waited for a car in a small city. At five to ten in the evening, I knocked on the door of the nearest house and asked whether they could give me shelter for the night. The people were quite obliging and allowed me to sleep on the covered terrace. Unfortunately, their German Shepherd dog kept watch in front of the only door, which was understandable. After all, I could be a burglar or a murderer. When I wanted to go out for a natural need, the dog refused to let me out. I had a tormented night.

On my return, my mother decided to board our tractor again with Milli, who was then pregnant with her first child, Meggi and Buttel, and to settle in the Rhineland, near Milli's in-laws, 22 miles away from Bonn.

To move from Schleswig to the Rhineland (as was the case for any change of location beyond the limits of the city or village of residence) you had to have a written permit from the military government to leave and from the sector where you were transferring to, the authorisation to arrive and settle there.

There was no more government, no laws, and no rights for the Germans. The occupation troops were all-powerful over us. The Americans were fair and very nice; they even distributed food and sweets to the children. The British were very correct but impersonal and hard. The French were feared, in particular their Senegalese regiments who seemed to be everywhere. They were almost as poor as we were and raided at the slightest opportunity. Our frontiers had shrunk to such an extent that there was a popular joke among the Berliners, famous for their sarcastic minds:

'After the war, what will you do?'

'I'll make a bike tour of Germany.'

'What about the afternoon?'

Count Roch zu Lynar, c. 1580

WILHELM GRAF VON REDERN

*Königl. Pr. Kammerherr, Gener-Intendant der
Königl. Schauspiele und Ritter mehrerer
hohen Orden.*

LEFT: Count Wilhelm von Redern (1802–83)

BELOW: Redern Palace in Berlin (building on right)

Gorlsdörf

Lindenan

ABOVE: The author's mother, Princess Victoria zu Lynar-Redern, with her eldest daughter, Milli

RIGHT: The author's father, Prince Ernst zu Lynar-Redern, c. 1920

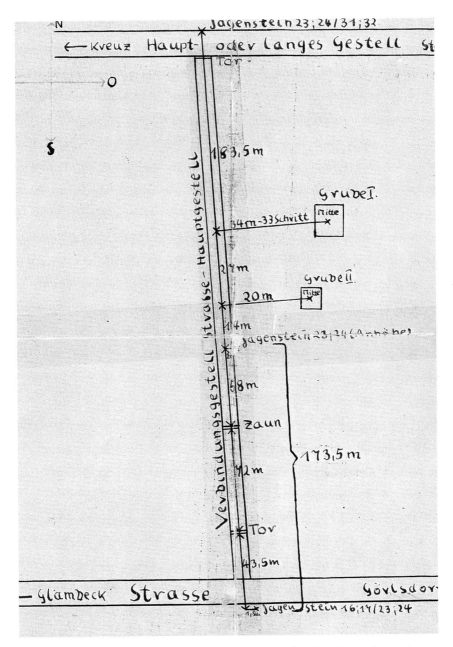

The map made by Alexander Lynar in 1945 showing where the
treasure was buried

Gregory Mills, of Geophysical Survey Systems, recovering some of
the treasure, June 1995 (courtesy of Sotheby's)

The treasure laid out on the forest ground (courtesy of Sotheby's)

ABOVE: Two early nineteenth-century tureens by the French maker Odiot – part of the 120-piece service (courtesy of Sotheby's)

RIGHT: A selection of the silver and porcelain (courtesy of Sotheby's)

The auction at Sotheby's (courtesy of Sotheby's)

The author with his wife and son

The journey took us four or five days. Our tractor, although with a lighter load than on its first trip, was travelling at no more than seven to eight miles per hour. The Reventlows were kind enough to give us diesel. Our drivers were Lix and Wilhelm who took turns. They had told Mother that they were experts in tractor manoeuvring. Actually, while everybody was asleep, they would rendezvous at the tractor and try to understand whatever they could and practise. They must have done a good job or the machine was exceptionally strong and good willing or both because we never had any technical trouble on the way. We stopped at friends or relations. At the stopovers, each one gave or received news of members of such and such a family, for all the homes had been blown up in every direction, the men still alive came back from the front as they could or were taken prisoners. We stopped at the Ratibors, where Mother got news of Ernst-Wilhelm. They told her he was in good health and was residing with friends of his in Bavaria. She didn't even know he was alive, he didn't know where we were . . . Towards the end of her life, Mother wrote to me:

I left my homeland probably forever, and I would have gone on my knees to Görlsdorf if I had been allowed to go back home but in the end, the thing that matters most for me is that all of my children are alive and well. You have all given me plenty of happiness and no sorrow. I remember that in times past, when I had kissed all of my children good night, I already felt like bursting with joy. With you all around me, my dreams are fulfilled.

When I was born, the midwife, Mrs Linde, tried to hide the general disappointment by crying out bravely: 'Oh, what a pretty little girl!' At the time, boys were greatly valued and a lady's reputation gained in prestige with the birth of a boy.

My mother particularly wanted boys, she despised girls and said they ought to be drowned like kittens. That did nothing for my self-esteem. Unfortunately, she was tragically chastised, not only by bearing four daughters and only one son but also by the loss of him.

In 1914, the terrible Great War began. My brother then came back from the Argentine on board a ship that was captured by an English war vessel. Bubi was taken prisoner to London. He was released and was able to re-enter Germany a few weeks later. He was killed in combat in the first months of the war. He had been afraid that the war would be over without offering him the possibility to fight for his country, enlisted immediately and fell in the Ypres battle, in Belgium, at the very moment when he was launching an assault.

I will never forget the moment when we stood at the park gate,

Mother resting against a tree, all of her strength drained away, waiting for the carriage bringing back the casket . . .

Today, I do not have any task or any responsibility any more and I am satisfied and grateful to God, to have you all and I thank Him and you for your kindness toward me.

She added a postscript at the age of 90:

I feel that senility and death are racing each other in me. I am eager to know which will win!

On our way, in the city of Marburg, we had to leave Buttel in a hospital to be operated on for the removal of a tumour in the intestines. She was terribly sick and had to stay in hospital for eight weeks, and my mother stayed with her part of the time. When she recovered, she went to stay with the Wittgenstein family in Westphalia, where we had all spent a night a few days before. I joined Buttel there a little later.

The Prince Wittgenstein brothers were two tiny old gentlemen, rather eccentric. They had never married or produced any offspring. They had adopted a nephew who had married a Bismarck girl we knew very well. The nephew had warned us that one of his uncle's favourite pastimes was to eavesdrop behind the doors.

After dinner, the young Wittgenstein stood up, careful not to make any noise, went briskly to the door and opened it abruptly. The old uncle was there, hat in hand (!) bent over, his ear to the keyhole. His face turned red with embarrassment.

The old brothers had not hunted or fired a shot in all their lives. Nevertheless, they had bought trophies in great quantities: stags, reindeer, elk and wapiti, which hung in all the endless corridors and halls of their enormous and horribly ugly castle.

My bedroom was located at the other end of the castle. I had to cross a good part of the house, which was very dimly lit. All these big stuffed animal heads stared at me in the twilight and more than once, at the turn of a corridor, I stumbled on one of the little uncles. He stood there, in the dark, without a word to me, as I passed him. It was rather creepy.

When we were all there on our first visit, one of the old gentlemen came to me with a conspiratorial look and whispered: 'I have looked you all up in the *Gotha*, but I could not find any reference to Wilhelm Messenger.'

'You wouldn't find his name there,' I answered, chuckling. 'He is not an aristocrat.'

The old gentleman pondered my words for a while, then said pensively: 'Oh, I see . . . But nevertheless, he seems quite a nice fellow!'

One day, as I was walking along the road below the castle, a British soldier in uniform, riding a motorcycle, passed me. He came to a halt a few yards farther away and couldn't start the engine again whatever his frantic attempts. When I arrived alongside him again, he addressed me: 'Do you want a motorbike? I'm fed up with the bloody thing, you can have it!'. He then proceeded to stop the next military truck that came by, climbed in and left me the proud owner of a motorbike. I wasn't even old enough to be allowed to drive it, although at the time regulations of that kind were not much enforced. I then tried to sell it, which proved very difficult, as there were no spare parts available for repairs. I got only a few marks for it and my pride was short-lived.

One day we made a stopover at a castle belonging to friends of ours located near a farm. A firm from the neighbouring town had stored in the farm about 50 metal drums containing several hundred gallons of alcohol at 98 per cent proof. As there had been no alcoholic drinks for a long time, our friends had made tiny holes, first shyly in one barrel, then a few more in other drums, and would draw alcohol when occasion demanded a celebration. Mixed with water and fruit juice, it became . . . inebriating. There was need for a celebration when we arrived and we toasted heartily. Everybody, me first, had forgotten I had just recovered from a vicious hepatitis. The adults didn't remember the effects of alcohol consumption and I hadn't had much experience of it. We were stone drunk at the end of the evening.

The next day I awoke with a sensation of tons of sawdust in the stomach on top of a very classical urge to bump against the walls to soothe the pain in my head. Wilhelm told me right then that the Americans had dropped an atomic bomb on Japan. Hardly emerging from my alcoholic stupor, I repeated over and over: 'It can't be true! It is not true! I learnt in my physics lessons that the atom can't be split!' We had to acknowledge the contradiction . . .

When we arrived at Milli's, her mother-in-law told us she couldn't have us in the house as she had invited us to do because the occupation troops had methodically ransacked the place and they were without furniture. We found a pavilion with three rooms in the garden of an old house, in the little town of Unkel. The housing office had declared that pavilion uninhabitable. Still, the state the rooms were in can't be described. I found some wallpaper in a corner and went to work. As I couldn't find glue, I made some with flour, taken off our food ration, and water. After one week of hard labour, I was rather proud of the results, but not for long. The paper started to fall off the wall, partly because of the quality of my glue, partly because the walls were so damp that the water was running everywhere. It was there, nonetheless, that Mother had to get settled. For my part, I was there only at weekends during the whole of that especially cold winter. We had only an open chimney to procure heat and I would feed it with what wood I could find in the forest. There was no bathroom, no running water except cold water in the kitchen.

It was so cold in the house that one morning, as Mother was washing in her room, some water fell from her bucket on the floor. It instantly froze and Mother slipped and fell heavily. She endured hardship without ever uttering one complaint, however. She was 57 years old. But we bore whatever misfortune with a rather serene mood, glad as we were that the war was over and, paramount to everything, that Hitler was dead and we had escaped from the Russians.

We listened to the radio from morning to night in the hope of hearing at last some good news, especially during the Potsdam Conference, in July 1945.

The Conference took place from 17 July to 2 August 1945, in the Caecilienhof castle, between Joseph Stalin, representing the Soviet Union, Harry Truman, the United States, Winston Churchill, Great Britain and, from 29 July, Clement Attlee instead of Churchill who had lost the premiership in the election.

The topics of the Conference were: the creation of the Allied Control Council (government); the war damages and the dismantling of the industry; the territorial settlement (north-east Prussia to go to USSR and all the territory East of Oder-Neisse to go to Poland); the definition of the occupation zones; the expulsion of the German population from the territories in Poland, Czechoslovakia and Hungary (around twelve and a half million people).

In May 1945, at the moment of the capitulation, the feeling that prevailed in me was relief. Relief from the nightmare of the war, from Hitler, from the Nazis. Whatever the cost, it would not be our honour or our life that would be at stake. I no longer faced having to die for an infamous, unjust, mad, hopeless cause. The fear of the thugs in power, of the provocateurs, of the bombs, was over. The war, the terrible war that at the bottom of our hearts we didn't dare win nor lose, was over. My brother, our relatives, our friends were coming back. Unfortunately, only one in four came back, mourning submerged every family.

We were full of hope, however, and that hope fired up unending commentaries among us: surely, the Allies would not give an entire half of Germany to the Russians. They were going to force them to retreat behind the Oder River. But the Allies decided that Germany, east of the Oder River, would definitively belong to Poland. That gave the Poles the right to expel the millions of Germans who lived on that land. Moreover, the limits of the occupation zones were defined. We learnt that all of Germany, east of the river Elbe, was falling into the Russian occupation zone. We had to surrender to the evidence: there was definitely no hope of going back home. That conclusion was confirmed by the news that the German authorities in the Soviet zone had expropriated without any compensation all land from the owners of 250 acres up.

Dorothee Löwenfeld's mother, Sybille, widow of Bill Bismarck, the second son of the Chancellor, was ordered to evacuate her estate of Varzin, in Pomerania. She firmly declared that she had no intention of leaving either her house or her land. She came out on the porch when the military car with the Soviet officers appeared at the gate of the castle and shot herself in the head. She was 81 years old.

In August 1945, 30,000 refugees per day were pouring into the 59 refugee camps in Berlin. The official estimations from Bonn have noted the disappearance of two and a half million people during the expulsions.

It was decided at Potsdam as well that the Mecklenburg and Thuringe provinces would go to the Soviets. The fear of the Soviets was such, in Germany, that the inhabitants of those two provinces had greatly rejoiced when the Americans occupied them. Without warning the population, the American troops withdrew during the night and on the next morning, the poor people found themselves under the Russians.

Misinformation took the proportions of a propaganda against the 'people's oppressors' as soon as the Soviets occupied the territory. From newspaper cuttings that would reach us from the east, we learnt that Mother had been a tyrant who used to gallop around her estate, cracking her whip (riding a horse, a whip? In Mongolia maybe, not in our country) on the back of her peasants.

In fact, I would like to point out that there were probably not many occurrences where a whole population would be relieved at the thought of losing a war! The ones who lived under the rule of those bloodthirsty tyrants who were Hitler and his gang of Nazis without being indoctrinated and are still there to testify, will understand. We Germans are very patriotic, even bellicose, and that has been our downfall more than once. Therefore, the feelings of humiliation and defeat could have prevailed. But what was left of the German people at the end of the war consisted mostly of old men, women and children to whom the sense of honour through victory meant only pain and death. As far as I was concerned, I was fatherless so the militarist side was lacking in me and I had rebelled since my teens against the slaughter, the raids, the sirens blasting, the reign of terror and despicable actions which followed my father's death. Having had no part nor any possibility of heroism during that dark period, I feel, nonetheless, the remorse and the shame which is in every German worthy of that name and I must today explain to my son why he must share the burden of guilt of the Germans. He already feels a touch of hostility against himself in certain circles abroad and must face it without rebelling, this is his (only) heritage.

*

Meggi and Buttel had stopped hitchhiking to join their fiancés in Oettingen, Bavaria, at Lix's parents. They had promised to come back for Christmas. On 24 December 1945, Mother, Ernst Wilhelm – who had come back a short while before, to our greatest joy – and I had prepared everything for the evening . . . except a meal, as we had nothing to eat except a few sausages carefully saved since Görlsdorf for the occasion. At 11 p.m., we were still alone. I signalled to Mother that we should start thinking about eating our sausages, just the three of us. Although we were starved, we were in no mood to eat heartily, even such precious food. My sisters materialised suddenly just then. They were literally collapsing under the weight of suitcases and packs, loaded with food, sweets and presents.

Lix had tried to bring them back here in his old banger that ran with a gas-driven engine. On the back of the car was fixed a great stove in which a fire burnt, fed by small pieces of wood. The wood burnt without intake of air and generated gas to make the engine work. You had to stop every hour to shove wood into the stove. It was a two-seat car, they were three. With the luggage, the gifts and the wood to go and come back, the vehicle was heavily overburdened. First the two girls had had to get out at every slope to push the car, then the car, exhausted, stopped dead at mid-distance. Poor Lix, who had undertaken that trip just to bring my sisters back home, was left alone at the roadside, with his old jalopy definitely out of breath, and he somehow had to be back at his place in time to spend his first Christmas after the war with his parents (he eventually made it). My sisters started waving wildly to try and get a lift from passing cars. It was a long and tricky operation. Although at that time everybody considered solidarity as a duty, they had the hardest time to find a vehicle with enough room inside for them plus their load. A US military truck obliged with wishes of merry Christmas and we hailed our sisters as heroines.

We all had a wonderful Christmas, indeed merry and cheerful and, because we were together, it felt warm.

In 1945, before I left the F.L.A.K., the Ministry of Culture delivered a certificate to all young people testifying that they had graduated from 'Baccalaureate' but without an examination. As could be expected, in the summer of 1945, with the war just over we were told that this certificate had no value and in my case, it meant that I had to prepare for the examination. Special classes were organised for the ex-soldiers or ex-parasoldiers who had to study in seven months the class work of the three years they had missed. Then they were authorised to pass a very selective examination as, given the fact that most universities had been destroyed by the bombardments, there were very few places in the ones that were still standing.

I remember once walking across the town of Düren in 1945. It was a city of 100,000 inhabitants before the war. I covered the distance in three hours, on foot, as there was no transportation any more. I didn't find one single building or one single house standing.

I succeeded in entering one of those speedy classes in Bonn. It was a course in the sciences (maths and physics) while my field was Latin and Greek. I had to get organised for a seven months course. Near Bonn in a fortified castle lived an old friend of my family's, Baron Albert von Boeselager. For years, he had shot stag at Görlsdorf every autumn. He seemed delighted to reciprocate by offering me his hospitality. He gave me food and lodging for seven months with great kindness and simplicity. Philipp, his second son, who had been so helpful to us at the end of the war, had come back from the war with the grade of major at 28. I knew that he had played a major role in the attempt against Hitler. He hadn't been discovered, fortunately. Not to compromise his family or friends, he had always carefully hidden not only his anti-Nazi activities but also his reservations against the regime.

He had the kindness and the patience to answer my questions about the 20 July 1944 plot in which he had taken part. I had been quite shaken to learn how many friends and relatives of ours had been arrested in the round-ups by the regime and I was eager to get a clearer picture, to gather as many details as I could, reconstructing the puzzle little by little. At that time, survival was so tough for everybody that I did not dare to add to my entourage's burden with questions which brought back painful memories, still too fresh for some or which encountered only a shrug without comment in others who had different cares at the moment.

On 22 May 1996 Karl Feldmeyer wrote in the *Frankfurter Allgemeine Zeitung*, on the occasion of a military contest, the 'Colonel-Baron Boeselager Contest'. This is what the article said:

Philipp Boeselager handed over the cup in the name of his brother Georg, who was killed at the front, heading a brigade in 1944. He was one of the participants in the conspiracy against Hitler and was never caught. His memory is associated with the tragedy that has become the fate of the German soldiers of the Third Reich, whose mixture of integrity, courage and willingness to stand in the way of crime still left them unable to prevent it.

Georg and Philipp Boeselager had both been young officers under the flag. Both recognised the Hitler regime as criminal through their personal experience. Both took part in the Army's clandestine resistance against Hitler.

The inspection of the Central Army Group [of the eastern front] by Hitler, escorted by Himmler, was announced for 13 March 1943. Colonel Henning von Treskow, stationed there as first officer of the General Staff, sketched the plan for an attempt in which Hitler and Himmler would be killed at a signal given by Georg von Boeselager, firing his pistol at a gathering in the officers' mess. At that time, Philipp was aide-de-camp to Marshal Kluge, Commander of the Central Army Group. He accepted the mission to inform Kluge even as it was known the best he could hope for, on the part of Kluge, was his neutrality. 'While I was talking to him,' remembers Philipp Boeselager, 'he kept nodding without uttering a word.'

At the last minute, the conspirators were advised that Hitler would come alone. Kluge then forbade the attempt, as he feared a civil war if Himmler survived Hitler.

One year later, Stauffenberg, together with Treskow, prepared the 'Wolfschanze' plot. A special task was assigned to a Cavalry Regiment of rapid interventions that Georg Boeselager had created.

Six of the squadrons were brought back from the front and covered in 36 hours the 125 miles that separated them from Warsaw, in a hair-raising cavalcade. The plan was to transport them by plane to Berlin when they arrived to ensure the taking over of the most important ministries. Near Warsaw, Rethel, Georg's courier, succeeded in intercepting them. 'Everybody in the old shelters!' he said. It was the password in case of setback. The horsemen went back where they came from. It was only by a miracle that the regiment and the Boeselager brothers escaped the Gestapo investigations. One month later, Georg was killed in East Prussia. Philipp is still living. He is now 80 years old.

Outside, it was chaos. The huge mass of refugees from the part of

Germany that was given to Poland was pouring over a ravaged and drastically shrunk country. The Poles had solved the ethnic problem with simplicity: kicking out all those who lived on the lands that had just been attributed to them. As the bombs destroyed about 70 per cent of Germany's houses and buildings, one can imagine the piling up of people inside the walls, which were still standing.

I arrived at the Boeselagers' in the beginning of September 1945, later joined by my brother. Ernst Wilhelm didn't have the luck I had of being able to enter the crash course for the Baccalaureate in seven months. He had to wait for months to get admission to a course that lasted one year. I was sad for him in as much as we all had to earn a living as soon as possible. Ernst Wilhelm was the eldest and most deserved to get a job immediately as he had been four years in the war instead of going to school.

Inside the castle, at least 30 people were put up the best way possible. There was really no good way. For three years the radio announced every week how many calories our food coupons allowed us. It fluctuated between 1,000 and 1,500 calories per day. It was not much, for it included non-filling food such as skimmed milk, which was very nutritious according to the authorities.

There was no coal. That winter was the coldest we had in years and the central heating could not be operated. We all lived and took our meals in the living-room, as it was the only room in the house that a smoking, starving stove heated, although poorly. Our hostess made valiant efforts to feed us but seldom succeeded in appeasing our hunger. In my case, at 17, I was constantly nagged by hunger. There was the problem of daily transportation as well. We were nine miles away from Bonn and there were two buses a day, one at seven in the morning, the other at seven thirty in the evening. My classes lasted six hours, alternately from 8 a.m. to 1 p.m. or from 2 p.m. to 7 p.m. Actually, the only school not destroyed in the town was used in shifts twice a day for different classes, morning and afternoon. As I had to spend six hours in town, either before or after my classes, I had to find a place to go and do my homework while waiting for the bus. My hosts pleaded my case with a hairdresser in Bonn who obliged by letting me use his daughter's tiny bedroom while she was working outside during the day. There was a small bed in the room and fortunately a table and a chair. That allowed me to work. There was no heating, the temperature varied between 1° and 10°C, depending on the winter months. After six hours and notwithstanding the fur jacket the Boeselagers lent me, my teeth were chattering. But I did not have much time to brood over it because I worked at least 14 hours a day to swallow in seven months three years of schooling. I was the youngest in my class of about 25 pupils who were a colourful bunch from a teacher's point of view. Their ages varied from 17 (me) to 25, quite a few had been military officers, one of them a major. Some had studied law or natural sciences at the university for several semesters; one had been a young genius at physics and was more knowledgeable than our teacher. They all had to graduate again because their first diploma was not recognised. I presume that the sight of these fully grown-up men, dressed mostly in old recycled uniforms, crouching more than sitting at shabby desks much too small for them, was rather grotesque. One of them had a severe eye injury brought back from the front and was almost blind. All of us were determined to succeed and we all did pass with flying colours the very difficult exams, except the poor chap with the bad eye, who had tried even harder than we had but couldn't overcome his handicap.

I graduated with an 'A' in April 1946 and breathed a sigh of relief. Mother had moved once more. My diploma in my pocket, I went to rest at her place in Bavaria.

In the spring of 1946, after a dreadful winter, Prince Oettingen, Buttel's father-in-law, gave Mother the use of the little castle of Kreuth with a farm, in the surroundings of Nüremberg. It was perched on a hill looking down on the little mediaeval town of Heideck. For years, this charming manor had been used for only one month per year. Therefore, the latest modern commodities didn't exist. Hot water was provided by a stove, the telephone worked with a handle and the sanitation was basic. For us it was home again. The rooms could be heated with reliable stoves, there was a real kitchen with a range and we had a garden where it felt like paradise to take the sun during the summer. And, above all, there was enough room to welcome family and friends.

Outside, it was a taste of the Middle Ages. Nobody had a car; the trains were rare, slow, irregular and full to the brim. So when you were visiting, it wasn't for the day. Our guests stayed the week and, thanks to the little farm, we had food.

I had it in mind to study law at Frankfurt University. I would move into an apartment with Meggi and her husband, Wilhelm, a law student himself.

I was terribly disappointed to learn that I hadn't the slightest chance of gaining admission into the university because I was too young. As was understandable, priority was given to the older ex-soldiers. I would have to wait at least three or four years. Goodbye studies, then . . . I comforted myself with the thought that the faster I could find a job, the faster I could earn a living and help my family instead of being a burden.

I found a job as an apprentice in a bank but with a salary of 60 marks per month (12 dollars), I wasn't in a glorious position. We were beginning to lack funds. Mother decided to divide her jewels equally between her six children so that they could survive, at least until the time when they could make a living.

Wilhelm was put in charge of the operation. Therefore, he made the trip from Bonn to Munich, Bavaria, to the jewellers where Mother wanted her jewels valued and divided into six lots of equal worth. Crossing the border between the British and American zones, Wilhelm was checked by a giant black GI who made him open the briefcase with all the jewellery which constituted our only fortune. Seeing a gorgeous set of emeralds, he took it in his hands and let it go again: 'Pack away your junk, man,' he said, laughing. Had he taken the jewels, poor Wilhelm would have been defenceless, as he had no right to prevent him from doing so.

Mother, pleased with her sacrifice, called it 'an excellent investment'. She gave each one of us a small purse containing one lot. In fact, selling my lot, I was able to live a few years until I could find a job that supported me. I can say that we all survived the most critical moments thanks to Mother's jewels.

*

In 1946, to get an apartment in a big city, you had to look for a building which had been half destroyed by bombs, but not entirely damaged.

We finally found an attic in Frankfurt and had it checked for safety to make sure that it would not crumble in the immediate future. Then we signed a contract with the owner, specifying that he authorised us to make repairs in the apartment, and that we would have the right (!) to pay a rent when the works were completed. In six months, Wilhelm and I, without the help of any professional except for the plumbing, succeeded in making the place habitable. There was no central heating but we had hot water from a woodburning boiler. In spite of our skilful (!) repairs, once, while we were having dinner and while Meggi's baby was sleeping in her crib near the table, the ceiling came down on my niece and on us. Fortunately, apart from some cement in the mouth (Meggi was flying all over her daughter, uttering threats at us), the baby was all right and, as we were toughened by now, we didn't take the incident too seriously and proceeded to do the repairs.

One day, we ended up with having nothing at all to eat except some 'dry eggs', a yellowish powder which, diluted in water and thrown into a frying pan, was supposed to convert into scrambled eggs (ghastly!). True, we had a piece of meat that Mother had sent us and that we had just received but, as the mail did not operate too fast, the parcel gave out an impressive stench on arrival. When we opened it, we saw a sort of slimy carrion whose colour varied from black to greenish. We needed courage to eat it . . . but heroism to throw it away. We didn't choose to be heroic. We went to bed cheerfully, our stomachs at last sated. We promised one another that the first one to be woken by stomach cramps or hints of paralysis in the legs – sign of serious food poisoning, we had been told – would shake the other ones awake and call the hospital. We slept like hibernating bears.

As soon as our activities gave us some free time, we jumped into the train to get away to the countryside, at Mother's. There, we were assured of relative comfort and of food, if not abundant, at least sufficient and edible. Today I have a hard time understanding how we gathered the courage and the energy to undertake journeys as we did then. To begin with, Kreuth was two miles away from the Heideck station. On the trip back to Frankfurt, we not only had our luggage but provisions of food to improve our staple diet. Given our heavy load, every step was a torture by the end of the road. There was only a symbolic schedule for the trains, which came and went as they fancied. In any case, there were very few of them and always packed with people. There was never any chance of having a seat and we had to make three changes to reach Frankfurt. Nothing stopped us at the time and we took in our stride, merrily even, the shortcomings and travelled at the slightest excuse. We had been so severely deprived of the freedom to move around, what with the army, the alerts, the bombs and the raids that the most hectic trips were exhilarating and fun.

Having no refrigerator in Frankfurt we had to gulp down fast what we had so strenuously brought back, happy when it was not rotten before our arrival. The menus of the two first days were consequently luxurious and, until the next trip to Kreuth, we lived more on the memory of those two days than of what we had on our plates. So, we would make plans to go back as soon as possible. At Mother's, we were pampered and her old servant, Lieschen Schläfke (the daughter of the Schläfke who was in charge of the stud for my grandfather), spoilt us. In the summer, we had the garden where we spent the day and sometimes the night. What rapture, all that space!

We often played cards because the lack of transport kept us confined at home. So, I became an almost average bridge player, or so I thought until the day I was invited for two weeks to an old uncle's and had to play during my entire stay. At my uncle's, the bridge game was hard labour, up to eight hours a day. Nobody would make any effort at conversation except to shout at me when I made a mistake. I made more and more mistakes as the days went by. I think they were not too sad to lose their fourth player and when I left they patted my back slightly too cheerfully. I have never sat down at a card table since then, except with children who, by the way, yell at me worse than the adults ever dared to.

I gave my first parties in Kreuth, with boys and girls from the neigh-bourhood. Pimply and wispy-bearded, dressed and shod according to unusual criteria of elegance, the girls still found us irresistible, pretended Mother. The truth is, they hadn't seen a boy, except in a military uniform, since they were little girls. Luckily for me they lacked material for comparisons.

Buttel came to get me from Kreuth once. She wanted me to escort her to Hamburg, I can't remember for what reason. The way I know her, it was probably to go to a horse auction, as she has always been a horse fanatic. We took the train from Frankfurt, the most important town in Germany at the time, to Hamburg, in the heart of winter. The trains had no schedule, the number of carriages was not fixed and sometimes you had to wait for an entire day at the station. When a train did finally show up, it was mobbed and the seats each had at least three contenders. In Frankfurt, I was able to push my sister into a carriage. For my part, I had to stay on the buffers for eight hours, as there was no connection between carriages. It was several degrees below zero and I was afraid that my hands would get numb or that I would fall asleep. Thinking about the consequences kept me wide awake, if not warm.

Safely arrived at our destination, we succeeded in obtaining coupons for a week's food in advance. We rushed to get all the stuff at once and went to wolf it down, all in one go, in a bistro where we ordered a simili-coffee. From the neighbouring tables, the comments rained aloud, almost threatening. They thought we were dealers on the black market. We had to extract our used coupons and show them to prove our good faith. We were so young, had been hungry for so long, and after all, tomorrow everything would be better . . . or we would not be hungry!

For many years after the war, the Allied occupation forces forbade the Germans to own any sort of guns, which had to be delivered to their military quarters. Many an ardent hunter hid their guns, as they would never part with their treasured hunting weapons.

When I arrived in Oettingen, at my brother-in-law's estate, we started very soon to stalk deer and to shoot with a small calibre gun that made almost no noise. In the evening it was taken out of its hiding-place, we went to the house of a trusted forester, assembled the guns, hid them under a huge cape and crept into the forest, feeling like poachers. Should we spot a deer, we had to get very close as the guns only had power for a maximum of 40 yards. You had to be almost a top marksman to score.

We had constantly to look around to verify that nobody was watching us. Should we notice anyone in the vicinity, then I had to take charge, hiding my gun quickly under my cape. I started to whistle while walking away, making as much noise as possible so that those people we met would not suspect that we were hunting. It was a lot of fun, reminding me of mischievous schemes I plotted in my childhood.

During the years after the war, there were large numbers of hares in Oettingen as nobody shot them. Every now and then, an American officer asked politely whether he could come to shoot hares, and whether we could organise a shoot with beaters (men, usually recruited among the local peasants, who would beat the bushes while shouting to chase the prey in our direction). The American officer then arrived with a dozen shotguns, distributed them among the would-be hunters in my family and our foresters and off we went. In the evening, the officer collected his guns again and drove off. However, there might be a shortage of American officers wanting to shoot. So, soon after I first arrived in Oettingen, we concocted a scheme. I was to play the role – as nobody knew me yet on the precinct as a member of the family – of the American, although I had to settle for civilian clothes much to my chagrin, for lack of a uniform and decorations.

Early in the morning, everyone who still had guns took them out of their hiding place. Lix and I collected them, put them in a car and we drove to our meeting place. There, Lix introduced me to the foresters who were in on our plot and to the beaters who were not. I played my role of the benevolent American who brought his guns, distributed them with generosity and would let his hosts and whatever guests they had shoot hares. I was supposed not to speak one word of German because it was too difficult to pretend an American accent all day and to duck embarrassing questions about my unit, my apparent young age, etc. I had to stay on guard not to betray that I understood German. It was hard not to give myself away, chuckling as I was when people made fun of me. So, we had a very good shoot, after which I made a little speech in English, which nobody understood, graciously accepted an invitation to dinner by my brother-in-law, and collected the guns again. It had been great fun but a rather dangerous pastime. If we had been found out, we could have been sentenced to ten years in jail, which really happened to people we knew, although in the end they were released before the end of their time. Still, facing two to three years in jail was a serious matter. Paramount to all, I became too familiar a figure in the population from which the beaters were recruited for our trick to proceed smoothly.

In November 1948, I was blessed with a magnificent pay rise at my bank in Frankfurt: ten marks more. My salary was now 70 marks per month (14 dollars at that time). The working conditions were . . . exotic. Three quarters of the building was destroyed; the rain and the snow had free access. All the employees piled up in one big room, except the president, who had a tiny personal office. I wrote the mail on a machine which dated back to 1915 and our calculators could only add and subtract and we had to operate them manually. Still, I learnt how to do the job rather quickly and, after two years instead of three, I was entered for the examination of the Chamber of Industry and Commerce. That examination also served as a diploma for the end of the commercial studies for the classes I had followed during those two years. I passed with an 'A'.

The bank manager often invited me for dinner at his house. He had two daughters and I suspect he sized me up as a potential son-in-law. I must say that the young ladies were quite pretty but I had no intention of contemplating marriage for a long time. I wanted first, before any kind of settling down and as soon as possible, to look the planet over.

Chapter Nine

STARTING MY LIFE

If life until 1948 was cheap, it became very expensive after the monetary reform and the creation of the German mark. In the years after the war, inflation became spectacular. Money was plentiful but there was little to buy. Everything was strictly rationed and the quantities of food and other necessities that we could acquire with the coupons decreased every month. The daily food allowance went down to 1,100 calories per day per person. The black market was flourishing now that it wasn't punishable by death as it had been before 1945. Everybody was resorting to the black market for one special thing or another, depending on their financial means. But for everyday necessities it was too expensive for a great number of people – and we belonged to that category. The shops were empty; there was no trace of the extras that make life more enjoyable for some, more endurable for others. I had an irresistible lust for oranges, we hadn't seen any in years. I was used to being rationed for everything as some articles of current consumption had been rationed since as early as 1937 and I didn't know anything else. In 1948, I declared to Mother: 'I can well imagine that before the war you could buy everything, even oranges but I can't believe you could buy as much butter as you wanted!' All I knew as fat was a homemade mixture: a tiny trace of fat, onions and flour mixed in water. I thought it was delicious!

In that atmosphere of deprivation, a monetary reform was announced, without details about the conditions or the date. On the eve of my 20th birthday, on 20 June 1948, D-day arrived, announcements were shouted over the air and in every newspaper. The old Reichsmark was dead, the bank accounts were blocked and every single citizen received 40 units of the new currency. From one day to the next, the Reichsmark was taken out of circulation. All of a sudden, the German people were told that the change was ten to one, with a maximum of 40 marks. On that day and only for one day, 65 million Germans became equally wealthy. There was not a soul in the whole country who did not possess 40 marks. There was not a soul who had more than 40 marks, at least in cash. On the next day, the police arrested a dealer of the black market at the Frankfurt railway station. He had 10,000 marks in his pocket, earned in 24 hours.

The German mark was born. To keep the whole operation secret, the Allies had the banknotes printed outside the country and had brought them in sealed containers. Instead of the dirty old paper bills, we all had now the same amount in beautiful crisp new bills. A feeling of great scepticism prevailed concerning the future of the new currency. Few believed the words uttered by Erhard, the Minister of Economy, in his speech although later he was branded 'the father of the German miracle'. He said that, within a few weeks, our lives would be changed. He had planned and organised the reform single-handedly as Konrad Adenauer, our Chancellor, showed more interest in foreign policy than in the internal economy ('we can starve, for all he cares,' was the general feeling).

On the first day, I wracked my brain to figure out what best investment I could make with my 40 marks. I risked them on a carton of cigarettes, the unofficial but safe currency, which was worth exactly that sum in the black market. I already pictured myself as a millionaire in a few weeks with the firing up of the prices. Actually, after one week, my carton was worth 300 per cent of what I had paid for it. I felt like an important businessman but three weeks later it was worth only the official price, ten marks. What disillusion! And I didn't even smoke. I started then.

I immediately received my salary, already a mere pittance, in new currency. When I went to my customary restaurant, where I had lunch from time to time – a big kitchen with a huge oven in the middle, in the basement of a destroyed house, with a few tables along the walls – I handed out food coupons when I ordered my course but the waiter told me: 'No need for coupons any more.'

I knew then that times had really changed. It was hardly noticeable at first, then the action gained momentum. The shops were filling as if by magic with the articles most difficult to find for years. Trust in the mark was growing in the public, then prices went lower and the goods became plentiful. It really was a miracle!

At the beginning we had more mistrust than confidence towards the new currency, especially we people from the countryside, who would still gladly resort to swapping and bartering: one ton of potatoes against 25 pounds beet, that is the language we talk and understand best, genetically!

113

In Frankfurt, we knew a guy who made a living out of the black market. He was a simple, likeable man. He lived in a more than modest apartment, partly destroyed. We would often go to him to buy some butter or coffee and he always invited us to drink a cup of coffee and a schnapps. At the time, he declared philosophically: 'This situation won't last, the black market will disappear soon, you will find a good job thanks to which you will have a good flat whereas I will go back to my trade as a plumber and I will stay right here.'

In fact, two months after the monetary reform, the black market had ceased to exist. For the 'good job', we had to wait much longer but for his lodging, our friend was proved right: he stayed.

The political and administrative situation under the occupation was chaotic for the Germans, after the war. But at least we were protected, generally, against dictatorial and arbitrary dictatorship. Life was difficult, we had no money, no home, very little to eat. The future was more than problematic but, as I read once in a newspaper article, 'who is afraid at 18?' I was not afraid, rather I was curious and impatient to learn about life and the world, new life, young world, or the other way around. After all, our material fate could only take on a better course, it couldn't get worse.

I was young and in good health, I had no doubt I would find my place in life. I had no idea about what I would do but I was heading toward a future that would bring me success and an exciting life.

At the very beginning after the war we still hoped that the differences between the Soviets and the Western Allies would give us the possibility of going back East but after the Potsdam Conference it became clear that we had not the slightest chance of returning home. I then shook myself, turned my back on the past and looked firmly towards the future.

The development of West Germany, in the economic field as well as in the political and artistic, was more surprising and faster than we would have ever dared to dream, and proved us young people right.

In 1948, after the monetary reform, we liked to entertain. After years of deprivation, we could at last buy food, clothes, even alcoholic beverages and we were anxious to get distractions.

One day, in Frankfurt, Ernst Wilhelm and I had organised a small party and among the guests, had invited our two favourite young ladies. My brother's had arrived, mine had stood me up. The evening dragged on and I tried to find solace in alcohol. With too much conviction, as on the next day I did not wake up until noon. Meggi had shaken me to no avail at seven in the morning, knowing I had to report for work. I was petrified about being so late but it was even worse than I thought. I couldn't set foot on the floor for five days. I had a severe intoxication, due to the atrocious quality of the liquor I had swallowed. Santa Hepatitis was hurt and was reclaiming her prey. I was cured forever from liquor . . . sweet liquor, that is. The doctor ordered me complete rest for two months, with a severe diet. Buttel and Lix offered me, with their usual kindness, an invitation to come to their place in Oettingen and to stay until I was in shape again. They took care of me so well that this time I fully recovered.

I was always very lucky with my sisters Meggi and Buttel and their husbands and I harbour in my heart an enormous gratitude for them. Meggi and Wilhelm took me in in Frankfurt for three years, Buttel and Lix opened wide their door for me and Oettingen became my second home.

*

I spent 1950 in Hamburg, in a small private bank, to learn import-export. I had a friend, Klaus von Amsberg, two years older than me, who studied law in Hamburg. He had resolutely great social ambitions. 'I want to marry a princess, preferably a reigning one,' he used to say. He married . . . Beatrix of Holland.

During that period, I received a phone call one day from Prince Otto von Bismarck, grandson of the Iron Chancellor. He asked me drily:

'Have you got a dinner jacket?'

'Yes,' I answered, slightly put out.

'Then come for dinner at my place. Friedrichsruh, Friday.'

I learnt later that Mother had called him to ask him to receive me. The problem was not the dinner jacket as I truly had one, handed down to me by some uncle. It was the lack of a car. Friedrichsruh was 12 miles from Hamburg and I had no intention of walking.

A friend of mine lent me his Volkswagen and, on the said day, all properly dressed up and spotless, I arrived at Bismarck's castle. Everything was grand there: the army of servants headed by a majestic butler in white gloves, magnificent reception room and very chic guests.

The menu was refined and the wines were surely high class. The elements of comparison I had had access to until now didn't make me a good judge but in any case I ate and drank heartily and spent an excellent evening, indeed had great fun.

I took my leave around two o'clock in the morning and found the intimidating butler, still in spotless white gloves, on the porch. He shouted my name and a valet brought me my car. Upon seeing it, the shadow of a disdainful smile distorted the factotum's pompous face. However, he opened my door and I started the engine. After a few yards, in a nightmarish 'boo-oom!', my poor little saucepan stopped dead. My sense of accuracy must have been altered by the exquisite wines I had been served at dinner and severely at that. Instead of seeing double as any inebriated bloke would expect, I saw zilch! Nothing at all. The huge fountain, right in the middle of the drive sprinkled shiny cascades of water and I never saw it. I had bumped onto the stone platform and it looked now as if I had attempted to climb it. Not surprisingly, the car refused to budge.

At my side the butler materialised and dropped a disgusted glance on me. Dark purple in the face, I extracted myself from my seat and went out to check the damage. The only solution was to lift the Volkswagen and to push it aside. Whether with goodwill or not the guy had to cooperate, as there was no way I could manage on my own. When finally I was in a position to start the car and leave, the door on my side was showing a deep and inglorious wound. The butler's face had a blunt expression of fury despite the handsome tip I had just slipped into his now black glove, which amounted to the price of my next week's meals.

Happy and relieved to have finally left, it was only after a few miles that I started to think about my poor buddy, the car owner. I didn't have a cent to make the necessary repair and I would have to save for months in dire deprivation. Furthermore, I was to expect a serious showdown. Well, nothing of the sort! My friend dealt in insurance and was fully covered. He almost thanked me.

I bought my first car, a small convertible sports car, branded BMW, dating back to 1932. It gave signs of weakness from the start but could still run. My friends called it 'the Rolls'.

One day my bell rang: it was a representative of a film production company. He wanted to rent my car for a film. He took it for two weeks, brought it back and came again for it for another week. He had paid me a modest price in the first place and I didn't show a great sense of business the second time around either. I could have asked three times the price, as they needed that one and only that one. Anyway, when my friends saw the Rolls on the screen, my car and I could command more respect than before.

When I left Hamburg, I sold my little car to a garage mechanic who offered to trade it against a big 1928 Bugatti in perfect shape. What would I have done with that petrol-thirsty tank? I sensibly refused and pocketed the 500 marks the guy paid me. Sensibly? Ten years later, the Bugatti was worth several hundred thousand dollars.

Chapter Ten

TRAVELS

In 1950, Buttel and Lix decided to make their first trip abroad, It was still very complicated and rare to travel in the aftermath of the war. They chose Italy and invited me to go along with them, taking care of all my expenses with utmost generosity. I was choking with joy and immediately asked for time off at my bank where I earned hardly a bite of my bread.

To go to Italy, you had to undertake an obstacle race between queuing up and paper work. You had to have: a visa to leave Germany, from the military government; a visa to Italy; a transit visa for Switzerland; a transit visa for Austria; a certificate from an Italian, attesting that we would be his guests in Italy – we had to cheat, there, as we had no intention of residing at anybody's place, but it was forbidden to take our currency out of Germany. Nothing could stop us and we complied with all the necessary requirements with a light heart.

What a privilege to be able to travel abroad (in normal conditions the Germans are frantic travellers), to lead an international life, to be tourists! Our tour took us across many of the most beautiful cities in Italy, culminating in Rome where the Holy Year was celebrated and we obtained a private audience from the Pope. Everything seemed a fairy tale and I returned home not only grateful to Buttel and Lix but with the inebriating sensation of being a citizen of the world!

One year later, Buttel and Lix made reservations for a cruise on the Mediterranean. I couldn't believe my ears when they told me they had made a reservation for me to come along. I shall never forget their kindness. I was delirious with joy! We were to go on a cruise, on a real ship, for two weeks and we would see all the sites in Greece and Egypt about which I had dreamt during my Latin and Greek lessons.

We left from Venice and arrived in sight of the Greek coast after two days. When we crossed the canal of Corinth, we three were sitting on deck, in the moonlight. We passed alongside an island and I asked a sailor what its name was. 'Ithaca,' he answered. Ithaca! Ulysses' homeland, where he came back after 20 years to find Penelope, his wife, sewing and unsewing patiently, surrounded by crowds of suitors, waiting steadfastly for her husband's return . . .

In Athens, when I contemplated the Acropolis, proudly spreading its beautiful vestiges of the past in the sunshine, I pictured in my mind Germany with its ugly ruins. Would they stand as proof of the godless misery inflicted and endured by modern time's humanity?

In Egypt, we were greeted by a pasha, a high dignitary when Egypt was still a monarchy, a friend of the Lix family. Like many upper-class Egyptians, he was of Turkish origin, blond and white-skinned. He spoke a perfect German and was a frequent traveller to Germany, usually attired in Bavarian leather shorts, and nobody suspected he was an Egyptian.

The pasha assigned to us as a guide the best-known Egyptian archaeologist. The latter took on the job with the grimmest good will. He warmed up after a while, seeing our eagerness to learn and our fascination with what we saw, flattered that we had studied much of what we were to visit months in advance. We stayed four days with him and he told us many of the secrets he had uncovered. We corresponded with him for a long time afterwards.

We left Cairo for Port Said to join our ship. It was a night of full moon. The railway ran alongside the Suez Canal for most of the time. We had a view of the ships but not of the water. It was an eerie sight, this endless file of enormous ships, sailing quietly, apparently on the desert sand. We were only a few months before the revolution that would depose the regime of King Farouk. The Egyptians were already very volatile, hostile to all foreigners, particularly to the British and the French. In fact, we felt quite uneasy as a small crowd gathered outside our compartment and shouted at us in Arabic. Then a police officer rushed in and kicked them away. We heaved a sigh of relief when we were back on board our ship.

*

After my years of work in the banks in Frankfurt and in Hamburg I decided to realise my dream to learn three foreign languages and to visit the world. I began by taking classes for six months at the Alliance Française, in Paris. To visit Paris was already a wonderful experience but to live there was a fantastic adventure that I was about to undertake.

I fell under the spell of the city and under the charm of the Parisians, the way of life of the French in general. After two months, I could manage enough French to allow me to make friends with boys and preferably girls very quickly. As usual, my major problem was money. The regulations in Germany would only let me change 300 marks per month. Having no other source of revenue, I bought a big loaf of bread every day and I ate it with margarine ('better than butter' said the publicity; 'much worse than butter,' said the customers) spread on it. As I was constantly hungry, this diet seemed to me excellent and I used to wait impatiently for my meal. A friend of Mother's – very well off – passing through Paris invited me to lunch at a restaurant. I ate two entire menus, to his greatest pleasure.

My friends and I – we were all penniless – would stay for hours on end at the terrace of the cafés in Saint-Germain-des-Près in front of a single *petit noir* (today's espresso).

I was living in a furnished room on Avenue de la Bourdonnais, without bathroom but my landlady allowed me a jug of hot water on Saturdays. If I still had a light on after nine o'clock at night, she would knock on my door!

Judging that I deserved a minimum of consideration, I went to live at the hotel de la Scandinavie, a small hotel for students, on the left bank. There was no bathroom there either but a sink in the bedroom: luxury!

Living now in great style, I thought it was time to invite a few friends to a party. We could not be more than six; the room would not accommodate one person more. As there was only one chair, we sat on the large bed. It was a hot summer's day; I had prepared a few sandwiches and put some bottles of white wine in ice in my sink. Later, when I let the water run out, I didn't realise that all the labels had come off the bottles and they went down the drain. On the next day, the whole drainage system of the hotel was clogged. When I came down the hotel owner was growling: 'If ever I catch the s . . of a b . . . . who did that, I'll wring his neck!' He never did.

One of my friends, a Swedish student, had brought a bottle of whisky, a rare treat in France in 1952. We had a toast to it. So, I passed the whisky around, everybody pushing and shoving in this tiny little room. Not paying attention, I didn't realise that I seasoned the whisky with red wine. I was going to throw the wasted beverages away but my Swedish friend said: 'It really would be a pity . . . such good whisky!' So, we all drank it as it was, with catastrophic consequences. On the next day I could hardly move.

Mother came for a visit. I reserved a room for her in a nearby hotel with a little better standing than mine and off we went touring the town, eating in the bistros of the left bank. Mother had never been to Paris before and she tremendously enjoyed discovering this beautiful city with me. She was always so full of energy that she would stand up like a geyser spouting and I never had time to hold her chair for her. I was lucky when the chair didn't drag me down in its fall.

A German friend of mine – today leading an important law firm in Frankfurt – and I undertook a big journey across France, hitch-hiking. We have memories from that time that we still like to recall when we are together.

Not very sure of the reception we would get, and fearing that we would be left to take root on the roadside, we were rather cowardly sometimes and pretended we were Austrians. We spent a night in a school in Brittany once. There was an eerie atmosphere in that manor, I'm almost sure I saw a ghost floating in the garden when I glanced through my window in the middle of the night.

One incident is engraved in my memory. A tiny French Renault car stopped to take us on board. The driver very politely came out to put our bags in his boot. It took him an unusually long time to wriggle out of his machine. He was about six feet seven. To enter in and come out of his diminutive vehicle was a feat he accomplished with good humour under our amazed eyes. We started to chat and I asked him if he knew Germany. 'Yes, but I didn't get the opportunity to tour it,' he said.

En route, we came across a big truck, dipping miserably in a ditch. Our driver stopped, saying: 'I have to see that, I'm curious.' He said hello to the truck driver who didn't look too glorious and seemed to stiffen in a sort of 'stand to attention' way when our friend introduced himself. They talked for a while, then he came back and we left. The giant drove us with the utmost courtesy and kindness where we meant to go, then left us with a friendly smile, a wave and a 'Bon voyage!' Several months later, I saw his photograph on a newspaper stand, on the cover of a magazine. I made my inquiry and learnt that he was the president of the Renault Company, a leading French car firm. He had spent several years in a concentration camp as a *resistant*. Still today I salute this great businessman and gentleman who treated us, Germans, with great friendliness and helpfulness and who travelled in the smallest and least flashy car of his factories. This incident would never occur in Germany, I bet.

I went on an extensive tour of Spain after my stay in France and in 1952, thanks to the recommendation of a friend who had been David Rockefeller's roommate at Harvard, I obtained a post as trainee at the Chase National Bank in New York. It was agreed that I would go through all the departments to thoroughly learn the American banking system. I was very enthusiastic and full of expectations at the thought of spending a year in New York City.

I left Hamburg by ship on 3 December, 1952, on the MS *Italia*. Mother and a few friends came to wave their handkerchiefs at the pier. A crowd was massed there when we arrived. An orchestra played 'Mussi denn, mussi denn . . . ' and everybody cried. I was moved and it was hard to leave. I saw my mother on the pier, it was the first time that I was leaving her for another continent and for so long, as I would be absent for a whole year. She left when the ship cast off the mooring ropes. I went down to unpack and get settled and when I climbed back up on deck two hours later the ship was still 30 feet away from the pier, the crowd was still there, still crying. Most of the passengers were emigrants, for them it wasn't a trip, it was exile; they had no return ticket. Thank God, Mother had left!

We made a stop in Southampton. I had the luck to be able to see in the harbour the three biggest ships in the world, the *Queen Elizabeth*, the *Queen Mary* and the *United States*. Huge, regal, silent figures in the mist, brightly illuminated. They filled my dreams that night.

On our arrival in the Americas, after a six-day crossing, a thick fog greeted us. It was only when we were practically inside the harbour that I saw the skyscrapers surge from the haze, as if floating over the water.

Magnificent America! The people – cheerful and caring – the television, the supermarkets, the refrigerators, the drugstores serving snacks! And everything was already cheaper than in Germany, with an exchange of one dollar for four marks (today it is one dollar for one and a half marks).

In the beginning I lived on the West Side, in a modest apartment organised into eight rooms, all of them individually rented, with one kitchen, two bathrooms and no living-room. There was no cleaning woman, which probably explained the filthiness that overpowered the place.

I had some trouble adjusting at first but a merry conviviality reigned in the house and everybody was very nice to me. A Jewish German couple who had emigrated in the '30s rented the room in front of mine. They were charming, cultured, and they would often invite me to join them. He was a writer and one day, after I admitted to him that New York was a town that intimidated me and that I didn't like much, he answered: 'I under-stand how you feel, but three to four months from now you will find yourself in some drugstore in the company of a charming young lady and all of a sudden you will realise that New York is a cheerful and exceptional town.' He was right, of course, about the part of the young lady too.

I was among his guests on one of the numerous evenings when he received a group of German immigrants. They were all intellectuals, mostly writers and philosophers. It was heartbreaking to see how those people would still cling to their country which had treated them so badly, how they were lost in the United States where, however, they had been greeted with a generosity they were very grateful for, and up to what dramatic point they depended upon their German language to write and make a living.

I was in awe of the high standard of living of the Americans compared to ours in Germany, seven years after the end of the war. I marvelled at being able to buy clothes of excellent material for so cheap a price. The American fashion style somewhat had me in awe, though.

The apparent familiarity with which the employees addressed their superiors produced a light and friendly atmosphere, baffling for me. I realised immediately, however, that mutual respect was present there as much as anywhere else but expressed differently.

I made friends with Joachim Stresemann. His father, German Foreign Minister in the '20s, had been the instigator, together with Aristide Briand, his French counterpart, of the first attempt at reconciliation between France and Germany. We both lived, at that time of our youth, in a very Russian environment – from the former Russia, not from the one we dreaded in Germany – probably because, uprooted like us, they were very hospitable and loved socialising. Once, in the middle of the guests of all ages who ate, drank, sang, talked in Russian, Joachim tapped me on the shoulder and whispered in my ear: 'Out of this whole crowd, I'm the only one who has ever set foot in Russia!'

I was invited to a Cossack dance with Russians. The evening went on evenly, somewhat stiffly until one of the guests, in Cossack uniform, suddenly rushed on another one, brandishing a knife, visibly set on the worst intentions. The ladies went into action and tried to interfere. After inquiries we learnt that the first Cossack had thought he recognised a member of the *Tcheka*, the Soviet secret police. If the Cossack uniforms were costume uniforms, the vodka was apparently authentic.

Although I had arrived only two months before, I received several invitations for Christmas. I have kept a grateful memory about it as it relieved me greatly of my nostalgia. Christmas is a family celebration and I missed my family very much. After six months in New York City, in that town which has a reputation for being tough, I had invitations practically for every day of the week. What a contrast to Paris!

A couple of lawyers had made friends with me. They were black and had a wonderful apartment in Harlem. They often invited me to their place. The meals at their table were a delight for the stomach of a young man always hungry. They invited me to the annual ball of the Association for the Advancement of Coloured People. The participants – very few whites – were all in evening attire. The women were beautiful. My friends must have known I was penniless because I could never pay for anything. They discreetly took care of all the expenses.

I once went to visit Yorkville, the German district of New York City. Practically no one spoke any English. The signs over the shops were in

German, as were the menus in the bistros, the beer was imported, the food was German and everybody complained about how different from the Germans the Americans were. Surprised, I asked candidly: 'Why don't you go back to Germany? – '*Ach nein*! Not that!' I still haven't understood.

Earning 150 dollars per month, my living conditions required an iron hand on my budget. I allowed myself an evening out once a month with a girlfriend. I would choose her with care, for her beauty and her conversation, and take her to a restaurant. One evening, one of them didn't judge me worthy of a break in her diet and nibbled at her food, spreading it over her plate, although she had ordered the most sophisticated courses on the menu. I was fuming and never invited her again.

Towards the end of my stay, I lived in the apartment of a Russian friend, Yuri Anitchkoff. He lived in a very big apartment and sub-let several rooms. He was a nice fellow, a bit of an eccentric and he had a good sense of humour. He was always impeccably dressed, with a black umbrella hanging over his arm. One day, we were strolling down the street together and it started to rain. I asked him to open his umbrella so that we could take refuge underneath. He looked at me, half embarrassed half mischievous: 'I can't, it is full of holes!' We burst into laughter and became friends.

Yuri could have rented a small flat for much less money but, as he admitted himself, he would have hated to live alone.

In the room next to mine lived Vera Romanoff, the last Tsar's niece, a middle-aged lady, gentle and charming. My host had a curious attitude towards her, one day he went 'Your Imperial Highness' all over the place and the next he would dress her down not so politely about the untidiness in her room (always in a shambles): 'But you have German blood, you should be more organised, take Lynar for an example!' I was most surprised to receive a compliment I was far from deserving . . . and he knew that.

Once when I was alone in the apartment, the telephone rang and I picked it up. A male voice asked me in French if I knew that language.

'Yes,' I said.

'Am I at Her Imperial Highness, Princess Vera Romanoff's residence?'

'Err. . . yes.'

'Are you her butler?'

'Not exactly,' I said, in an even voice.

'Is she there?' my correspondent was beginning to get impatient.

'Nope.'

'May I leave you a message for Her Imperial Highness?'

'Yes.'

'I am the Court Marshal of His Majesty the King of Greece. His Majesty will visit New York shortly and would like to give a gala dinner in honour of H.I.H., his cousin, at the Waldorf Astoria.' He gave his telephone number so that she could call him back. I didn't tell this high-ranking dignitary that his boss should instead give a small allowance to his cousin who slaved for 50 dollars a week in a fashion shop.

The Russian colony, extremely generous and helpful, passed the hat around to buy a dress for Vera, who hadn't fled Russia with her paraphernalia and hadn't the first cent to be decently attired for a regal evening, especially one given to honour her. But I think she preferred the gala to years of a slightly less tight budget. She was back for a few moments in her country as it was before, in the pomp and protocol of times past. But all of her people had disappeared, wiped away in a storm of which she, poor modest employee since she was an adult, was a survivor who did not understand too much what had happened although it had cost her everything but a cheap little life.

Before going back to Europe, I was lucky enough to make a long journey across the United States, thanks to the help of the Chase and to a little donation from the 'Rockefeller Foundation'. I travelled through New England, then Chicago, Detroit, Denver and Colorado, Texas and the Southern States by train but mostly in Greyhound buses, which cross the country in every direction. What gigantic and sumptuous landscapes ran before my eyes! Distances seemed unreal (16 hours by bus to complete the crossing of Texas) to me who bumped against a border where I had to show my identification and authorisation papers every five minutes when I had left my homeland.

I came back to New York to pack and embarked to Germany in mid-December 1953, happy to see my people again but my heart full of melancholy at leaving America. America had welcomed me with so much generosity and cheerfulness, allowing me to grow up and at the same time it gave me back the carelessness of childhood that the war made me lose a little too soon.

*

After my year in the United States was completed, I spent six months at home, at my mother's place. She had moved to the Rhineland after the monetary reform, as the little farm in Bavaria was now too expensive to maintain and did not produce any income.

We found a small house for Mother, near Cologne, and she was – as usual – delighted with it, especially because she would be near her two sisters and her eldest daughter, Milli.

I left in June 1954 for South America to learn the third language that was in my programme. Through friends of Lix's, I had found a job in a bank in Lima, Peru.

Mother waved me an emotional goodbye, shedding a few tears, for in her mind I was leaving for a land of cannibals and she thought I would never come back. This woman had seen me endure the dangers of a world war without any excessive apprehension but the beautiful and exotic journey I was undertaking gave her more fears. I think that in her mind to die for one's fatherland was a natural hardship that had to be expected and happened to many men of her kin all down the centuries but journeys exposed you to contact with wild warriors without any uniform or discipline, who sized you up as a potential meal.

Lix and Buttel took me to La Rochelle by car. I embarked there on the *Reina del Pacífico*, an English ship, for a three-week journey. The *Reina* was an ocean liner in the old English fashion, with an impeccably British service but, unfortunately, with British food as well. Lix and I had resolved that I should travel first class. In that fashion I would arrive in style in Lima and I might make a few acquaintances on board who could lead to friendships on arrival. In the steerage which my means could have afforded less painfully, I might have made more colourful friends but with no future following up as they didn't even have a fixed address.

Life on board was rather monotonous. The bar closed at 11 p.m., actually at 10 p.m., as the clock had to be wound back an hour every night to reach the local time on the day of arrival. The band would tuck in at ten as well because of the orders of their union back in England. I relied on two merry bachelors, the doctor and the nurse, to help me exhaust my nightly energy. We would prolong our evenings in the doctor's spacious cabin, amply equipped with a variety of spirits.

Sometimes, after having drowned our boredom slightly too generously, the doctor thought it was his responsibility to see me to my own cabin. Arriving in front of my door thanks to his help, I would find it my duty to take him back to his sleeping quarters as he would need my help even more than I had needed his. We would make the trip back and forth up to five or six times, hanging onto each other for dear life, more desperately at each journey. Thank God the corridors were deserted! I just hoped for my friend that he did not have too many early sick calls in the morning.

The boat made several port calls en route, one of them in La Havana. I recollect an animated town, full of charm, whose population seemed to enjoy life. I readily believe that Cuba was then corrupt with its dictatorship and mafia but it showed less than what I witnessed, 25 years later, right in the middle of Castro's regime. La Havana had become a sad town, dirty and poor, all traces of the joy of living had vanished. People would hug the wall and avoid foreigners in public under strict orders of not making contact with them. To take a cab, I had to wait until the indefinite thug who had followed me around since the airport would hail one for me, show my passport to the driver and give him the name of my hotel. He came along for the ride, uninvited and not much of a conversationalist.

Before arrival in Lima the traditional costume party took place in the ballroom. It was a great success, the boys were good company, the girls were pretty and seductive (not one Peruvian among them, though, too bad, I could have gladly pictured myself disembarking with a local fiancée on my arm). On the next day there was an announcement at breakfast: a pair of men's trousers had been found under a couch. Everybody started laughing and teasing one another. My laugh choked in my throat when, back in my sleeping quarters, I realised that a pair of my trousers was missing.

The arrival in Callao, Lima's harbour, brought me back to hard reality. Callao was a dirty place, reeking of such stenches you would have thought all the goods were foul, the ones embarking as well as the ones coming in.

Lima's climate is awful for eight months of the year. It never rains but the air is so humid that you have to use the windscreen wipers day in and day out when you are driving. The temperature, during the day as well as during the night, stays around 15°C (60°F). Enough to freeze, for only a few villas belonging to local lords are heated.

Within a couple of days I found a room in a small boarding house and there I spent my evenings sweating (!) over my Spanish books and dictionaries, shivering in the old fur jacket I fortunately had brought along. I had had a few Spanish lessons in Germany before coming over but I still couldn't make out one word. I went to work on it every night and every weekend, praying for the summer to show and warm up the atmosphere.

I was more than disappointed by the salary the bank gave me, as they had me working painfully hard from the very first day.

It had been difficult to judge from Europe whether the amount I was offered would be enough to live on and on what scale. I had decided it was worth trying. It was too much to die but too little to live.

This bank, managed by Germans, recruited its staff around the world on rather demanding criteria: the new employees should not be more than 26 years of age but must have ten years' banking experience, speak five languages fluently, be single, ready to work four to five hours' overtime a day with no supplementary pay and have management capabilities. Salary: 100 dollars a month.

The manager of a corresponding English bank through which the

Peruvian bank had tried to recruit quipped: 'With the salary you offer and the qualifications you require, we might have some problem in finding anyone willing to work for you.' Nonetheless, my bank would always find suckers like me, who wanted to see the world. When they had had enough they would go back home or would find a better position in Peru.

Generally two to three years would pass between arrival and departure of the young recruits, which says a lot in favour of their motivation and their endurance. So much the better for the bank which had no second thoughts about having us work, at certain periods of the year, until midnight.

After two months, I was told that the adaptation period was over. From now on I must deal with the mail in Spanish and in English and personally type the letters. My knowledge of Spanish being still limited to say the least, it was panic at first but I improved rather quickly.

I would still shiver in my little freezing room, alternating bronchitis with sinusitis, but after three months I read an ad in the newspaper, promising me my dream in my price range: 'A flat in a private villa.' I had to reduce my dream in view of the two tiny rooms and shower, cold water only. However I was in my own place, I could receive my friends and I had a small portable stove on which I could fry my eggs.

Towards November the weather improved greatly, the sun shone and from December on I could go swimming in the Pacific Ocean. The sea, bordered by beautiful beaches, was only 20 minutes by bus from my place.

Earthquakes were frequent. I experienced my first in the countryside, at friends'. We were having lunch when a deep rumble was heard and the earth began to shake. In a flash, everybody fled to the garden except me. I thought to myself: 'What a bunch of nut cases they are in this country, they flee for a mere train passing by!' I proceeded peacefully with my meal. As there was no railway in the vicinity, at the next rustle I beat everybody to the door.

The house – no way could it be described as a villa – where I lived, was built of wood – decrepit by now – sheltering termites. Once a year, in January, those insects grow wings and come out to fly in millions for their frenzied weddings. After a few days they come back home, having shed their wings on the way, under my despairing eyes and notwithstanding my wild twirls, armed with a wet towel. On certain days, the remnants of their evening dress would be half an inch thick on the floor.

Soon after the home-coming of the termites, they and I had my first earthquake in the apartment. It was 11 o'clock at night, I was in the shower as I was just back from the bank. I heard a thundering noise that seemed to last forever and the floor started to shake. Knowing that the termites had already munched away most of the wooden beams, I pictured myself crumbling underneath, along with them. I made a beeline for the garden, stark naked. I had to retreat shamefully and fast under the interested stare of the female house servants who had arrived even sooner than I had.

My work and my financial situation were not making much progress despite my persistent requests for a raise, which the bank stubbornly rejected. But my social life had taken on momentum. I had made the acquaintance of two boys, Peter, a German, and Lazlo, a Hungarian. Both had been living for many years in Peru and Peter had married a Peruvian girl. We became inseparable.

Peter had a house in Chosica, a small town 30 miles distant from Lima, where the climate was totally different due to the 2,500 feet altitude above sea level. From the 15th mile on, every single day of the year, the sun, always a no-show in Lima, would spring out. The sky was forever blue, it never rained, to the point that the fields had to be irrigated. It is rumoured that Pizarro, the Spanish Conquistador, looking for a site to build his capital city, asked a wise old Inca to name an appropriate location. To get some revenge, in view of his homeland being taken over, the Inca pointed to the place where Lima stands today, the only spot out of the whole coast where a beastly climate reigns. A few miles away in any direction, it is far better.

The atmosphere in Peter's house was cheerful and warm. His pretty wife and her girlfriends would play the guitar and sing the catchy Peruvian tunes. Thanks to the hospitality of this charming couple I was introduced to the merriness of Latin-American parties and to the friendliness of its inhabitants.

I went to see my first bull fight in a 16th-century plaza, the oldest on the continent. The Peruvians had a new one built, bigger, even grander, in the '40s. But the architects got mixed up in their calculations on the direction of the wind. It proved impossible to fight in the bullring as the wind would have the *muleta* – the tiny piece of red cloth which is the sole protection of the bullfighter – float too high, fully uncovering the man's body and leaving him defenceless in front of the murderous horns of his opponent. I went to see some cockfights as well. They seemed very cruel to me but I was fascinated by the crowd going crazy to the point of betting astronomical sums which would probably leave the unlucky one as well as his family without tortilla the next day.

In spite of my hard labour, I managed to go to numerous parties. I was a living corpse on waking up in the morning but young as I was I would hang on. Once, coming back home from a party around two o'clock in the morning, I was stunned by such overpowering tiredness that I went to sit down on a bench in the park I had to cross to reach my house and fell asleep. I was woken up a few hours later by a benevolent cop who advised me to go and finish my sleep in my bed. Today, I don't think I would so easily get away with it, not even in Europe, and definitely not with my wallet still in my pocket.

At another party at friends', everybody was thrown into the swimming pool in the small hours, including me. Some friends took me home and left me at my door. Only when they were out of reach did I realise I must have left my keys at the bottom of the swimming-pool. I hung on to the bell but didn't succeed in getting anyone from the inside interested before an hour passed. During all that time, a cop would go on with his round, passing one way and then the other way before me, as I stood soaking wet. He would simply shake his head without a word.

On one weekend we went on a boat excursion to see the guano islands, near Callao. I wonder who on earth got the silly idea to visit islands of s . . . The expedition did not come out as very poetic, the billions of birds would shriek like no bird of proper gender education would dare and their droppings would unload an incredible stench. Alongside us in the water, jellyfishes three to nine feet wide floated everywhere in sight. I would have hated to capsize.

Peruvian politics of the time were interesting. The President of the Republic was a general who had made his way to that position a few years before by a very classical *putsch*. Routinely, a new *putsch* would make an attempt at overtaking the regime every four to six weeks. The leader would then be put on a boat and sent to exile with no more sanctions. He would receive his retiral pension from the Army. These attentions were because the President in charge would expect the same favour returned when his time to be demoted came.

I met my President once, at a party at his palace. The invitation card stated that 'el exelentisimo Señor Presidente Constitucional de la República del Peru, General de Division Manuel A. Odria was soliciting the honour, etc'. He was a diminutive *cholo* (half breed), with a cunning and mischievous look. His tiny slanting eyes, deep sunk in his face, sent piercing beams. He would straighten up so as not to lose one inch of his height, that is, when he remembered to correct his natural tendency to sag. The rattling of his medals resounded like a cavalry trumpet. He was skilful in defending himself and the people, was a good manager and his country was prosperous while he was in power. He was dethroned in favour af a 'democratic' regime that left Peru bloodless.

One day after a party at Peter's, I went back to Lima with a husband, his wife and her lover. I was the only one unaware of the triangular situation, at least until then. The husband was driving a little English bug on high heels, too light for the road. It didn't matter, as the driver, rather tipsy, decided on the way, that he was fed up with his cuckold's part. 'Have a good look at that tree, over there,' he said suddenly, with a devilish snarl, 'that's where we're going!' He swerved at a sharp angle only inches from the tree and the little car rode for an instant on two wheels. The husband started driving from one side of the road to the other, roaring mad, feeding on our panic. Our supplications had no effect on him. As I was starting to have an insight on the Latin-American psychology, I whined that I was car sick, could he please stop the car. He braked and stopped sharply, a despising smile on his lips. I went out, opened all the doors and his wife and her sweetheart sprang out as well. With a stern tone of voice I stated that we would start again only if I would do the driving. The husband finally surrendered . . . on the condition that it was his wife's lover who took the wheel. That guy certainly placed his varied trusts on the same bad horse. The lover knew less than barely how to drive, so danger was still lurking. We finally made it to Lima at walking pace. When I took my leave, they seemed delighted with one another, with the party, even with me.

After one year of hard labour, I had two weeks' holiday. Peter and I resolved to make a trip to the Amazon and braced ourselves for the test that we didn't expect to be a bed of roses.

We left by the Andean railway, the highest in the world, which climbs up in five hours from sea level to 15,000 feet. On arrival at the top, I got up and collapsed. Everything was whirling around me. You had to move slowly and were not to make any effort so as not to succumb to the *sorroche*, the mountain sickness. So much so that inside the train, very primitive comfortwise though it may have been, oxygen devices had been installed in every compartment.

The cold was biting and the panorama of the Andes, which culminated 6,000 feet above, was magnificent. Everywhere around us, llamas were grazing peacefully between the stones of the rocky ground and, crowning our heads, impressive glaciers blinded us with their diamond lights.

We left our train – built by the British around 1880 and still a technical wonder – at Cerro de Pasco, the end of the line and pursued our journey in a bus, a big truck with an awning as a top, inside which wooden benches had been nailed.

The dirt roads we had to drive on were seeded with holes 20 inches deep and we would proceed at 20 miles an hour. Thus we went down to 2,500 feet and there we stopped in a little town named Tingo Maria, a centre for coffee plantations, bordering the jungle. It was raining. What an indescribable delight I felt to see rain for the first time in a year! I stayed outside for a long time, getting slowly drenched by a thin, warm rain that totally enraptured me.

We were greeted by a friend, an Italian *marchese* who made me realise how life in the deep forest could change a civilised being. He was a guide to us in the jungle and he told us that after about two years he knew how to feel the presence of an animal, just like the natives, foresee the changes in the weather, translate noises and smells, recognise animals and plants, manufacture his own medicines, feed himself, find drinkable water and protect himself against insects and snake bites.

He used to mesmerise us with his descriptions of the dangers in the Amazonian jungle, the most fearful of all forests. Supposedly, one could not survive more than 24 hours alone in that jungle. First, no way could one have a swim in the Amazon because of the swarms of piranhas, the little fish with razor-sharp teeth, which can eat a cow in ten minutes.

Other small fishes, two inches long, assault people or animals careless enough to go swimming. They make their way into the body of their victim through any aperture and proceed to eat it from inside. If one is not in a position to be operated on immediately, it will be certain death as the fins of those little monsters form hooks and make them impossible to remove.

Then there is the infamous *chuchupe* to be feared. It is a green snake up to 20 feet long, with a head as big as a dog's. It curls up in a tree, stalking its prey, invisible because of its colour. It is the only snake which chases its quarry and is faster than a man. Its venom is very powerful so, when it catches its prey and snatches away a chunk of its flesh, the victim dies before the snake takes another bite. I don't know why, but this story about a snake with the head of a dog, moving faster than its prey, sounds today not too convincing a horror tale.

From Tingo Maria on, there was no public transportation of any kind. We had to negotiate a seat in a truck, in the back, with the load. We had no problem in finding a vehicle as the whole city already knew that downtown roamed two crazy *gringos* who, instead of taking the plane and arriving safely in Pucallpa, the end of the 'road', would rather make the trip in three days in a truck without seats, swallowing the dust, to reach the same spot.

The journey was indeed picturesque. The road first goes up and, at 6,000 feet, hugs breathtaking ravines. Our driver, an Indian who munched coca leaves non-stop (not to fall asleep and not to feel hungry, poor chap, but that we knew only later) fell asleep all the same and we ended up in the ditch, on the mountain side by sheer luck. The front axle shaft was damaged and the Indian attempted to repair it with whatever he could get his hands on.

We still had four hours' ride to the next village, four stretching hours with the unattractive choice of the axle shaft falling apart or of the driver falling asleep. From where we were stuck in the back we could not evaluate the situation, much less control it. We arrived safely and rushed out to change vehicles.

We reached Pucallpa, on the border of the Ucayali, a tributary of the Amazon. It might have been the end of the road but there was no doubt that it was the end of civilisation.

We spent the night at the Gran Hotel, the only hotel in town, an old wooden shack in which there were no sanitary facilities and where you had the feeling that it was tumbling down when anyone was walking upstairs.

In the morning, we embarked on our ship, a rusty 100-ton tub about 50 years old, which thought nothing of transporting 200 passengers. We were in first class and that gave us access to a tiny cabin with two bunks. The passengers in the second-class section slept on deck. I must admit that the trip wasn't expensive: seven days on board, food included, cost five dollars per person in first class. To start with, the meals were almost edible. However, as it was impossible to get any supplies on the way, they fast became rather monotonous. It was rice-frijoles (red beans) at lunch, frijoles-rice at dinner. We adjusted philosophically but could never keep that nonchalant attitude towards the savage assaults of trillions of mosquitoes that had decided to do away with us before we left the ship.

As the boat was a steamboat, it had to stop every four hours to load wood. At one of those stops, a white man approached us. He was German and had been living for 50 years in this hole of a place. He was 73 years old and looked ten years younger. He hadn't set foot in Lima in ten years and the last time he was in Berlin was when King Edward VII visited Kaiser Wilhelm II.

At the next stop, an Indian approached me. He wore a live anaconda around his neck. He insisted on selling it to me, progressively lowering his price until it was 20 cents a metre (39 inches). The snake was five metres long. The Indian could not understand why I didn't want to give out a mere dollar for the whole beast, alive at that.

Our captain was skilful enough to avoid the sandbanks while we were his guests. Not infrequently, we were told, he would run aground and stay stranded for a few weeks until the high tide came in and delivered him. We crossed the point where the Ucayali joins the Amazon and the river became a sea.

We reached Iquitos, a rather important town, in the middle of the jungle, with no access road. Before the regular air service between Lima and Iquitos, mail, cargo and passengers were routed on British ships. They would sail down to the mouth of the Amazon, 3,000 miles away. They would then follow on to Liverpool, in England. From England they would go back the other way to Buenos Aires, Argentina, and then around Cape Horn to get to Lima on the Pacific Ocean. This sea voyage would take three months when the distance from Lima-Iquitos is 1,500 miles as the crow flies.

Not so long ago, the Iquitos lords would send their children to Europe to study, as it was a shorter trip than to Lima. Parents could give their offspring the opportunity of this golden education for they had made great wealth during the rubber boom at the end of the last century. At that time, they even had an opera house built, where Caruso came to sing.

The local governor invited us to his house and we made a dim impression, I'm afraid. The guests were all in white dinner jackets in our honour and we showed up in jeans. They entertained us lavishly though during the few days we spent in Iquitos.

We returned to Lima by plane in a five-hour flight when the journey to Iquitos had taken 15 days to complete. But the trip back seemed to last much longer than the forward one because the plane cabin was not pressurised. As we climbed up to 14,000 feet, we had to endure the flight with oxygen tubes in our mouth to suck some air. I tried to avoid the other passengers' eyes as each time I glanced at them, I would start with laughter and I would choke on my metallic straw. Peter was less than happy, though. He felt he was tasting a preview of the treatment he was sure to get at the hospital on the crash landing we were bound to make.

The financial gap between the wealthy and the poor was appalling. I knew a family who owned the biggest hacienda in the world, extending to the size of Belgium. They had their private police, manufactured their private electricity, extracted their own water on the grounds and lived in absolute authority. The revolution put an end to those huge private domains 20 years later but the poor people didn't get any better off. They are still miserable. The powerful are different people, that's all.

Probably in order to forget their damnation on earth, the Peruvians multiply the festive days. National Day lasts all of four days, the Race Day is celebrated all over Latin America, the 87th birthday of an obscure marshal is celebrated, the anniversary of a war against Chile (I noted later that the Chileans celebrate the same anniversary, only with a little more justification – they won that war).

For a modest overworked employee such as I was, those non-working days were a godsend and there could never be enough of them. I had acquired the mentality of those poor Peruvian workers who could not earn a living even if they killed themselves with work, so they prefer not to work at all.

We had our own private celebration: Bank Day. A celebration we were slightly ashamed of, however. Contrary to the other enterprises where the executives would invite their employees, ours would present us with the bill and there was no way we could object, it was taken off our salary.

Numerous celebrations would refer to the war against Colombia in the '30s over a piece of jungle whose location nobody knew exactly. Lima sent an expeditionary force to the area but the military found it extremely difficult to encounter the enemy as it is impossible to engage in combat inside the jungle. They could only confront one another on the rivers. The belligerents on both sides could count a little on one or two small boats. The Colombians decided to send their air force to back the sailors. It consisted of one single-engine airplane which spat, in the absence of real bombs, a few tins filled with powder. The tins missed the target and fell into the water, along with victory.

Peru was constantly at war with its neighbours, Ecuador and Chile. Chile, often called 'South American Prussia', always had an excellent army which would enable Chile to win the war and snatch away one Peruvian province after another. Peru would take repayment from Ecuador, from whom it stole a few provinces as well, to compensate for its loss and their humiliation, as Ecuador was even less able to fight for itself than Peru.

After my last fruitless request for a rise, I slammed the door and left my bank for good. It was 31 December 1955 and that decision gave me the opportunity to have a great New Year's Eve with my pals instead of sweating that special night away on my accounting books the way my employers had planned for me.

From January on, an American friend of German extraction asked me to work for a few months in his small fishing company, first in Lima, then in Guayaquil, Ecuador. I accepted with enthusiasm, ripe for adventure as I felt. I immediately bought equipment and food supply for the boat that was still in Callao and was due to get under way for Guayaquil a few weeks later.

In mid-February, I took my leave from my friends in Lima. They gave a number of *fiestas* to wave me goodbye and I gave a few as well to celebrate the fact that I was sorry to leave. The whole process of those celebrations was very pleasant indeed, I had no idea I was that popular.

When I went to get my ticket at the company's office, I was told there was no money for a plane ticket. By then, I was used to that sort of answer and took the bus for a 20-hour journey with no qualms. My boat arrived one day after me. It was an old American minesweeper, modified to fish shrimps, creatures that abounded in the territorial waters of Ecuador at that time of the year. The deep-freezing and packaging of the shellfish were done on board prior to exporting the lot to the United States.

Guayaquil is located approximately 75 miles from the sea on the Guayas, an important river which flows up or down at the rhythm of the tides. On the Guayas, a few piers had been built for offloading cargo in Guayaquil from the boats going upstream. It was the only so-called harbour for the whole of Ecuador. On the Guayas, lush green islands covered with multicoloured flowers were drifting, formed by dead trees and scrub torn out of the jungle deeper inside the country and inhabited by all sorts of snakes, birds, rats and insects. Those islands, measuring up to several hundred square feet, would pass up and downstream as the tide commanded and seem to stay permanently in front of the town.

Until ten years ago, the Guayaquil climate made the town feared because of the frequent epidemics of typhoid fever and endemic malaria. The toughest crews sometimes refused to make a stopover in Guayaquil.

Very few houses were made of stone, most were built of rotting wood. Swarms of bloodthirsty mosquitoes, specialising in human blood, would invade everything, day and night and you had to stuff yourself with quinine to prevent malaria. Surging from the floors, the ceilings, the walls, and the kitchen pipes, *cucarachas* would creep around and infiltrate everything. They were bugs as big as the palm of my hand, armed with prodding, quivering antennas thin as hair, which measured one and a half times the length of their body. I would find them in my tooth glass, inside my sheets at night, in the food, in my pockets, in my shoes, I still shudder with nausea at the mere memory. They were not the most revolting roaches. Their cousins, the water *cucarachas*, reached four inches in length and had wings. They were as clumsy as mosquitoes are in our countries, exploding on our car windshields when we drive at night. Those ones would arrive with the buzzing of an electric fan and splash! They would squash against my head or my chest.

In January, other bugs joined the party. There were giant moths that invaded the atmosphere in droves and finished their life in the streets where they would pile a couple of inches thick. They made a strange 'shshsh . . .' sound when cars ran over them. On the roof of the highest building on the Gran Plaza, a big board showed the image of a *cucaracha* with the warning: 'Kill it before it kills you.'

The piers in the 'harbour' were permanently strewn with cocoa bags which would spread a sickening smell and with huge banana bunches, the two main exports. You could buy a bunch of 100 bananas for one dollar.

I settled in a decidedly shabby small hotel, low class even considering the local standards. Schools of young boys would wait for the rich foreigner (me) to come out in the morning, carrying enormous live lobsters that they would let crawl on the pavement for me to buy, half a dollar apiece. I would refuse heroically as I had neither kitchen nor stove.

Every morning at dawn I went down to the harbour and embarked on a rowboat manned by an Indian. He took me to my ship, which was anchored in the middle of the river. I had to buy food supplies, organise the export of the shellfish, soothe the tensions among the crew members which consisted of a captain and a German engineer plus a few sailors of undefined nationalities.

The captain and the engineer were at each other's throats over the most insignificant detail. They would join forces, however, to turn against the shipping agent on the ground, although neither of them spoke one word of Spanish.

The boat would stay three or four days at sea and then come back to unload its catch on shore. It was supposed to have a full hold on arrival but the shrimps would elude the captain and the catch was rather meagre.

While the boat was at sea, I had the opportunity of enjoying my tropical paradise. It was the rainy season and the water poured down from the sky in curtains with a crackling sound and lightning that added some spice to the general boredom of the area. It was pitch dark in daytime, which was a pity, as the electricity system would collapse at the first thunderclap. Forget about staying dry. It was raining as much inside as outside but there was less risk of drowning. The sewage system was non-existent, torrents of rain crashed down from the hills in muddy whirls, overpowering the city.

An elderly German worked at our shipping agent's office. I enjoyed his company as he was the only person around with whom I did not have to keep a constantly watchful eye on my pockets and my wallet lest they vanish. I asked him how on earth he could endure life in Guayaquil for 42 years without shooting himself through the head. Slightly surprised, he answered: 'You don't like Guayaquil, eh? Funny. Of course you need approximately 20 years on the spot to get used to it but after that you come to love it.' I hoped not to have to stay that long.

Our bizarre working team was completed by a Canadian female secretary, 30-some years old. She had married an Ecuadorian: 'I was in love with life and South America,' she would singsong, putting her head back and closing her eyes on her memories.

Her Latin lover kept her sequestered for seven years, locked in a house, draped in local rags, with no contact with the outside world. He would make her endure severe beating sessions when he was drunk, that is to say every night, and got her to bear five children in seven years.

As her family was searching for her everywhere during the whole time, the Canadian consul finally found and freed her.

When she tried to obtain financial aid for the children from her

Valentino-type husband, taking him to court, she was told bluntly that he had sired and given his name to 45 children before hers and was penniless.

She was blonde and fair-skinned and easily found another husband on the spot and gave birth to yet another child after one year. Then that husband left for Argentina without a second thought. He just informed her, laughing, that he had not married her at all. A chum of his had played the role of the minister. And it had to be at my company that this dimwit had run aground at the end of her tiring journey in dreamland.

I met a few of the local high-society families, all of them banana-cocoa-coffee planters, who would go from riches to rags depending on the cocoa or coffee stock market. They proudly lined up in front of me some of their glamorous daughters to no avail. I was on my guard concerning the senoritas' fathers and cautiously chose my girlfriends from among the foreigners, not eager to lock horns with the coffee lords.

One evening I invited an American girl to the movies. I planned to court her as romantically as the film star courted his partner. On the door to the cinema was nailed a warning: 'Be cultured, don't spit on the audience and don't use obscene words.' I had such a fit of laughter that the charm was broken, especially as I couldn't bring myself to translate the placard to the young lady, my education forbidding it adamantly. Every time I started chuckling she wanted to know what was so funny, she thought I was making fun of her. The evening had been a disaster, it ended up worse.

I took my ex-girlfriend home and after a few steps on the way to my place, I heard some whispers behind me. I turned around and saw four Indian teenagers following me. I accelerated my pace but it was too late. As soon as they were upon me, one of them slid his arms under mine and joined his hands in a strong lock on my neck, projecting my head, chin first, on my chest, two others faced me and each one took hold and hung with all his might to one of my arms. The fourth one emptied my pockets. 'We don't want to do no harm to you, *señor*,' they whispered, 'we just want your money.' Half my size though they were, there were four of them and I couldn't move. Outraged and humiliated, I was dumb enough to kick one of the scum in the stomach. He answered by slicing the palm of my hand with his knife. They fled with my wallet. The cut in my hand was not serious although bleeding profusely as usual and I never carried much cash in this country. But the loss of my documents, ID and working licence included, was a catastrophe. In South America, it was almost impossible to replace them. Civil servants drowned in paperwork and did not understand anything about it, as they were not chosen because of their competence but because of nepotism and connections. Their best defence was to answer 'no!' to whatever you asked them.

I envisaged the future gloomily when, two days later, I received a parcel through the regular mail. My wallet was inside, not with the money, to be sure, but with all of my documents. A note was clipped to it, which had me in stitches: 'Por favor, señor, I would like a job on your ship.' Juvenile delinquent, maybe, but rather witty. If I had had a job free, it would have been for him, he would have blended nicely into my team.

My ship was a disaster, as it didn't fish any shrimps. I could see bankruptcy lurking ahead and I was probably not the only one to interpret the future in such a way, judging by the mood of my crew. My boss then decided to send the boat to Chile where he hoped to find at last those elusive gambas that every fisherman except him would fish anywhere.

For me the orders were to go to Mancora, a tiny village in Ecuador where another boat from my company was dipping. Two days before sailing, when I arrived at the pier to take the rowboat, I saw a corpse floating in the water, head split in two. Nobody paid any attention to it and when I came back two days later to leave for good, the corpse was still afloat at the same spot. Human life was apparently not worth more to the police than to the criminals.

I sauntered one last time over the evil-smelling cocoa bags and the banana bunches and my Indian assistant and I made our way for the last time together among the floating islands to get me aboard my vessel.

Mancora was located in the desert and the local life revolved mainly in the frame of a dirty shack, sheltering a tiny bar and two bedrooms. The walls of the cabin were pasted with American posters exhibiting blonde and white *gringas*, well-groomed and clean – 'encounters of the third type' – no doubt, for the saloon patrons of Mancora.

The shack had an appropriate sign outside: 'Hotel Crillon'. True, it prided itself on a jukebox that would bellow non-stop. And the beer was cool. Considering that there was neither water nor electricity in the village and that each drop of water had to make a journey in a tank wagon from a point 35 miles distant, I think that the shack well deserved the stars of a Parisian palace. Even if the sign in the lavatories did read: 'Be cultivated; don't stand on the seat.'

Although it was burning hot during the day, it was cooler at night and I slept better than in my two months' stay in Guayaquil where neither my millionaire friends nor I had air conditioning, as it did not exist at the time.

I went on with my round to Talara, in the north of Peru, where I got busy obtaining the visas for Ecuador for another crew. This time around, the sailors' nationalities, as ill-matched as usual (five different nationalities for seven men), were more problem-prone than before.

I had a German from Stalingrad, without a passport, who had served as versatile mercenary at times with the Soviets, at other times with the Germans, probably with both sides most of the time. When he tried to seek refuge with the Americans against his ex-buddies who were starting to get fed up with his two-cent intrigues, the Americans pretended to deliver him back to the Russians. Boris wisely fled. Excellent at mechanics, speaking four languages, he couldn't read or write.

Boris was not my biggest obstacle to get permission to navigate legally; it was a bunch of three Peruvian sailors. Ecuadorians and Peruvians loathe one another. I succeeded in extracting all of my visas from the Ecuadorian consul, though, swearing that I felt a profound antipathy towards Peru and its inhabitants. I think that, in order to look convincing, I sort of spat on the floor to seal my words.

The filthy palace into which I moved this time was even smarter than the one in Mancora. The notice on my room door read: 'Under no circumstance will breakfast be served in the bedroom as it is more ethical to eat in the dining-room.' On the bar counter, downstairs a sign advertised proudly: 'Cold drinks, sometimes'.

Having fulfilled my contract, I made a long detour back to Lima and visited at leisure Chile, Bolivia, Brazil and Argentina.

In July 1956, I left Lima for good and took the plane to Panama. I had always dreamt of seeing the Pacific Islands and, as I was already halfway, I decided to pay them a visit before going back to Europe and finally getting to work seriously on a career. The only way to reach Tahiti was by sea. I embarked on a French ship from Panama for the 15-day trip that would get me there. There were three classes on my boat. I was in the third. I slept in a dormitory, which had ten bunks. There were neither windows nor air-conditioning and the vicinity of the engines allowed us to share their suffocating heat and the noise . . . well, I had to get used to it, I had plenty of time.

I was introduced to the captain. 'How's the stew, young man?' he asked me with a teasing smile. 'Very good, sssir!' I said, sailor style, standing to attention. He immediately provided me with a pass for the deck and another one giving me free access to the reception rooms in first class. I then enjoyed the use of a deck chair for my nights in the open, eagerly tasting the salt wind and blessing my benefactor. The journey was magnificent and, upon disembarking, we were greeted in due style by beautiful young girls (*vahines*) offering us fragrant collars of flowers among songs and dances of welcome.

During my stay on board, I got acquainted with a few Europeans who lived in Tahiti. The Chinese and the Tahitians, who then lived in harmony with one another, as well as the Europeans greeted me on arrival as an old friend. They all did their utmost to offer me their paradise. Thanks to one of them, I quickly found a small bungalow to lease, three miles away from Papeete and rented a motorbike so that I could explore the island.

Riding my motorbike, I toured Tahiti leisurely in four days. The only road was the one that circled the island. It was 75 miles long, not counting the 13 miles, which fence each side of the peninsula, on the part of the island farthest away from Papeete.

Papeete, Tahiti's capital city, was still a very tiny town, whose straw huts blended harmoniously with the colonial style of the last century. Tourism was non-existent because of the isolation due to the difficulty in getting there. One ship every six weeks and two seaplanes a month from New Zealand were the only bonds with the rest of the world.

There was no newspaper in Tahiti; the only means of communication with the outside world was the radio that broadcast two hours a day, relayed through Brazzaville, in Africa. The seaplane from Auckland brought the urgent mail every two weeks. On that day, the crowd gathered in front of the post office and waited for hours, without showing any signs of impatience for the mail to be handed over. It was a good opportunity to meet everybody, laugh and chat as the Tahitians love to do. I never missed that appointment either for it allowed me to get acquainted with the young girls. Although corresponding only slightly to the classical beauty features, all of them were smashing. They let their splendid manes entwined with flowers slip onto their shoulders, twisting it from time to time over their head in a gracious movement which displayed their perfect arms and let it splash back while shaking it and rolling their thighs in their brightly coloured *pareos*, the local version of dresses. The fragrance of the perfumed oils they anointed their skin with, mixed with that of the flowers in their hair, was intoxicating.

I became friends with a solitary sailor, renowned in his time, Eric de Bishop, a Frenchman who had sailed around the world, alone in a small boat. He was getting ready now at 64 to cross the Pacific from Papeete to South America, in reverse from the route of the famed *Kon Tiki* expedition headed by the Norwegian Thor Heyerdahl.

I visited Eric every day and followed with fascination the building of his raft, made solely of local material and totally devoid of nails, as the ancient navigators had built their boats. When the raft was ready, I waved him an emotional good bye. He succeeded in arriving in front of the rocky coasts of Chile but found his doom there when the barrier reef tore his raft apart.

Shortly after my arrival, General De Gaulle appeared on an official visit. He wasn't then in office nor did he occupy a formal position, not being prime minister any more and not yet President of the French Republic.

There was however, a huge reception, which took place in the gardens of the governor's mansion, and everybody was invited. As I made for one of the long buffet tables, I saw a jolly old fat Tahitian woman grabbing one of the plates filled with sandwiches. She emptied it into her voluminous handbag. She didn't appear to be embarrassed at all when she caught my surprised look: 'It's free, might as well take it all!' She said with a wide grin.

I left to explore other islands, big ones, small ones, and ventured as far as the Australes in the Southern hemisphere, with picturesque means of transport. I travelled with song and laughter, in the company of the children, the fishermen, the matrons, the pigs, chickens and goats more often than with the *vahines*, the beautiful girls of whom so many travel books rave. I had the best time, for I made more trusted and dear friends in Polynesia than in many other places where I rested my suitcases in 35 years of my career. It is there that I left a piece of my heart and I still go to visit it as often as possible.

Chapter Eleven

RETURN TO EUROPE

The trip from Tahiti back to Europe was a long journey around the world. I left on a French ship from Papeete to Sydney, via the New Hebrides and Noumea, the capital city of New Caledonia. I already knew quite a few people among the passengers and I made numerous other friends on board during the crossing of the Pacific, which made the voyage unforgettable.

We made a stop in Port Vila, in the New Hebrides, for a couple of days. This wild land was the kingdom of luscious vegetation and of a very tropical and rainy climate, which accounted for all sorts of exotic diseases, among them endemic malaria.

In the more remote islands of the archipelago, the population remained practically untouched by civilisation and very few people had ever seen a white man. The tribes had their own chiefs and applied a strict ritual law. Whoever caused severe damage to the community was put to death. His body was cut up and the pieces shared by the injured parties. These would enjoy a roast of his flesh and bones in a merry gala meal. The fiercest wars among tribes gave way, for the victors, to lively cannibal festivities. At these festivities there was plenty of palm wine, followed by songs and dances, in a rejoicing where everyone challenged the others with assaults of elegance, complete with high-feathered multicoloured coiffures, painted faces, pierced ears and noses ornate with bones, necks burdened by collars of human teeth.

I had the luck to touch ground while they were celebrating the 50th anniversary of the British–French condominium, an original form of colony, where two administrations existed side by side, each with its own civil servants, laws and schools.

'Our ancestors, the Gauls . . . ' intoned the young Kanaks on the French side, 'God Save the Queen . . . ' screamed the little natives on the English side. It has to be said that French and English were far busier fighting their petty local wars than educating the so-called savages. Thanks to their non-involvement, the country had kept and has retained all its charm and character. And I had ample time to compare the ceremonial uniforms of the Savages and the Civilised, as well as their rituals of songs versus brass bands and dances versus marching parades. For the speeches, they were equally solemn, pompous and boring in either category.

New Caledonia, our next stop, made me quickly catch onto the damage that civilisation could impose on local populations. The country, populated originally by Kanaks, served as a convicts' dump for the French in the middle of the last century. Then its wealth in nickel mines had attracted their greed and incited them to claim the territory as their own. At the time when I set foot on the island, the Europeans already accounted for half of its inhabitants. While the Kanaks seemed ugly in their facial features by our standards, the Europeans appeared to be conceited, arrogant and recently monied. Indeed the Kanaks themselves, a Melanesian people, show far less good nature and gentleness than the Polynesians, as I had the opportunity to study in the 15 days of our stay.

There was a small colony of Tahitians living in Noumea. Probably intimidated by the ruthlessness of the locals of either community, they had lost their natural jollity and gathered rather gloomily in the evenings in a nightclub. I had a rendezvous there with a Tahitian girlfriend I had known in Papeete and who lived permanently in Noumea. We planned to spend the time of my stay together. Unfortunately she had an appendicitis crisis on the second day and had to be rushed to the hospital to get an operation. She was so pathetically sad that I spent my two weeks on hospital visits.

*

After another week at sea, I disembarked in Sydney, Australia, and settled in a hotel for ten days, waiting for another ship to take the passage for Europe. I was supposed to board an Italian boat, very spacious, which, on the way to Australia, transported Italian immigrants and returned more than half-empty to Europe. Consequently, the ticket fare was very modest and the passengers very young, for most of them were students or serving in the army.

In Australia, alcohol consumption was still strictly restrained. You could drink in the pubs only from five o'clock to six in the evening, except on Sundays, when . . . it was forbidden altogether. The way the ceremony unravelled every day had me wide-eyed and I would not have missed the show for anything.

At five to five in the afternoon, the gigantic bar counters were littered with hundreds of huge beer mugs, in rows as straight as soldiers on inspection. Armies of barmen started pouring ice-cold beer into the mugs. In front of the closed door of the pub, an endless queue of men waited sheepishly for the signal. At five o'clock sharp, someone opened the door wide and gave passage to the crowd. Every man started drinking, methodically, meticulously, without losing too much time in conversation which was limited to a few grunts punctuated by burps. Everyone would swallow the 15 to 20 beers he was determined to stuff down in such a short time and, at five to six, everyone would order three more beers and pay his bill for the total of his intake. Those were savoured at a rather less rushed pace after the 'dry' hour, allowing the poor stomachs to somewhat unfreeze. Not too much, however, as the gentlemen had to find their way home before the effects of alcohol so quickly gulped down made them forget their address.

This rule about alcohol consumption may seem loony considering the way it was applied, and all the men would gladly have voted for its abolition. But the wives opposed the change of hours, stating they would rather have their husbands come home early and drunk than late and probably just as drunk.

Upon disembarking in Sydney, the news about the war between Israel and Egypt was splashed over every newspaper. The conflict was gathering momentum on an alarming scale for the British and the French, shareholders of the Suez Canal, had every intention to fight for their investment against Colonel Nasser, the Head of the Egyptian State, who had nationalised the Canal. They had sent troops and Nasser had retaliated by sinking the ships harboured in the Canal, which was subsequently clogged like an overworked pipe. The Russians, always keen on blowing on ashes, threatened to jump in on Nasser's side.

A third world war was feared. Lix, always full of solicitude for me, immediately sent me a plane ticket so that I could rush back home. However, the shipping company informed me that the ship would sail around the Cape instead of through the Suez Canal. The usual voyage took three weeks; the new one would add two weeks without costing me a dime more. I went for it.

I embarked in Sydney harbour on 20 November 1956. On board, we listened with fervour to the news on the radio and commented hotly on it.

I was becoming a seasoned navigator and studied with interest the strategy of the different officers toward the solitary travelling (young) ladies. Many of them, whose parents resided in overseas colonies, were returning to them or going back to Europe in tune with the rhythm of the college holidays. Or they were unaccompanied wives who went one way or the other, depending on family weddings or deaths.

I had learnt that, at the start of a long journey, you had only the first evening to find a girlfriend on board. You had to act tactfully as well as swiftly and be everywhere at the same time on that very first evening so as to be introduced to as many ladies as possible. To make a choice on the spot and obtain a date for the next day was mandatory. Indeed, by the second evening, every solitary lady under 50 was already committed. The unlucky guy who could not get a head start on the first night was banned from female companionship for the rest of the voyage.

It seemed to me that the approaching moves had more to do with the nationality of the hunter than with his personality.

The Germans, always correct, would stop dead in their track in front of the ladies, stand at attention and bow low, one hand stiff behind their back. In their mind, an extravagant courtesy was the key to the interest of the ladies if not to their heart, although it had more to do with servility than with politeness. The ladies, however, would jump up every time and seemed more startled than conquered.

The English, a few young midships excepted, did not waste too much time in female company.

The Italians were the wittiest and made a romantic courtship complete with declarations of eternal love followed by 'Eye wille giv' you Italiane lezziones so as I can introduce you to mye parents on arrivale in Genoa.' They made every effort to attract the girls to their cabin for the 'lezziones' they had in mind. If they were rejected, they would not insist, retiring gracefully from the competition with as much dignity as they had left on one hunting ground to start stalking another prey immediately on another.

The French were formidable. They targeted a prey and pursued, persecuted, literally suffocated the poor quarry who, losing her head, and barely able to remember her own name, succumbed hopelessly to the demands of such skilful hunters. I never witnessed an instance when the French tactic did not end up with the complete surrender of the prey.

There was competition from the naval officers as well. In their spotless white uniforms enhanced by golden ornaments, they had the most beautiful female passengers blush with emotion under their conquering stare. Those fearful rivals worked during the day, though, bless them.

Our only stop was Cape Town, where we stayed only two days. It was a pretty town, with an ideal climate and very nice wine. However, the apartheid spoiled the fun for me, forcing still too fresh and painful memories to surge up. Segregation was aggressively everywhere, in restaurants, public transport, hotels, theatres, you name it. However, the proximity of the blacks was more required than tolerated in lifts, as long as they were among the whites, to operate the elevators.

I was unloaded in Genoa a few days before Christmas and took the train to Cologne where my mother met me at the station. After such a long absence, that particular Christmas warmed my heart.

I spent a month at home, time for me to see my family and my friends. Then I had to face up to an appointment I had been postponing since my return. The time was ripe for me to decide what my future was going to be and I could not avoid the self-confrontation any longer.

I wanted to leave Germany. I wanted to get away from that land which was everything but a shelter for me. There was no room for me in a country that had stolen everything away from me, whatever the government, and left me in the situation of a poor relation in my surroundings. Besides, the banks offered me only a modest position for a start, in spite of my experience and the four languages I had now mastered fully.

Not having a college degree I could not become a diplomat, like my father and my ancestors. I was at this stage of brooding when my friend Peter, back from Peru a year before, called me and suggested that I join him in Lufthansa, the new airline company he had entered. Lufthansa was created in Berlin in 1924 and dissolved by the Allies in 1945, as the Germans were not allowed to have planes any more. Lufthansa had been re-emerging since 1955, its headquarters settled in Cologne. It was still a small company, owner of a few planes of not too recent vintage, with about 1,000 employees dispersed around the world. Lufthansa certainly did well as there are now 60,000 employees. At the time, it was looking for people like me, who spoke several languages, had already travelled extensively, and were ready to move often, mostly abroad. The company was willing to promote them rapidly if they showed aptitude for management and adaptability.

I reported at Lufthansa headquarters and was engaged on the spot.

Chapter Twelve

LUFTHANSA ASSIGNMENTS

I trained for four months in Hamburg to learn the subtleties of the trade. Hamburg was a small office, the employees were few and the environment was cheerful. There was a party at the close of the office every day for everybody, the general manager included. It has to be said that we worked until very late at night.

I noted in my files that, in June 1957, for the first time, all the airline companies put together had transported as many passengers over the Atlantic as all of the shipping companies, that is to say one million people by air versus one million people by sea. A few years later, when the number of flying passengers reached ten million a year, the number of ship passengers was down to less than a hundred thousand. Today, there is no passenger ship crossing the Atlantic on a regular basis.

After Hamburg, I was transferred to Cologne where I was assigned a vague position in the charter department. There were only two employees but I was the only one supposed to be part of the team of the 'stud stable', as we were derisively called, a picturesque ensemble of young people who were supposed to be able to shoulder responsibilities and reach higher positions. We were waiting for the call, with more or less patience.

One day, when I arrived at the office, my boss, a good fat man who held me in sympathy told me: 'Starting next week, you will be our manager in Bonn.'

Startled, I asked him to fill me in on the job, admitting sheepishly I hadn't the faintest idea of what it was about, and what I was supposed to do.

'Don't worry, my boy, I haven't a clue myself. But you'll see, everything will work out fine. All the managers are as much in the dark as you are.

But you are all young and so is the company. Together, you will acquire experience and craftsmanship. Come on, now, let's drop the subject and tell me about the restaurant you had dinner at last night, who you were with and what you ordered, that's more solid ground.'

At the time of the Cologne Carnival, renowned for its madness, the female staff reported an incident to me that had everybody in hushed stitches. During Carnival week there was a 'Women's Carnival Day'. On that day, everything was granted them, whatever the demand and it was expected to be outrageous.

We had a general manager, a native of northern Germany, who was rather stuffy. Stubbornly disregarding the warnings of all of his staff, he stayed in his office on that day instead of tiptoeing home like the rest of his male colleagues.

He was sweating feverishly over his files when a group of cleaning women, already rather intoxicated, crashed into his office.

'Hey, honey, have a drink with us!' they shouted, handing him a half-full bottle of wine.

Indignant, he showed them the door with a theatrical gesture and blurted: 'OUT!'

A fat woman, with very red cheeks and messy hair, swept everything off the desk, sending papers, ashtray, records, pencils flying across the room. She pushed the manager forcibly back on his armchair and jumped on his knees.

'So, baby, how about that drink, now?'

Having lost all of his flamboyance, he obeyed meekly. He left as if the house was on fire as soon as she released him and took her attention away from him, trying to look as inconspicuous as he could. He told me years later that it was his very last taste of any carnival on earth until he retired.

A week later I was in Bonn.

The 'office' consisted of a large room where the customers came and went and a tiny adjoining room, my kingdom, which I had to share with a secretary. On the first day, we had to squeeze our bodies even tighter into this box as the guy I was replacing was still there supposedly to try and show me the business in 24 hours. I had precise instructions from my boss:

'Stay with him as little as possible, he will only teach you rubbish.'

As a matter of fact, the guy's only concern was to show me where I could find the sand to cover the visiting cards that tourists' dogs were bound to leave one day – which never happened, by the way.

Next day I was on my own, with no idea what was expected of me, but feeling invested with a burdening responsibility which would have inflated me with pompous pride had I not been deflated by anxiety. Fortunately I had friends at headquarters and I could call them to fill me in. Besides I had a small team, young and efficient, who gave me full support when they realised I did not intend to reign by terror as my predecessor had done.

I had a visit from all the travel agency directors, who assured me of their full collaboration and the Ministries would lend me a favourable ear. Soon, though, I was confronted by my competitors in an all-out commercial battle. The ones from KLM, the Dutch airline, and those from SAS, the Scandinavian Company, among them, gave me a hard time, as they were fearfully competent and experienced. Although we had our swords on the table in business matters, out of the office we were the best of friends and still are.

During my two years in the Bonn office, I had the opportunity and the honour of organising a few charters for Chancellor Conrad Adenauer who would receive me every time with great kindness. I went along once in a charter with the Finance Minister, Erhard, and a delegation of dignitaries and political figures on a five-week tour in the Far East.

As Lufthansa, still a very small company, did not have any representatives in the countries we visited, it fell on me to make contacts with the local airlines and with agents to organise all technical needs. We were received with all the decorum generally reserved for a head of state.

Our plane, a Lockheed Super-Constellation, had a special, all-first-class configuration and, besides the Minister and his staff, there were a dozen journalists and five members of parliament. We landed at night in Calcutta, India, and took transport to the hotel. We had to go across the town and our seasoned chief hostess, who had seen the war, broke down in tears just looking out of the car window. The miserable huts, the beggars in the streets, the corpses alongside the road, the heat and the smell just floored her.

Our next stop was Saigon, not yet overcome by the Communists and still a very French colonial city, then Seoul where the best offices and our hotel were housed in the only modern building of the town. We went on to Tokyo and Colombo in Ceylon – now Sri Lanka – and then Karachi, the capital of Pakistan.

On our second day in Karachi we were all invited – the crews as well, and we had two full crews for extra safety – to the presidential palace. A huge buffet was awaiting us in the gardens. I went ahead of the guests on my checking tour and had a glance at the buffet. At my approach, a swarm of huge black and gold flies rose from the plates. I could not say anything, as it would have been a diplomatic incident if my party didn't eat the meal. I couldn't bring myself to touch the food, however, but everybody else ate heartily.

After the meal, I went to the beach with the crew. A Pakistani came along with a camel and sold a ride to our chief captain, a heavily-built and tall man. The saddle girth broke under his weight and he fell on the wet sand, hard as cement, and broke three ribs. We took him to the only hospital in town, where beds of sick people were crowding even the corridors. The captain was more or less attended to and his ribs temporarily bandaged. He was told he had to wait for the doctor's inspection. By that time, the rest of our party had gone on to merrier grounds and I was alone with the victim. He implored me to get him out of the place and fast. So I smuggled him, two hours before our scheduled departure, on board his plane and accommodated him in one of the crew beds where he remained until our arrival in Germany, 28 hours later.

Our passengers arrived, along with the rest of the crew. They were green in the face, dragging their feet, breathing with difficulty. They were prey to violent diarrhoea that turned later into severe dysentery. I was the only healthy one on board. Sharing the food with the flies did them in, obviously, and I felt a pang of remorse.

Our second captain – sick as he was – barely managed to do the take-off, which was particularly tricky from Karachi. Immediately afterwards he collapsed into the second crew bed and left the co-pilot at the controls for the next eight hours.

Meanwhile, I was running up and down the aisles, distributing the pills I had taken the precaution of bringing along. I calculated that I had to be stingy with the medicine, as my supply was meagre. I reserved it, without telling anyone, for the people most useful to our situation, namely the ones responsible for getting us back home. I gave the pilot three times the dose recommended. I had to pretend everything was in order in the cockpit, which was almost stripped of its occupants. In Istanbul, I had the second captain on his feet again, just in time to take over as the co-pilot was now rapidly weakening. The welcoming committee in Cologne saw a sad-looking bunch of personalities tumbling down from the plane.

I marvelled to see my career take on the turn I had dreamt of and the extreme modesty of my salary was not even a shortcoming, this time. Besides, I had been used to cutting down on my needs for such a long a time that it didn't matter much any more.

I had the priceless opportunity of being able to plan my future outside Germany with no obligation to settle anywhere for long. I could frequently come back to see my mother and my family as I travelled free or for a nominal fee. I could also send for Mother with a special fare and all through my career, she often came to join me. Lix and Buttel were more than willing to travel, so they showed up frequently too and I never felt exiled from my loved ones.

After two years in Bonn, I was sent to open the office in Caracas, then in Madrid, then in Athens.

I was not yet an expert in the management of an airline office but the head office seemed to consider that my experience was still better than what the new recruits, more numerous by the minute, could offer.

In November 1960, my boss told me: 'Here is a company car, take it, drive up to Sweden, then take the ferry to Finland and open up a new office in Helsinki.' So I packed a bag and went off the next day, driving through Germany and Denmark for two days before arriving in Sweden. There at that time you had to drive on the left side of the road and I had never done that before. Sweden is a vast country with few inhabitants and therefore the traffic was not too dense. For hours on end, I didn't come across more than three or four cars on the road. After a coffee break, I forgot all about left-hand driving and ended up facing an oncoming car. I narrowly avoided a collision but felt some panic about the possibility of repeating the experience. So, I fixed a large cardboard sign in front of the steering wheel with a big 'LEFT' written on it. Thus safely arrived in Stockholm, my car and I boarded one of the large ferries to Helsinki.

For some reason, my car was not loaded in the inside of the ship, but on deck. I spent a happy evening on board (Finns and Swedes often take these boats only to have a good time, i.e. get drunk, as alcoholic beverages are extremely expensive in shops because of restrictive taxes, and tax-free on board). So, we spent the time eating and drinking. On arrival at my destination in the morning, I noticed that during the night, the temperature had fallen way below zero and it was raining. I recovered my car buried under a sheet of ice and when discharged on the pier, it refused to budge. Two bright employees of the ship came up with the idea of pouring warm water all over the car and I was able to drive off. Once in the centre of the town, with the temperature still around 10 to 15°C below zero, the water froze again and all four wheels locked. There I was, alone in an unknown town, stuck during rush hour in the middle of the street, facing the prospect of being frozen to death myself. I couldn't communicate with anybody as I did not know a word of Finnish and the car could not be pushed out, as the wheels would not turn. While I was wondering what to do next, two big burly men got out of their car and approached mine, mumbling vociferously. When they realised it was to no avail they hailed two more guys in another car, strongly built as well and grabbing the car at each corner, lifted it and dropped it on the sidewalk, me still inside. They mumbled something I hoped was 'good luck' and bolted. I proceeded on foot to a hotel and had the car lifted off to a warmer place.

This was my first encounter with the Finns, burly-looking and cold in appearance, in fact warm-hearted and cheerful. About 15 per cent of them are of Swedish origin and speak that language at home. Their ancestors settled there centuries ago during the Swedish occupation of Finland until the Russians took over in 1809. They control the largest part of the economy. Until the last war united the entire population, there were tensions between the two groups. You still have to be careful when you talk to a Finn to distinguish between a Finn (Finnish speaking) and a Finlander (Swedish speaking). With the Finns, you refer to their capital as 'Helsinki', with the Finlanders as 'Helsingfors'. They thus have differing names for every city in the country.

I was often invited out by Finlanders as they are extremely hospitable. My first invitation for a week-end including a big dinner-party, was at a beautiful 18th century manor house built entirely of wood, situated on one of the country's 1,000 lakes. They made me take a sauna on arrival and as a joke set its temperature at 120°C instead of the usual 90°C but regulated back the temperature before I started to boil. It was my first taste of a sauna and it was quite an experience, as you had to roll stark naked in the snow which was -20°C. I liked the whole procedure and got hooked on it but on that night, I had to sit up a few times in my bed, gasping for air.

The party was on the Saturday evening. Dinner was served early, around seven o'clock. Enormous quantities of food were brought to the table and we had one or two whiskies before sitting down. Then there was a different wine for every one of the seven courses. The poor hostess had to toast (skal) every single one of her guests and the guest had to empty his glass. I was sitting on my hostess's left side, the place assigned to the guest expected to make a speech. I thought I would be excused, not speaking the language, but everyone spoke English, even when addressing one another, just because of me, that evening. So, I did my best to comply. By the time dinner and after-dinner cognac was over, I had absorbed as much alcohol as I would in a week. The general atmosphere was rather merry. At midnight, to my bewilderment, we all went back to the dining-room and another full meal was served, complete with wines. I guess the cold up there gives you a sound appetite and helps you digest the alcohol. They usually dedicated a toast to 'the king'. They have been away from Sweden for 200 years but they nonetheless are still steadfast monarchists.

There were about five or six airline representatives in Helsinki and we had lunch together once a month. Each of us bought a drink before the meal and a cognac afterwards. As we had wine with our food, we thought it wiser not to show up at the office until late in the afternoon.

One day Aeroflot, the Soviet airline, invited us all, after one of our luncheons, to the Soviet embassy. The senior member of our party, the manager for Panam, the American airline, drove to the porch of the embassy but forgot to brake. He crashed into the door and found himself, slightly bewildered, still in his car, in the middle of the entrance hall. He was immediately surrounded by half a dozen guards, machine-gun at the ready. They were less of a threat, such as it was, than the Finnish police. If you were caught intoxicated by the cops, you were jailed for two to three months and had to do manual labour on public projects, such as roads or the airport. The general manager of the largest chain of travel agencies had disappeared for three months on such grounds. So, nobody in his right mind took his car to go out in the evening. In fact, the first time I arrived at an official cocktail party, I thought it was the wrong day as there were no cars in front of the house.

I had a great time in Finland. I was invited out all the time, the girls were pretty and friendly and as there was not yet a Lufthansa flight to Helsinki, the work was not overpowering.

One evening I went out for dinner with a young lady who had told me she was divorced. I drove her home after dinner, stopped in front of her house and before I had time to get out of the car to open her door, a man sprang to do it, flung it open and swung a hammer on my head. The girl reacted quickly, as if she were used to that kind of incident. She pushed me aside so that the hammer only grazed my head, then shoved the man (her husband) back and left the car, shouting: 'Go!' She did not have to repeat the injunction. My wound was not serious but still needed a few stitches as the blood gushed onto my face. Meanwhile I must have been a frightening sight on my way to the hospital.

There was still snow at the end of May but summer finally came and the country sparkled in all its beauty. On weekends in the countryside we went swimming at midnight in bright sunshine, the parties went on all night as no one felt sleepy in the daylight of the night.

After nine wonderful months, I had a phone call from the head office in Cologne, ordering me to move on to Lisbon, Portugal, where I was supposed to open another office. I mentioned in passing that as I spoke Spanish, not Portuguese, 'wouldn't it be wiser to send me to Madrid, instead?' 'Get going!' was the insensitive answer.

So, I had to adjust to a delicious climate, a beautiful city, palm trees, sunshine the year around and the sea nearby.

I rented a small house – the first time I had a house all to myself – and hired a maid. The maid was a cheerful and witty old lady who mothered me. She was excellent at washing and ironing but didn't know a thing about cooking. So I learnt how to prepare my food and cooking became a hobby that my friends and I appreciate to this day. 'Good thing you didn't take up stamp collecting,' is my wife's comment.

The opening of a Lufthansa line was repeatedly postponed, so I had no planes coming in and no quota to fulfil and the one and a half years I spent in Portugal were the happiest and most carefree time in my life – especially considering the frugal years of war and post-war. I had an extensive group of good friends of various nationalities and we often went on excursions to the various beaches practically empty of tourists then, enjoying picnics or lunches in the harbour where we treated ourselves to fresh fish and lobster. I learnt the language correctly, as I find it a normal courtesy towards the local people to at least give it a try when you live more than a year on their ground.

In October 1962, I was called back to the Lufthansa headquarters and told that I would be the next general manager for France, as I had the required qualifications and could speak French. I was overjoyed. Since my student days in Paris, it had been my dream to go back one day to live and work there. Now I was getting an excellent and important position complete with independence and a good salary. My determination to be fluent in three languages had paid off.

The beginnings were strenuous, though. I had a lot to learn during the first year before things began to work smoothly. I remember sitting in my hotel room in November 1962, having not yet found a flat, and listening to the radio news about the Cuba crisis, saying to myself: 'Good grief! I've got my dream job and already the third world war is about to break out!'

The '60s and the '70s were a wonderful period for a bachelor to live in Paris. It was hard in the beginning to squeeze myself in among the French, as they are not particularly warm people. However, speaking the language fluently helped me in a short time to make friends with a nice crowd, through young and unattached young ladies.

When the students' and workers' outburst erupted in May 1968, I had the full staff at work and it was a feat for each one of the staff members to report to the office. As there was a general strike, we had no planes coming in and one bus a day to Brussels in which we would stuff our unfortunate passengers to catch a plane out of Belgium. For us, there was neither bus nor subway. I organised that those of us who had a car picked up any staff member willing to come to work. Soon the petrol stations were closed, on strike or hopelessly empty of petrol.

I asked my future sister-in-law, who lived in Belgium, to come over with petrol. She drove a diesel Mercedes and filled the boot with containers with my precious petrol, although at the time it was not legal to bring petrol into France. When she arrived at the border, a customs officer opened the boot. He reacted immediately: 'You can't enter France with petrol except in the tank.' She retorted with dignity: 'As you can see, I'm driving a diesel, this is diesel for my return trip.' So the officer let her cross the border with her load and we, at Lufthansa, had enough petrol for two weeks. Nonetheless, it took us up to three hours to get to the office. The streets of Paris were jammed with cars. At the office, it was a challenge for me to find enough work for my employees so that they wouldn't have time to think of joining the strike and the class war that was paralysing the country. All around our office there were endless street demonstrations with the strikers carrying red and black flags. I pictured in my mind my beloved adopted country falling prey to the Communists, which I did not appreciate greatly. Fortunately, the Communists turned their back on that opportunity. Apparently, they prefer to head a revolution rather than follow it.

Then came the day of De Gaulle's historic speech. He asked the people to help him reestablish order and called on them to make a counter-demonstration in favour of the Republic.

At 6 p.m. on that evening, I was standing on the balcony of my club on the Place de la Concorde with friends and we waited anxiously. Would the people of Paris come in sufficient numbers to impress the anarchists? They arrived, young and old, thousands, tens of thousands, waving blue-white-red flags, until there was a human sea covering the huge square and the two miles of the avenue Des Champs-Elysees. They marched, quiet and resolute and their appearance reversed the trend. Order was resumed soon after.

That same year I married Claude de l'Arbre, a Belgian girl. For many reasons, the marriage did not work out and we separated three years later, remaining good friends. Claude died tragically of cancer in 1973 at only 36 years of age.

I tried steadfastly to remain in my Parisian post, clinging to it with grim determination, surviving a good number of attempts at transferring me to any other spot on the planet. Then one day in 1975, my general manager made the trip to see me. 'Look, you surely realise you were very lucky to stay so long in this very coveted place, I have run out of good reasons to give to the other managers for you to keep your post any longer here. An average assignment abroad lasts five or six years, you've been 13 years in Paris!'

I was transferred to Munich in January 1976. Nineteen seventy-five had brought two very important events in my life. One was a happy one, when I met my future wife, Lolita Merlin, who came from an old and distinguished French family of scholars and writers, and the other an extremely sad one, the death of my best friend, my brother-in-law, Lix

Oettingen, who died within three hours of a heart attack, at 55. He left an emptiness which can never be filled and I still miss him every day.

I wasn't too happy about being transferred to Germany. Although my job was important, I wasn't as independent as I was abroad and my salary was significantly lower. However, Munich is a pleasant town to live in and at least I was near to Oettingen and could often see my sister Buttel and support her somehow in her grief.

I had met Lolita at a party. She later told me that she had taken me for a Frenchman, which I took as a compliment to my knowledge of the language. We had just met when my marching orders came in. I wanted to take a souvenir from Paris with me and hesitated between an Impressionist painting and a French wife. The painting was beyond my financial means. It took us some skilful manoeuvring and about three years before we were finally able to live together. Lolita was divorced and lived with her two daughters who were going to school in Paris. So, during the three years of my stay in Munich we had a 'shuttle marriage'. We saw each other during the weekends and the children's holidays when they would go to their father's. One of us then made the trip to join the other. This was one more reason to get married, so that she could have free plane tickets and I wouldn't have to do all the travelling myself!

While I was in Munich, I let my general manager know more than once that, although everything was all right in my actual position, I wouldn't mind being considered for a good job outside Germany. After three years, the least duration required for a German assignment, he called and asked me if I would like to take the position of general manager for Mexico and Central America. I agreed with enthusiasm and by Christmas 1978 I was settled in Mexico City, with my wife full time, as there was a French lycée in Mexico for her girls.

I had a wonderful job, very independent as nobody in head office spoke a word of Spanish or knew anything about Mexico. I travelled extensively around the country and Central America, a fantastically interesting region.

When I visited Mexico City for the first time in the '50s, it was a charming, mostly colonial city of two million inhabitants, with a very good climate, surrounded by a chain of snow-capped volcanoes. Twenty-five years later, there were almost 20 million inhabitants and the pollution of three million cars and innumerable industries had altered the climate beyond repair. You couldn't see the volcanoes any more, except three of four times a year. A thick layer of smog covered the city which is located in a valley at an altitude of 8,000 feet.

We made the best of our stay, had a beautiful house, nice friends and were happy. Then, after four years of marriage, my wife told me she was expecting a baby. We soon learnt it would be a boy; the only Lynar of the next generation as my brother has three beautiful daughters but no son. Although I put on a big grin, I was troubled deep down. My son would be the first Lynar without his land. I wouldn't transmit to him what generations of my forebears had passed on to me. He would have to make his way in life with no other heritage than being a German abroad, a foreigner wherever he settled. I wiped these sombre afterthoughts from my mind; there was nothing I could do about it. I'd do my best to transmit to him our sense of values and duty, our history, our traditions. After all, the moral heritage will always be with us and there is no risk that anyone would want to steal that!

Upon hearing the news, Mother was overjoyed once she understood that modern science could determine very early the sex of an unborn child. She told me repeatedly how much she looked forward to the birth of her grandson. Then she died suddenly, at the age of 92, three months before the birth. It was very sad; until the end she was the central point of the family, not only for her children but also for all my cousins. She had lived all these years in the same small town in southern Germany, near Ernst Wilhelm and his family. My brother had settled there many years ago. After his studies, he had found a job to his liking as general manager of one of the largest private art collections in Germany.

When one of your parents has reached such an old age, you should be prepared for their passing away. But when it actually happens, it is a shock as well as an acute pain. You have been sharing love, affection, and experiences for so long, that a part of you dies with her. A part of me has died with her, but, strong as she was, a part of her is still very much alive with each one of us.

After the first one or two months of sheer bewilderment at the sight of this tiny baby of mine, not knowing too much how to behave towards him, I came to thoroughly enjoy having a son. Meanwhile the pollution in Mexico City was reaching a critical level. When we were playing with the baby on the terrace in our home we were covered with black, greasy specks. The economic situation of the country, in full growth when we arrived, collapsed and it became harder to live there. Even dairy products would sometimes be missing for a week, causing inconvenience for us but sheer misery for the poor. It was time to think about moving on. When the president of Lufthansa came to Mexico for a visit I brought up the question. He asked me where I would like to go next, and I answered 'Rome' without much conviction. My wife and I had that dream in the back of our minds but I had not pushed for it, thinking I had dried up the goodwill of my superiors with what I had been accorded until then. To my astonishment, the president replied: 'All right, but you will have to wait another 18 months, until the manager in charge there now goes into retirement.'

Lolita and I took advantage of this waiting period to study the Italian language. When we left for Rome, we had spent seven and a half years in Mexico, spoke fluent Italian and our son was four years old.

We were very happy in Rome during our four years there. It is a splendid city, the mild climate is very enjoyable and the Romans are kind and very hospitable as well. I had to travel a lot within the country for business purposes and really got to know it well. Our son, already speaking fluent German, French, English and Spanish, learned Italian in no time and enjoyed his crowd of little devils, as the Romans give endless parties the year round for the children, whom everybody treasures.

Rome was my last assignment and in 1989 I retired. We had an emotional parting from Rome and our friends there and settled in Nice, in the south of France.

Chapter Thirteen

RETURN TO GÖRLSDORF

On 9 November 1989, at eight o'clock in the evening, my wife and I were watching the news on television at home in the south of France. The Berlin Wall had opened its gates and they showed on the screen tens of thousands from the east side flooding over the border to go to the west side of the city for the first time in 30 years. On the western side, there was a tremendous atmosphere of jubilation; people were hugging in the streets. I never thought I would see that day and suddenly I had the hope that I would be able at last to go back home soon.

For all of us, it was a door opening and we saw a future again for the old country. Ernst Wilhelm – who had retired a few years earlier – and I were sketching detailed plans of how we would rebuild the old estates and considered ourselves lucky that it came at a moment when we both had the time to dedicate ourselves to this task. Things were to work out differently as we had not taken into consideration one party, the German government, which immediately proceeded to usurp our place.

My wife and I resolved to leave for Berlin the next day, taking our eight-year-old son with us. We wanted to be there to experience the historic days of the fall of the Berlin Wall. We had to wait four days as all the planes to that destination and all the hotels in Berlin were full.

Very late one evening we left our luggage at the hotel and went out immediately, braced to wait hours for a taxi and to make our way across the thick crowd. In fact, we reached the Brandenburg Gate in record time. There were very few cars on the way. A thin rain was falling and the sky was preparing a storm. If all the media were already present, the tourists had not yet appeared. No one knew how the situation would develop.

The Berliners, maybe to have more freedom to move, had walked and they were there, silent in the dark. Everybody made way for our cab to advance up to the limit of the discreet fence set by the police.

The policemen helped the taxi driver to get through, insisting that we stay inside as far as possible. We were a hundred feet from the wall when we got out.

A viewing platform had been erected. It was narrow and not more than two to three people could stand on it at one time. Politely and tactfully nobody stayed long, just the time for a glance and then you would leave your place to others, without waiting to be asked.

Not a sound revealed any presence. During daylight, however, people had been all over the Wall, climbing, talking, shouting. Now, on our side, men and women with tense, worried faces, talking in hushed voices to the strangers around them let out, in jerky voices, fragments of their story. They were East Germans, transferred West years before or just now. They all waited, hoping to be reunited with their family. But, fearing infiltrations from their secret police, they didn't confide many details. From time to time, a television projector would light up, flash in the night a blinding light and subside. There was nothing to see. A call, a shouted question, a moan, a sob, an exasperated shout burst out and quickly the entourage would silence the culprit. Everybody wanted to avoid provocation.

We left around one thirty in the morning, against the protestations of Sebastian, my son, who was dizzy with excitement as well as with lack of sleep. The crowd was spreading away from the Wall in silence, a disappointed, discouraged silence, quite different from the silence of minutes before, when it was loaded with expectation.

We couldn't stay more than 24 hours so, early the next morning, we rushed back to the Wall. It was not as easy as the night before to get there, not because of the traffic but because of the extraordinary number of pedestrians.

I lifted Sebastian up on my shoulders and climbed on top of the platform. Beyond the Brandenburg Gate, far away, a compact crowd was visible in the distance. I understood the reason for the silence of the night before, in answer to the few choked calls from our side. The *vopos*, the dreaded policemen of the G.D.R. (German Democratic Republic), patrolling, gun in hand, were keeping the people as far away from the Wall as they dared. It was easier for them to do it in the cover of the night, without witnesses from our side, in the daylight they were more timorous.

'Look on the other side, in that empty corner was the Redern palace, where your grandmother was born, at the corner of the square and the avenue Unter den Linden.'

'Where, Daddy, where?' Sebastian asked, his eyes opening wide, searching.

'On the right, just behind the Tor.'

'Oh, it's a beautiful house, Daddy!' the child said, seeing nothing at all.

'It was, my boy, it was.'

Since the early morning, numerous bank trucks had been stationed all around Berlin. The government of what was still 'Western Germany' allocated an amount of 100 marks (60 dollars) per fellow countryman from the East, man, woman or child, so that he or she could have a sweet taste of the West. People rushed in droves through the open gates, came to cash their allowance and spread all over the city to spend their money. Very few dared risk putting it aside, they couldn't imagine that, from then on, they would be free to come and go as they fancied. The *vopos* were in front of every breach in the Wall. They didn't interfere but their very presence was a threat. Still, I saw some of them put their machine-gun at the foot of a colleague to go and cash (in uniform) the 100 marks offered by the ones they still considered as their foes.

We walked toward one of the breaches in the Wall to go to the other side. Some *vopos* immediately stepped forward and prevented us from crossing. I felt rage surging in me, so thick and violent that my mouth dried and I remained speechless.

With a determined pace I targeted another hole, very small, apart from the crowd. Two *vopos* were standing there, chatting amicably with three or four civilians from the West who were facing them. I recognised the smiling and benevolent *vopos* I had seen on the French TV screen, fraternising with the reporters. I went to them and had just the time to utter: 'Excuse me . . .' The *vopos'* faces froze instantly in an openly hostile mask, the civilians turned my way with a threatening face. I understood they too were policemen from the other side, together they were defending the border.

We went on with our inspection of the Wall. Another small gap, far away, freshly knocked down, seemed deprived of guards. We came forward, not to step across, we couldn't take the risk, but just out of curiosity. Some western policemen in uniform were standing a few feet away from us. From the other side we could only see the claw of a bulldozer, gathering the stones and the rubbish fallen from the Wall. Sebastian rushed forward to pick up a stone. A police officer stepped in to prevent my son going near the breach.

'I just wanted a little stone!' Sebastian said. The police officer hesitated, glanced apprehensively toward the roaring iron hand, went a few steps forward, and stopped. Then rapidly he bent down, picked up a stone and handed it to my little boy who thanked him with a radiant smile.

Immediately people surged out from nowhere and rushed forward. But the policemen made them retreat.

At school the next day, Sebastian took his piece of Wall out from his pocket to show it to the teacher. She brandished the humble little stone, with no paint, no sketching, just a plain, ugly little piece of cheap concrete, to the class, then handed it back to Sebastian, took his hand and led him to show his Wall to the whole school. The piece fell on the floor in a seniors' class and a small chunk broke off. A teacher picked it up and asked in a pleading voice: 'Could I keep it?' Sebastian was generous. He became 'the-little-boy-with-the-Berlin-Wall'.

*

From 1 January 1990, it was no longer necessary to have a visa for the other Germany.

My nephew, Albrecht, Buttel's son, organised our first trip to Görlsdorf since our flight, 45 years before. We had a Volkswagen bus, loaded with a picnic. There was Buttel, her daughter, Francisca, Albrecht and his wife, Angela, and me.

We left early from our hotel in West Berlin, on the morning of 4 January. We arrived soon at the Potsdamer Platz, one of the most frequented squares in Europe before the war but now a desert without any houses. Behind, was the border where a long file of cars was waiting, but the *vopos* were quite friendly and checked the passports fast enough. We were on the other side in a matter of minutes, and found ourselves in what is the most ancient part of Berlin, with the old city centre.

We drove down the avenue Unter den Linden which had lost nothing of its past splendour, passing in front of the hole where the Redern palace, later the Adlon hotel, used to be. The historic centre had been rebuilt and repaired fairly well under the communist regime, except for the Imperial Palace which they blew up in an attempt to try and eradicate the reminder of the monarchy.

There were numerous large, broad avenues, almost without traffic, except for a few big black limousines and now and then a Trabant – a 'Trabi' as we derisively called this caricature of a car made of plastic in East Germany. There were very few shops, one shabbier than the next one and one restaurant every two miles.

Everything was grey and lifeless. The town ended abruptly and we found ourselves on the freeway, the old one, the one I had seen being built when I was eight. It was now so run-down that we couldn't drive at more than 45 miles an hour.

We missed the old private entrance that Mother had obtained in times past and took the next one. We arrived in the little town of Greiffenberg where we had a big farm and Mother's central administration office. The buildings were all in an awful state, most of the barns and the stables in ruins, as well as the distillery. Everywhere, old agricultural machines, rusted and impossible to use any more, littered the place. The best of our farms, a prosperous enterprise, had been reduced to ruins.

Coming out of the village, we left the car to enter the cemetery and pay a visit to our ancient servants whose names are still so familiar to our ears. An old woman came to us and offered her help in finding the graves. When she understood who we were, she confided:

'I was a toddler when I arrived in the village with my mother and I often saw the Princess, up on her little carriage. She would address us always so kindly that I still remember it. During all the years of communist regime, we didn't even have the right to mention her name. But now everybody speaks again openly about her and only to praise her so much that the young people don't believe us.'

She gave us a few details about the villagers' life up to then, making comparisons with the 'people's oppressors' as the communists would describe us.

'Now, our employers spoil us a lot,' she said, ironically, 'for Christmas every comrade was given an orange!'

We said goodbye warmly, climbed up into our bus again and went on in the direction of Görlsdorf, on the route Mother had taken almost every day to go to the office. We arrived at the place where the big wrought iron park gate used to be. It wasn't there any more; neither were the two bronze stags that lay on each side. But the little caretaker's house was still there and in good shape.

We took the path of the Snake which I had gone down in the opposite way with the tractor on that fateful day in 1945. The path was in such a state that if the ground had not been frozen, we certainly wouldn't have been able to go on.

The park, designed by the famous landscape architect Linnè, so majestic and well kept, was a wild jungle, with fallen trees here and there and never taken away. I no longer recognised anything, I didn't even know where we were, and I couldn't get oriented. Then all of a sudden we came to the end of the park, I recognised on the right side the long white house, the stable, and the butler's little wooden house. But on the left side, where the castle had stood, there were high, thick bushes and nothing else. We stopped the car and explored the place on foot. We found some remains of the foundations of the house, completely covered with a thick vegetation. I spotted the traces of the winter garden because of their semi-circular shape. There were vestiges of the vault room still standing in spite of the dynamite explosions that the communists had orchestrated to prevent any accident that the shaky walls might cause.

My eyes searched behind the ruins, for the little lake. It had vanished as well. Only the river stayed, its water literally black with pollution.

In that jungle reigned an eerie silence. A pale sun made the snow sparkle. The landscape was so peaceful that I could not imagine that place being prey to war and fire. Nature had taken possession and given it back its primitive aspect. In my mind, though, the rooms of my beloved house filed off, filled with the people I loved. I remembered scenes so vividly that I almost heard the sound of the voices.

We went on with our pilgrimage. The stable had been cut in two for some obscure reason. The riding school was now a barn, Ehrentraut's house now sheltered a few handicapped children, the water tower and the little orangery had disappeared, and the church was run down.

The rest of the village, however, was almost the same. The *Krughaus* my grandmother had changed from its vocation of wine and beer bar had recovered its original designation, adjoining a small food store.

Mr Hahn's office wasn't there any more but the long houses of the workers were still in place, deserted, probably because their crumbling roofs and their unkempt interiors had discouraged the last occupants. Old agricultural machines were abandoned, bits of iron and rubbish littered the ground as in the districts where people are unhappy about their living conditions and have no chance of seeing them improved. The charming little village that was still in our memory had become a ghost village. We crossed the railway line and found Wiechmann's house, in front of which I had been photographed with my first stag. It was intact.

We walked into the forest which we found neglected, stripped of its highest trees and of its luscious bushes. On our way, we found a guide, an old man who had worked for 50 years in the stud and had recognised us from an old photograph. He climbed into our minibus with us and told us that our forest had for 30 years been the private hunting grounds of General Mielke, the dreaded chief of the *Stasi*, the East German secret police. Under his rule, the forest was forbidden ground for the villagers who could no longer go there for walks or to pick up wood, not even to go to the traditional harvest of mushrooms, as they used to. The General didn't allow the game to be disturbed.

It has to be said that the estate had become a far better hunting ground than in our time. Stags from Hungary had been imported to improve the stock and moufflons (wild sheep) had been successfully introduced. How much solidarity the high-ranking officials, who had taken away our land, had demonstrated with the people! 'The land belongs to the people' was their motto, we had been told. Apparently their people didn't want their land or didn't care for it if we could believe what we saw in the village as well as in the countryside.

We reached the stud. At last, a few buildings more or less in good shape. The sun was already setting when we stopped between two stables, in the alley that runs along the boxes. I was nine years old again, I listened to the hushing sound, soft, rhythmical, of the horses eating, I could smell their odour, and I heard the hissing of a rake smoothing the sand.

Except in three or four important towns, there were no hotels in East Germany. We had to go back to West Berlin to spend the night. Between Berlin and the Polish border, there was only one petrol station. We were therefore careful to fill the car before joining the freeway – 50 miles – to go back to Görlsdorf the next day.

This time we didn't miss the old private entrance that led us directly into our forest. This part of it was better maintained, there were tall, venerable old trees. We found a gate through which, they told us later, the game was chased so that it jumped out in front of the State dignitaries and their guests, among them Ceauscescu, who could take ostentatious poses to give what was only a mercy shot to the animals, under the frenetic applause of the flatterers . . . and their repressed laughs.

The forest was dignified and serene now, we were alone with our memories, Buttel and I. Nature was displaying an unusual splendour for a country so far north. We arrived in a clearing which had sheltered the little baroque-style manor house of Glambeck which my mother had set aside for me to live in once I became an adult and for as long as she lived. Glambeck was a charming house in the middle of the woods, encircled by a park full of tall and old trees, spreading their branches over a small lake.

We had known for years that Görlsdorf had burnt down in 1945 and had felt pain the previous day not even to find a ruin standing. When I was in the R.A.D., while poetically mending my socks in the evenings, I thought I would soon be tasting the wines in our cellar that had been lying there for so many years. Unfortunately, when I came back home in March 1945, I was still too young and I had a disease which forbids alcoholic beverages. If I had had the opportunity of playing the drunken sailor Görlsdorf might not have burnt down. I would have had to get help in my drinking enterprise, though. Actually, I do think that the wine was at the root of the fire that destroyed the castle. I am convinced that when the looters came in and got drunk with some of the enormous quantity of wines they found, they set the house on fire, on purpose or by accident. As the castle had two storeys entirely wood-panelled, it burnt like a torch.

There was no trace of the house here either. But why on earth this massacre? The little manor of Glambeck had gallantly spanned 200 years but had not survived 30 years of communism. We did not expect that. It was so far from everything, so pretty and innocent, why tear it down? Buttel and I were stunned, our eyes on the ground were looking for traces but all had vanished except in our memories. It is true that memory keeps forever our treasures. But it does not keep the smells. You have to find the same smells physically so that memory can recall the flavours. And then the joy that the aromas of times past procure is incredible. We smelt the surrounding bushes like hounds do, but the forest had wiped away the perfume of our past and spread her own, like an arrogant usurper.

A bang behind us woke us with a jump. Albrecht was making a diversion by opening a bottle of excellent champagne. We chased out the dark thoughts we had never allowed in before that day and toasted our joys of the present.

We returned to the road to find the entry to the path which before led to the spot where I had buried the 13 crates. I was happy to notice that my calculation of 45 years before was right, for the stones I had chosen for markers were still in place. I knew then that I had a fair enough chance of finding my buried treasure, once the communist regime ceased to exist and Germany was reunited. We were so confident about the future that we started making plans for the renovation of the estate once it was given back to us. It never occurred to us that our government would snatch away our property altogether, going as far as modifying the Constitution to do so. It was more of a plunderer in that matter than many eastern countries which, after the communist regime fell, gave back to their legitimate owners what belonged to them.

Back in the village of Görlsdorf we went to the bar and found there, unexpectedly, my childhood buddy Horst's brother. He was in charge of the place. In the small adjoining store he managed as well there were now only some essential goods. He showed us the catch of the day: green, hard, small, unappealing tomatoes. They came from Iceland and cost the equivalent of six dollars a pound.

Soon Horst appeared on the threshold, breathless because he had run to arrive. I was moved to find an old man instead of the young boy I had left when we were both teenagers, half a century ago. We exchanged souvenirs in front of a schnapps. The two brothers invoked the memory of their mother who, when she was alive, talked so much about mine that she had attracted the attention of the *Stasi*. Until her death, she had taken care of the graves of my father's sister, who died at Görlsdorf, and of Bubi, Mother's brother. The mausoleum that contained the remains of three generations of my family had been profaned and the coffins opened by looters in search of jewels. Horst had found the remains of Bubi, which he recognised by his uniform. Bubi's open coffin was lying among the ruins. He had buried him in the village cemetery.

We went to say hello to Horst's wife, in the house he had built with his own hands on ground that was ours before and which he always felt, rightly, was his as well because he belonged there. In the entrance, there was a photograph of the castle of Görlsdorf hanging on the wall.

Horst had been a prisoner of war in France until the end of 1945. When he came back, he began to work as a tractor driver in the state-owned farm that comprised all of our old farmland in Görlsdorf and the neighbouring villages. When we met again on my first visit, he was still in his old job and the continuous strident noise of the tractors had resulted in making him almost deaf.

'Why didn't you leave for West Germany before they built the Wall?' I asked him.

'I couldn't leave my mother here and I was engaged, then it was too late,' he replied with a sigh. So, he went on working all his life under the very spartan living conditions of the Communist regime. He was, like all the others in East Germany, used by years of war and its aftermath to lead a very poor existence. Not much to eat, never any 'luxury items' such as coffee or oranges. They didn't fully realise how low their living standards were until the reunification, when they travelled for the first time to the West. Not interested in politics, Horst had no difficulty with the ruling party. He made barely enough money to survive but was sure to keep his job. The highlight of his life was the building of his simple house. He was understandably proud of it. The propaganda spread by the P.D.S. – this is what the communist party calls itself nowadays – told him and the other modest proprietors over there that the ancient owners were back to snatch their land and houses away from them.

Horst is now a 70-year-old man, old before his time. We are happy to see each other every time I go to Görlsdorf and his wife always greets me with the nicest welcome. Buttel and I invited Horst and his brother to Oettingen. They came with their wives and we all had great fun discussing old and modern times.

We went together to the cemetery, to say a prayer at the graves of my uncle, my aunt and of the people and their relatives from the village we had known. Night was falling; its shadow added silence and mystery to that faraway place. I felt that my presence on the unchanged grounds of my past was unreal, as if I had crossed a mirror which sent back the reflection of times past and found myself on the other side of it.

In Angermünde, our little town where we went at the end, we visited an old lady who had been a servant at our place and with whom Buttel had always corresponded by mail. She hugged us tearfully and, as with all the other people we had met, she talked with emotion and sadness about my mother's time.

Several times during that excursion in search of our past, the people we met mentioned 'the treasure'. Apparently everybody knew about its existence but nobody knew the spot where it was buried. I offered a deaf ear to a few attempts in the style 'you can count on me to help you dig . . .' I could well imagine that if the treasure was still there, it would not be because it had been preserved for owners who had every chance of never coming back, but because nobody had had access to the place or knew where to dig. Later I heard that Wiechmann, the forester who had helped me bury the crates, would have had a map of the surroundings. It couldn't be. I knew Wiechmann's loyalty and besides he firmly believed we would be back soon. And he would not have kept in his possession such a document, which would have put him and his wife at risk.

I met the forester who had replaced Wiechmann and served under Mielke. He is a good and helpful man, who dug with us to find the treasure some years later and rejoiced sincerely when we were successful in our search. From my first visit in 1990 he had offered me his hospitality when I went to Görlsdorf, sometimes with my son, who became friends with his as they are the same age.

In any case, 'the treasure', which seemed to exert a true fascination on people, was not of great interest to us. In the event that we got permission to dig and then managed to find it, it would not change our lives. On the other hand, I was determined not to let anyone get their hands on it. 'They' would not get one little spoon on top of the rest if I could help it. It was that idea that made me bury the crates to start with. In fact, this fierce determination of a young boy to try to salvage from looting some plates and cutlery was rather pathetic but that was all he could do and he did it. I didn't have any longer the strong feelings of my youth and I felt much less pugnacious. I still did not want anyone to get possession of my hypothetical treasure, but I was in no hurry to recoup it. In fact, I would gladly have left it to rest there where it was best placed but someone, someday, was bound to find it.

It was enough for me to recall the desecration of the graves of my relatives and ancestors to react and find strength in my soul again.

I would come and dig out the treasure when the moment was

convenient and I would find it, even if everybody searched before without success.

*

We went back to Berlin. Buttel and I thought that if the reunification of Germany ever happened, the way of life of the people we had seen in Görlsdorf and the outlook of that region would change drastically. We felt great hope and excitement and thought we were exceptionally lucky to be alive to witness the days ahead.

I often went back to Brandenburg, to the grounds of our ancient estate, after this first return in January 1990. I visited every one of our old 13 estates as well as the 10,000 acres of our forest. In the beginning, I took my son along on those pilgrimages. I had described to him before the enchanted place of my childhood, I wanted him to see it with the same marvelling eyes, I wanted him to picture himself growing up here with me. But everything had changed so much. And all for the worse. Sebastian certainly could not imagine how it was in my time and I couldn't blame him.

I saw everywhere the same discouraging display of buildings abandoned, old rusted machines left to rot badly, uncultivated and unkempt fields. At the beginning, the managers of the L.P.G., the huge farming complexes that the communists had created in the 1960s, forcing the peasants to join their private little pieces of land together, approached us to offer their collaboration in what concerned the exploitations. To be sure, they never expected the West German Government to decide that *nothing* would be given back to us. The workers, among whom some still remembered 'the good old times', hoped that there would be a flow of investments through the ex/new owners, that would improve their living conditions.

However, in April 1991, the Government in Bonn testified in front of the Constitutional Court that one of the conditions Gorbachev had set in order to authorise the reunification of Germany, was the non-restitution of the land in the East to their former owners if they had been expropriated between 1945 and 1949, i.e. before the creation of the German Democratic Republic (D.D.R.). The Court obliged and stated that, in view of that argument, the interests of the State required that expropriation. The only exceptions concerned the former owners who had been dispossessed by the Nazis before 1945 (the executed *resistants* like my uncle, the Jewish families and the foreigners). What the Court ignored was that, at the beginning of 1990, the government had already decided to keep those possessions and to sell them to finance the skyrocketing cost of reuni-fication. The government succeeded in having the Constitution modified and to cancel for that occasion the constitutional right to private property.

Meanwhile, Michail Gorbachev, President of the Soviet Union, and Chevardnatze, his Foreign Minister, as well as George Bush, President of the United States, have stated that the declarations of the German Government concerning the matter were 'without foundation' – a diplomatic formula to say 'deceitful' – which set in motion a counter procedure, still being debated now.

In the same judgement, the Court ruled that all those who did not qualify for restitution would have to be compensated in money, but without defining how much. It took the Government more than three years to produce a law to that effect. That law is a striking example of bad faith. The more an ex-owner had in old times, the less he would get today, some of them – my family among those – would not get a penny of compensation!

I have now to witness, powerless, the sale of our land, piece by piece, and to see the proceeds swallowed by the Government budget in Bonn. So, in 1996, our stud was sold for five million dollars and we did not see a cent of it.

As time went by, the people who worked in our ex-farms were losing hope that we could again build a new enterprise together, for, even without restitution but with an adequate compensation, we would have invested in the East. The communist ex-government officials had feared for their positions in the beginning, now they could not believe their luck when they realised that our democratic government gave them more rights than to the legitimate owners. They were becoming increasingly arrogant and sure of themselves. They were staying at the head of their enormous agricultural enterprises that they managed insanely against the interests of the people, of the animals and of the grounds and when the ex-small owners asked for a compensation for the piece of land the communist government had taken away from them, they proved with falsified accounting that they could not pay.

The previous estate owners had already declared in 1990 that they had no intention of throwing out the little owner who had in good faith acquired his land or built his house. They just asked for the restitution of the lands in possession of the State. But the ex-communists, called now 'the Red Socks', spread the rumour that the estate owners wanted to throw people out of their houses, which created a certain panic, as one can well imagine.

In view of this situation in East Germany, I decided not to set foot there again. What good would it be to see the disappointed faces of our friends who had, as we had, hoped that we would be working together again, in the common goal of rebuilding a healthy, modern, well managed agrarian sector for the benefit of everyone concerned? Now they saw, as we did, that all our dreams had collapsed. It was a terrible disappointment for us all after the hopes that the events of November 1989 had awakened.

On my part, after having been badly shaken by the brutality of our losses and changes in material conditions, I must now, at the age of retirement, face the financing of the education of my son, the last one to bear the name of my family, with only my pension. A conservative estimation of my property in the hands of the State is in the range of 50 to a 100 million marks (between 30 and 60 million dollars).

This outrageous and totally inexcusable deprivation of our rights led me to not only fight it in court but to try as well by all means available to recover the 'treasure' I had buried myself in my own land in 1945.

For my family and me, it is not a treasure in the sense of a material fortune. For us it is tradition, a social past, something very private, belonging to a family as one link in a series of chains that cross one another along generations.

Had we had material ambitions, it seems obvious that we would have secured against hardships by transferring money abroad, as is currently done. We would not have relied on silverware and a few trinkets buried in a hole in an inaccessible forest to play the role of a Swiss bank. But over the centuries, nobody in our family on either side had ever invested in any place else other than in his or her country. We all meant to make our prosperity coincide with our nation's.

When I made the choice of which of our possessions to take along or to bury, I had to do it alone, as my mother had other things on her mind. The best proof that the treasure did not mean any material good for Mother is the lack of interest she demonstrated toward the treasure. Had it been otherwise, she would have been the guardian of the map. She hardly gave it a glance after that night. On the other hand, she was always careful about her jewel case and she took away as much cash as she could gather in the house, and that is what we all survived on for a time. Mother's management seems to have been excellent for she still kept some jewels for her children and her son's wives when she died. She even saw us go hungry and didn't budge with what she intended to keep as her heritage. She was so right. With two meals a day for each one of us, no jewel, whatever its worth, would have lasted a week in that period of galloping inflation. We all agreed with her.

At the time I buried the treasure, I believed I would come back in a matter of a few years, or, much more realistically, die in the general inferno of 1945. I pictured the plunderers stuffing themselves from our porcelain plates, armed with our silverware, and I boiled with rage.

Until summer 1994, the German Parliament had not passed the law concerning the destiny of the land in the East and we still hoped for restitution or at least compensation. Finally, by the end of 1994, the Bundestag (Parliament) adopted a law that confirmed our worst fears: a compensation was set apart of roughly 5 per cent of the taxable value of 1934. It would be calculated minus the sums we had received as help in the '50s and '60s. The landowners in West Germany, not the States, allocated and paid this help by way of solidarity. The ridiculous and petty scraps the State envisage paying for stealing our possessions will be paid in 2004, when almost all those who had known their land at the time it was prosperous will be in their graves. For the most extensive estates, like ours, by a complicated and intricate procedure, the State will have nothing at all to pay; therefore, we will not receive one cent! But, as the State can be generous with what does not belong to it, it allowed its victims to take back their personal belongings, providing, of course, that they did not include works of art.

It has to be said that, since Göring created the trend, the German State embezzles with gusto the works of art belonging to private people. Hypocritically, it is suggested that after 20 years of exhibition in the State museums without the least indemnity, they will be returned to their rightful owners . . . who will be dead and I seriously doubt that their heirs will ever recoup what is legitimately theirs.

What has happened to us has happened to many families and I know of many cases. Baron Axel von dem Bussche was sure that, after the reunification of Germany in 1991, his estate in the East would be returned to him. He was wrong because he did not meet the petty qualifications of the Government. The fact is that he had not been killed by the Nazis, as he had neither been reported nor been caught and they did not dispossess him. Therefore he did not correspond to the specifications designed and fixed for the restitution to people of what was theirs.

My uncle Wilfried had all the qualifications: he had been assassinated and the Nazis had confiscated his properties. Still, his heirs have to fight every step of the way to retake possession of their own land. It looks as if there is a lot more for them to endure and a long time to wait.

The 'law', in Germany, authorises the *resistants* to the Nazi regime to get their properties back. But a *resistant*, who was lucky enough not to have been caught and executed, had no right over what was legitimately his. Restitution was for the dead, and not always.

In 1992, Axel stated a claim in front of the Constitutional Court in Karlsruhe. He testified in these terms:

> I only did my duty fighting against the Soviets Hitler had provoked. I left my physical integrity in the process. I do not intend to stay passive while the communist injustice gets recognition as democratic justice. Can the State usurp the right to profit from the disaster caused by Karl Marx, taking hold of the possessions stolen by the communists? Must we provide our country with its spoils of war?

The Court decided against him in May 1996. Axel was dead meanwhile and did not see the shameful day when one of the bravest, most illustrious and notorious *resistants* to Hitler was definitely stripped of his land.

Von Mendelssohn Bartholdy was of Jewish origin and from the family of the famous composer. He had an important estate in Brandenburg. In the 1930s, in view of the turn the Nazi politics towards the Jews was taking, he registered his estate in the name of his 'Aryan' wife. He therefore avoided confiscation by the Nazis but not by the communists or by reunited Germany, although the law which stipulates that all that was Jewish property would be returned. The argument is that the estate was not expropriated by the Nazis and was not Jewish property.

Mr von Ribbeck is another case. He came from a well-known family in Brandenburg, near Berlin, and died in a concentration camp during the war, having been arrested as anti-Nazi. The State refuses to give back his land to his son because the Nazis did not themselves expropriate them. Does that mean that modern Germany punishes more than the Nazis and is more unfair and cruel than they were?

Another example is that of the von Putbus family who were great landowners on the island of Ruegen, in the Baltic Sea. The head of the family died in a concentration camp where he was imprisoned as an opponent to the Nazi regime. For him, the reason actually given for not returning his land to his heirs is that he was sent to a concentration camp only 'because he did not succeed in getting along with the local leaders of the Nazi party'.

*

The word *heimat* is the most German of all the German words. It does not mean 'nation', it rather designates the place or the region where you were born and where you spent your childhood. It is very important for a family, particularly in ours, which had more than 350 years of existence in the same place.

The relationship a family has with the land it has owned for 12 generations is, I realise, difficult for most people to comprehend, nonetheless it forges an extremely powerful bond which lasts for a lifetime. For my mother and for all the heads of families before her, the land was as important as the family members were, because it would survive them and all of their descendants. In my case, although I don't possess my land, I still feel the same bond with it. I acquired it when I was very young and I felt the amputation of it as a pain that has kept the same intensity ever since.

In 1945 after our flight, nobody among us thought about the material loss of expropriation – we thought about it later but it was never of great consequence because we were earning our living. But losing the *heimat* and the prospect of never being able to go back to it or live in it was a problem of major proportions.

Where does this bond with the land come from? Without my conscious knowledge, as I tried never to ponder over it, I always felt the lack of land as a void. I do not mean to have back all that we had, just some of *my* land. This need might originate in the fact that in agriculture as in forestry, you work for the future, without being able to harvest the product of your labour immediately. In agriculture, with the planning of the improvement of the land and the cattle, the change in cultivation, etc., you have to wait for years to collect the results. With the forest, you never see the fruit of your investment; you work for your children or your grandchildren. It strengthens the bonds with the land and with the family. Furthermore, when you consider yourself as a link in a long chain, living always on the same ground, generation after generation, inheriting the land, working it as best you can during an entire lifetime and transmitting it to the next link, it gives you a sense of security and helps you to understand death as a part of eternity.

As far as I am concerned, I have repressed these thoughts and feelings since 1945 to be able to face life better, as it was set to be a hard battle to fight for people already worn out by the war and its deprivations. I did not want to drag an eternal regret of the past. I did not want to complain. I wanted to build something new. The best way to reach that goal was to turn my back on the past. But when I went back to Görlsdorf in 1990 and during my successive visits there, all those suppressed feelings rushed strongly back and I realised they had been there, deep down in me, sleeping for 50 years. That explains the resentment we all have, we, the eastern families, for the Government in Bonn. We resent it for being neither respectable nor honourable and for not trying to reverse the great injustice done to us by the communists. The politicians had continuously claimed they would give us justice as soon as the country reunited.

We do not want money; we want the land, even if it is only a small part of our ancient estate. But a cold and calculating government grabs the sums it pays for the development of East Germany from the ex-owners, trampling on their special relationship with their piece of earth, their willingness to make sacrifices, and despite the favourable feelings which exist towards them in the population.

*

When I think back 50 years, to the first years after the war, I try to remember what my state of mind was at the time. I did not realise then what deep changes the flight from home would mean for us, the giving up of our land and the end of the war.

We slipped from a materially very comfortable existence to the extremes of poverty, from a freedom to decide over the important events of our life to an absolute dependence on other people, from a spacious house where servants rushed to meet our least wishes to no place on earth where we could have chosen to stay.

I was young, my life was ahead of me, but for my mother, my uncles and my aunts, already touched by old age or on the verge of it, who had lived most of their existence with the power to mould it and live it their own way, used to providing with pleasure and pride the needs and well-being of their children and the ones who depended on them, it was a huge and sudden pain that settled forever in their hearts, without any chance of healing as they were too advanced in years to start a new life.

With tacit agreement, no one evoked his or her problems, needs or losses. We talked solely about the everyday chores and the possibilities of the future.

Our transition to our new existence was made easier perhaps by our education. In the families of ancient extraction, nobody thought that privileges and an easy way of life were to be taken for granted. We conformed to the saying: 'You have to deserve what you've got.'

All through history, the families had had to endure ups and downs, natural or political catastrophes, royal favours or disfavours, bankruptcy or temporal or physical disappearances. The cataclysm of the last war has therefore not surprised these families as a lightning in a blue sky. Actually, the great majority of the people belonging to that social group have succeeded quite well in rebuilding an existence after the war, although the competence and knowledge of its most important members consisted mainly in knowing how to manage a landed estate.

Money, in the sense of finances, had no meaning for the landed families. We knew its value and significance but we never talked about it. It is easy not to think or talk about money matters when it is plentiful but indeed, this independent attitude towards wealth allowed us to dive into rough seas and swim from the start, with no second thoughts. I could even say we had an advantage due to the fact that our social climbing was behind us, and that was one mountain we never had to climb and never will have to.

On the other hand, the loss of the land was a capital punishment. It was felt as an amputation. The land represented our belonging to a certain space (not the other way around), to a house, to memories and traditions. We couldn't be dissociated from our land. Indeed, I was blessed in that field. In 1946, Buttel married Lix Oettingen who, in spite of an eight-year gap between us, became my best friend while Buttel and I had already always been very close. We became inseparable.

Secured from financial worries themselves, their solicitude for me was a great help and comfort to overcome the difficulties I encountered to find an orientation. Their house became my second home; I could come and go to and from Oettingen as I pleased. I appreciated the way of life they offered me even more as I now knew very different living conditions. Buttel and Lix took me along on their trips, they taught me what I know today in many fields and many of my joys and much of my happiness come from them.

Lix died in 1975, leaving an abysmal void in many lives, mine among them. His son, Albrecht, has inherited many of his parents' qualities on top of his own which are remarkable. Our friendship developed along the years as a person to person bond, independent of the one that bound his father and me and yet tacitly enriched from our memories. Albrecht and Angela, his wife, have gone on to make me feel in Oettingen as in my own house. I am very rich . . .

Chapter Fourteen

TREASURE HUNT

Towards the end of 1994, we officially asked for the agreement of the Government to go and get back our own belongings in our own forest. Fifty years of waiting were probably not enough, the officials had us wait another six months before finally giving us the permit to go and dig and keep our cutlery. They might have thought that, given the frenetic searches done without success by the Russians first, then by the German communists then probably by our own Government, I would certainly not have more luck than they all did. They could therefore appear to be generous without loss.

In the meantime, the State was beginning to sell, for its sole benefit and without any hesitations, our estate bit by bit for large amounts of money. I was advised of the finished business every time by official mail, without comment, from the *Treuhand*, the office created by the Government to privatise the State properties in East Germany. Thus they recognised me as the owner sufficiently to be worth a stamp on a letter, coldly and shame-fully announcing my deprivation.

My family and I found an American company that rents, by the day and for a very high price, men and devices to help find buried treasures.

In June 1995, Buttel, Albrecht, Gregory, the representative of the American company with his equipment, and I arranged to meet in Berlin.

On 28 June we left very early from Berlin and arrived at Görlsdorf to meet the forester at his house, as we had agreed with him.

Around 7.30 a.m. we entered the forest. I had my map and very quickly I found the first hunting stone which I had taken as marker to orientate my map. The stones were all still in place. Albrecht and I bent over the bonnet of one of the cars and proceeded to study the sketch. We had parked the cars in a depression of the ground so as not to attract the attention of possible passers-by on the road, about 600 feet away. Then I counted my steps on the ground. I had to bear in mind that at the time my legs were certainly a bit shorter than now (I haven't yet reached the age when they bend). For a while I felt slightly out of balance, as I couldn't find the second stone. It had been unearthed, in fact, and lay on the ground three feet away. I determined the direct line between the two roads and the place where I should leave the path and enter the woods.

In 50 years the aspect of the forest had changed completely, the trees had grown. I calculated the place of the first hole and found myself presently in front of a very slight depression in the earth, as the one formed when one opens a hole and covers it afterwards.

I signalled to Greg to go to work. His device is not a metal detector but a much more modern and sophisticated machine, portable, resembling a vacuum cleaner, connected to a screen on which it sends pictures of the earth down to a depth of six feet. If the earth has been moved, even 50 years before, the streaks in the earth will appear different from the other ones on the screen. Greg activated his 'vacuum cleaner' and swept the space I indicated, walking around, one way then the other. After 15 minutes, Greg pointed with his finger: 'You can dig here.' He showed us the very clear image on the screen of the modification in the earth under our feet. We were all slightly sceptical about the potential performance of his device but, obediently, everybody started digging.

After shovelling four and a half feet down with no result, I started to be invaded by doubt. I remembered I had not dug the first time, I was nauseated the whole time. So, I had some difficulty in evaluating at which depth the crates had been laid. I didn't remember it was so far down from the surface.

Then, a soft 'cling!' resounded under a shovel. With our hands, with infinite care, we swept the sand off to find a dozen plates, standing as slices of bread, directly in the earth, in excellent state. And all around, other plates, porcelain figurines and all kind of trinkets. Some objects were broken but relatively few. The crates had totally disintegrated, however. Only some little pieces of black and soft wood remained. What had saved the plates was that Ehrentraut, our butler in times past, had set them standing in the crates. That way the rain, infiltrating all along the years, had been allowed to run across and the pressure from the earth had not been too heavy on the porcelain.

It doesn't explain, however, that we found such fragile objects as figurines and crystal decanters intact. Ehrentraut was a true artist in his craft and deserves all the credit. He took the secret of wrapping and preserving to his grave as the Egyptian embalmers did for their mummies.

Once we had found the first pit, I did not have much difficulty in finding the second one, and Greg and his machine confirmed it at once. We dug with more faith and enthusiasm than for the first hole. The silver objects came out in an abundant harvest; they were far more numerous than I remembered. As archaeologists do, we dug the sand with measured and smooth gestures so as not to break the objects when they appeared.

The silver articles were black or black-green, depending on the purity of the alloy. Actually, if the silver is not pure, then the alloy is made with copper and the copper covers the objects with a green colour (*vert-de-gris*) when it stays moist for a long time. If the silver is purer, the objects get a black colour. All the silver was in a perfect state of conservation. Many objects still had pieces of newspaper stuck on them, and you could still read the titles and some lines of the articles. I could not look at them. Hitler's propaganda was not going to spoil that beautiful day and the Führer was not to be recalled here.

Piles were accumulating around us, and more was coming out, hailed by the laughs and applause of our team. They commented to one another how exciting the operation was and how privileged they felt to be there and to have witnessed in the flesh the successful conclusion of that long epic.

Greg, who makes fascinating excavations all over the world, told me that this treasure hunt in Görlsdorf was the one that caused him the greatest emotion because of its human value. Indeed this odyssey had a touch of unreality. The owner of the treasure buried it half a century ago on his estate. There had since been the total Nazi débâcle, the Soviet occupation, the Communist Government of East Germany and then the Government of reunified Germany and here I was again, having survived all of it and having toured the planet in every direction, picking up my own belongings, in what I can still call my land.

In the second pit, we found a little metal box I did not remember. I examined the map, intrigued. That must surely be Mother's coffer! The leather upholstery had rotted away, a few rags of indefinite material still adhering to the metal testified to it. The coffer, covered with wet sand, was locked. Did Mother really believe at the time that not having the key would have discouraged the looters? We had no difficulty in forcing the lock as it had rusted to almost non-existence. My sister and I opened the lid.

I was about to enter the private world of Mother, to see what were the things that counted most for her among her material possessions she was about to leave behind. I had no hint as to what they could possibly be. She had died only 14 years before and had never uttered one word about it to anybody. Some dusty fragments appeared, remains of letters and photographs indecipherable today. All the frames, the letters and the objects had decayed except for a few rare trinkets in silver or gold, solely the ones that had a special significance for one or other of her children. Not one of the photographs was recognisable. Mother had wanted to prevent the theft of her immaterial treasure, and of this one only, from the vandalism of the conquerors. Now, in front of my recovered possessions, hearing in the background the congratulations and the exclamations of pleasure from the members of my little team, I felt poor, definitively poor for the first time. I realised I hadn't grasped before that day the inner wealth Mother had. Now this humble little coffer was giving it to me, from the bottom of my mother's heart. So, while I was trying to rescue all the material wealth I could gather so that other people would not get it, even if I never recovered it, my mother, who did not want to know anything about it, had packed dreams and that is the treasure that will give warmth to my heart for the rest of my years. I bent down and took in my hands the little heart-shaped piano and the carriage whose wheels could still roll and I remembered I had wanted to take them with me on my flight in 1945 but could not find them. I pressed them against my cheek. I was back home.

*

While waiting for the truck from the transportation company we had called as soon as we had found the first objects, we had a merry picnic in the middle of a plunderers' cavern.

The truck arrived from Berlin around three o'clock in the afternoon. When night fell, the two pits were empty but the movers stayed at work until 10 p.m. to load everything into their vehicle. When it was ready, the motor refused to start. The battery was dead. We were all puzzled and so worn out that we could not think. There was no mechanic or garage open at this time within a radius of 20 miles.

Nobody dared imagine having to sleep on the ground. We had surmounted all kinds of obstacles to be there, we had been successful in our search, we had uncovered the treasure and now because of a ridiculous engine failure, we were running the risk of having it stolen right under our noses because we were not equipped to defend it. We sweated hard to operate the heavy handle to start the truck.

After numerous unsuccessful tries and only with the help of the forester's car battery, the engine finally emitted a welcome roar. This incident didn't dampen my exhilaration. How different was this night from the one of so long ago! We had nothing to fear, we had a truck instead of a cart to transport the same load and we were doing it now legally while last time we had risked our lives. We were at peace with the rest of the world now, which certainly was not the case then. And I had found the treasure intact, absolutely nothing was missing.

When I had seen coming out of the earth, one piece after the other, what I had laid down in it 50 years and two months before, I had mixed feelings. I saw myself as I was then on that doomed night, shivering with cold and fever, with my child's fright, my teenager's hopes and my man's worries. I felt compassion and pride to have guided this young man, who still lived in me, to the edge of that hole today, where he had given an appointment to himself on that dreadful night. I was also grateful to and proud of the three men who had never uttered a word about my secret which was theirs only by the affection that bound us and had been cemented by the bond that had united my parents to their grandparents and parents. We would have had a good laugh together, had we known that for a half-century the treasure had slept there under the boots of the hunters who had stolen our territory and strutted on top of it.

However, a moment before, as my sister and I stood motionless above those pits, so small, which contained all that was left of our past, I knew we shared the same bitter thoughts. We had needed a permit to come and take possession of what was ours and what I had myself saved for my people. Our land, our forest, our stud that we, like our ancestors, had so much loved, would they never be given back to us? Wouldn't we ever have a roof on our land? Won't we ever have a right to live in the place where we spent our first years and that was genuinely ours? What to do then with those remains of a past splendour which will never be revived and which are such painful memories?

Chapter Fifteen

THE AUCTION

The memories attached to the silverware and the china that we have sold are rather painful as they revive scenes of a time past forever. In London, Sotheby's had arranged a press conference before the auctions. It was an enormous success, which took us by surprise. We had more than 60 journalists, photographers, radio and TV people. All in all my treasure story was reported in 13 TV and 12 radio programmes and in 250 articles in newspapers and magazines in 18 different countries.

A noted English archaeologist, who studied the matter, told me that I was only the second known case in recorded history, where the same person buried and recovered his own treasure – buried to save it from the enemy. The other case had been in England in the 17th century.

On auction day, in Geneva, we were all there, all the generations, to wave a dignified goodbye to our past. We were like a battalion ready for inspection. Even the Bethmann-Hollweg ladies (granddaughters of Countess Reventlow who had given us such a warm shelter when we arrived on the tractor) gave us the honour and the pleasure of being part of our family on that day. The eldest of them, Isabella, was Sotheby's manager for northern Germany. That is the reason why we had chosen this firm to auction what we wanted to sell from the treasure. She very kindly opened every door for us and was a very valuable help. The very large Odiot silver service my great-great-uncle Wilhelm Friedrich had bought was sold in Geneva. It consisted of 116 pieces that had been used for the receptions in the Palais Redern in the 1800s.

Many people have asked me why I sold this beautiful service. The reasons are simple. Neither my siblings nor I live in a place big enough to house it. We don't have the staff to take care of it, and we do not give the kind of receptions where it would be suitable. And we could all use the money. So, after consulting with my sisters, with whom I would split the proceeds, I decided to sell what we couldn't use and which had no personal meaning. This consisted, apart from the Odiot silver service, of a large amount of silver and the Meissen porcelain.

Albrecht, who achieves in one week what we poor average humans achieve in one month, left his seat before the start of the auction and reappeared only at dinner. While we were all there eating, Lolita, my wife, mentioned that she would very much like to know who had bought the biggest piece of massive silver, a giant soup tureen. 'I would be sorry if it had been bought by a Japanese, he might intend to move into it,' she murmured. 'I would so much like it to decorate the table in a beautiful castle.'

Some family members had also bought several pieces, as well as friends of ours. The jeweller, who bought a store in the new Adlon hotel that is built in the place of the ancient Redern palace, had also bought some of the treasure to put on display in his windows.

The phone rang as we were going to bed. It was Albrecht.

'Tell Lolita she can sleep in peace, I've got the tureen!'

That was the most wonderful surprise and the most extraordinary present I could have dreamt of. We all rejoiced in the idea of our future visits to Oettingen when we will savour our meals – excellent and renowned cuisine in Oettingen – in our ancestors' silverware. I'm sure they would be pleased. So, the merry-go-round starts on another tour. I can hear Mother's happy laugh.

*

I have entered the winter of my life but I have looked the earth over and my home is the world. I may still have time, instead of putting my bones to rest in my *heimat* with my ancestors, to find a place where I can stop my wandering . . . on another planet.

APPENDICES

MAP OF GÖRLSDORF AREA

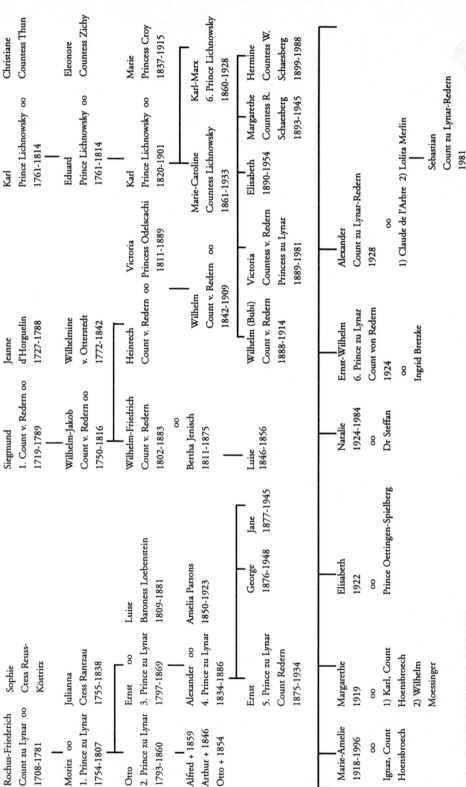

FAMILY TREE LYNAR-REDERN